HEALTH, HEALING, AND RELIGION

A Cross-Cultural Perspective

David Kinsley

McMaster University

Pearson
Education

PRENTICE HALL
UPPER SADDLE RIVER, NEW JERSEY 07458

Library of Congress Cataloging-in-Publication Data

Kinsley, David R.
    Health, healing, and religion : a cross-cultural perspective
    David Kinsley.
        p. cm.
    Includes bibliographical references and index.
    ISBN 0-13-212771-7
        1. Health—Religious aspects.   2. Healing—Religious aspects.
3. Medicine—Religious aspects.   I. Title.
BL65.M4K56 1996
291.1'75—dc20   95-25271
                                                                        CIP

Editor-in-Chief: Charlyce Jones Owen
Acquisition Editor: Ted Bolen
Editorial Assistant: Meg McGuane
Editorial/Production Supervision and Interior
      Design: B. Christenberry
Electronic Page Makeup: A & A Publishing Services, Inc.
Buyer: Lynn Pearlman
Cover Design: Bruce Kenselaar
Cover Photo: A Komokwa Mask from Village Island, B.C.;
      from University of British Columbia, Museum of
      Anthropology, A3588. Photograph by Bill McLennan.

©1996 by Prentice-Hall, Inc.
Simon & Schuster/A Viacom Company
Upper Saddle River, New Jersey 07458

Printed in the United States of America

10   9   8   7   6   5   4   3   2   1

ISBN 0-13-212771-7

PRENTICE-HALL INTERNATIONAL (UK), LIMITED, *London*
PRENTICE-HALL OF AUSTRALIA PTY. LIMITED, *Sydney*
PRENTICE-HALL CANADA INC., *Toronto*
PRENTICE-HALL HISPANOAMERICA, S.A., *Mexico*
PRENTICE-HALL OF INDIA PRIVATE LIMITED, *New Delhi*
PRENTICE-HALL OF JAPAN, INC., *Tokyo*
SIMON & SCHUSTER ASIA PTE. LTD., *Singapore*
EDITORA PRENTICE-HALL DO BRASIL, LTDA., *Rio de Janeiro*

To Dan and Estella Overmyer
and Becky and Mark Overmyer-Velázquez,
with appreciation and regard

Contents

PART THREE   MODERN MEDICAL CULTURE

Preface

The aim of the book is to illustrate that healing is related to religion and moral concerns in most cultures and that healers are often religious specialists. The book seeks to show that healing is often a symbolic and ritualistic process and that healers are masters at employing symbols and rituals in their treatment of illness. The book also demonstrates that modern, scientific medicine employs symbols and rituals and bears similarities to premodern medicine at many points.

The book is based on an undergraduate course I have been teaching at McMaster University for several years. I would like to thank the many students who have taken this course for their ideas and criticisms. They have contributed to this book in many ways. I would also like to thank Ted Bolen, formerly of Prentice Hall, for his encouragement in writing this book; Bobbie Christenberry for her help and good humor throughout the copyediting and production of the book; and my wife, Carolyn, for reading this many times.

Introduction

AIMS AND STRUCTURE OF THE BOOK

The book has two general aims. First, it explores the ways in which health, sickness, and healing are inextricably related to religious or moral concerns, themes, and practices in almost all cultures. Until recently, for example, healers in most societies were religious specialists of one kind or another. Shamans, priests, and spirit mediums dominated healing. Healing practices, furthermore, were typically religious rituals. Sacrifice, pilgrimage, prayer, and propitiation of spirits, for example, were common practices to bring about healing in most cultures. Concepts of health and sickness were religious or moral. A very common idea, for example, was that sickness came about because of the violation of ethical norms. Sickness was the result of sin, to put the idea in traditional Christian terms.

Second, the book suggests that the dichotomy between modern, scientific medicine and earlier or alternative forms of medicine (a dichotomy that is frequently insisted upon) is less than absolute: many themes, strategies, rituals, and structures present in premodern medicine are discernible in scientific medicine as well and still have important functions to play; in many ways, modern, scientific medicine is still traditional, drawing upon approaches, rituals, and strategies that are ancient.

The book has three parts. Part One presents important themes and characteristics in traditional medical cultures that illustrate the interrelatedness of religion, health, and healing. Part Two deals with Christianity and shows that many of the characteristics of traditional cultures apply to Christian materials. Part Three discusses modern medical culture and shows that it is characterized by many traditional features as well.

RELIGION AND HEALING

Healing is a central concern for most religions. Why is this so?

First, serious illness raises questions about human existence, about one's own existence. Like other fundamental human experiences—birth, marriage, sex, death, and so on—sickness unsettles a person. It interrupts normal routines and assumptions about oneself and the world. Serious illness can push a person to the edge of the familiar world so that he or she sees things with a fresh eye. The view of things from the sick bed is very different from the view of things from anywhere else. Serious illness raises basic questions about the meaning of life and the place of human beings in the cosmos; healing is often directly related to addressing these concerns. As we shall see, one of the principal roles traditional healers play is to frame sickness in a meaningful context.

Second, a basic assumption in many cultures is that bodily health is related to spiritual health, or that health is related to morality. Bodily sickness or health in most cultures is understood to be largely a reflection of one's relationships to various supernatural beings, or to certain overarching or underlying principles of reality (that is, to spiritual concerns), or to other individuals, both living and dead (that is, to moral concerns). One's well-being, in other words, is seen to be part of a whole web of relationships that impinge upon one in everyday life. Physical sickness is therefore a symptom of disharmony between the sick person and his or her wider universe of relationships. A well-known example of this idea is found in traditional Christianity, in which many people understand sickness to be related to sin. In Hinduism, sickness may be understood as the result of bad karma. Healing, in such situations, involves restoring harmony, correcting behavior, rebuilding fractured relationships (with gods, ancestors, or the living), all of which have moral implications.

Third, because sickness and healing are so closely related to religious or moral concerns in most cultures, healers tend to be religious specialists of one kind or another, and therapy tends to involve religious rituals or to have religious or moral implications.

In modern, scientific medicine these connections, interrelations, or themes are muted. The religious and moral ramifications of illness are understood to involve persons (such as clergy) or matters that are outside the boundaries of medical practice. Nevertheless, there are indications that important concerns of modern medicine continue to be the construction of frameworks of meaning and the relating of illness to patterns of human behavior (implicit morality). Throughout, the book stresses the ways in which aspects of traditional medicine and healing persist in modern medicine.

PART ONE

Traditional Cultures

INTRODUCTION

In looking at the ways in which ideas about illness and healing relate to religion and morality in traditional cultures, Part One seeks to delineate several broad themes or tendencies. Most of these themes and tendencies will also characterize the materials covered in Parts Two (Christianity) and Three (Modern Medicine).

At the most general level, it is vividly apparent in almost all traditional cultures that sickness and healing are closely associated with what we consider religious, spiritual, or moral ideas and themes and that healers themselves are usually religious specialists of one kind or another. That is, illness and healing are meaningfully framed or understood in what we might term a theological, mythological, or moral context.

In the first place, illness is often associated with spiritual beings such as gods, goddesses, ancestral spirits, demons, animal spirits, and spirits of locales such as rivers, mountains, or forests. These spiritual beings are part of a moral order that includes human beings. When humans offend them in some way, they are often provoked to send illness. In the most general sense, then, illness is frequently directly linked to morality. Moral transgression brings illness, often because it angers a deity or spirit.

Second, healers in most traditional cultures are usually religious specialists. This is not surprising. If illness is understood within a religious or moral context, then a healer must be familiar with the dynamics and mysteries of the religious and moral realms. If a deity or spirit is implicated in the cause of illness, the healer must be a person who can contact and influence these beings. Shamans, priests, mediums, herbalists, and other types of healers in traditional cultures are all knowledgeable in one way or another about the spirit world, about the moral order that connects human

3

beings with each other and with other species and spirits, and about the rituals, prayers, and incantations that are effective in dealing with gods and spirits.

Third, illness is typically treated by means of religious rituals in most traditional cultures. The shamanic seance, which we will discuss in Chapter 2, seeks to heal by contacting the spirit world. In the seance, the shaman seeks information from his helping spirits about spirits that may be implicated in the illness, the cause of their anger at the sick person, and the whereabouts of the patient's soul if it has been stolen by a spirit. In many cases, the healer is a priestly figure who knows appropriate rituals with which to appease angry deities. The healer often undertakes sacrifices on behalf of the patient to satisfy a disgruntled spirit or deity. Pilgrimage, or a journey to a sacred place connected with healing, is also a common therapy in traditional cultures. Often the preparation of medicines involves the precise knowledge, not only of local botany, but of the appropriate prayers and rituals that accompany the collection of herbs and their manufacture into medicine.

In short, in most traditional cultures, illness and healing are understood to involve religious matters. Theories of disease causation (Chapter 1) nearly always exhibit an implicit theology, healers are almost always sophisticated in spiritual and moral matters, and therapy is often explicitly religious, involving prayers, sacrifices, and sacred journeys.

Chapter 1 introduces healing in traditional cultures by surveying some common theories of disease causation and some common types of healers. Chapter 2 looks at the shaman as a religious healer. Chapter 3 gives a series of profiles of individual healers in a variety of cultures. Chapters 4–7 discuss specific healing scenarios. The healing dances of the Kalahari Kung of southern Africa stress the centrality of group solidarity in healing. The Navaho chantways emphasize the restoration of harmony by means of recapitulating and recreating sacred Navaho mythology and summoning the Holy People to be present at the ceremonies. Zinacanteco healing rituals feature the importance of a sacred journey in the healing process. The examples from northern India feature the importance of healers who are experts in contacting and influencing the spirit world (usually in the context of exorcism) and the importance of holy shrines as places where healing can be successful. Chapter 8 summarizes Part One by focusing on some major healing themes and strategies in traditional cultures. Among the themes discussed are confession and purification, sacred space in healing, framing illness in meaningful ways, and group solidarity in healing.

Chapter 1
Theories of Disease and Types of Healers

There is great diversity among what I have termed *traditional cultures*. Many different beliefs exist concerning the nature of ultimate reality, the nature of the divine, and the kinds of spirits that exist and impinge upon human life. Indeed, each traditional culture is in some ways distinct and unique. In terms of ideas about illness and healing, views differ from one culture to another. We will look in some detail later at several specific cultures to emphasize their distinctive characters. At the outset, however, there are some generalizations that can be made about ways of thinking about illness and healing and the kinds of healers who dominate in traditonal cultures. As a way of introducing traditional views and practices and providing an introductory framework for the individual cultures and healers to be discussed in subsequent chapters, it will be helpful to look at ideas that seem particularly common in traditional societies, at theories of disease causation that are related to implicit theologies, and at some common types of healers in traditional cultures, each of whom is a religious specialist of one kind or another. In some cases, these implicit theologies, theories of disease causation, and types of healers persist in Christian and modern materials.

"ANIMISM" AND PERSONALISTIC CAUSATION

An underlying assumption of most traditional cultures is that the whole world is alive. What we refer to as the "natural world" in our culture, what we often consider dead matter, is considered throbbing with life in traditional cultures. What we consider unconscious life (the plant world, for example) is often believed to be invested with consciousness, will, and divine power. Traditional cultures tend to perceive the world as filled with life, to attribute to all so-called natural objects a soul, an animating essence; this is usually referred to as animism (from *anima*, "soul"). Human beings, too, or human beings especially, are believed to possess a soul (or sometimes several souls) that underlies their very life and defines their essence.

Traditional cultures think of human life and destiny as involving the welfare of the soul and the harmonious interaction of the individual's soul with the souls of countless others, human and nonhuman. Historical, natural, and biographical events are often understood as the result of the interactions between souls, spiritual forces, or deities. Put in its most obvious form, earthly-human-social events are often understood to be reflections or consequences of what happens on another, spiritual plane; that is, they are infused with the dynamics of the spiritual dimension of reality.

Most traditional cultures affirm that the world is alive; that most, if not all, objects and beings have a will and personality. It follows that causation is understood in personal terms. Things happen because someone or something wills them to happen, usually for personal reasons. In the course of daily life, people interact with each other and with countless other beings, visible and invisible, during which a whole range of emotions and feelings are aroused: gratitude, affection, trust, jealousy, hatred, fear, and so on. Deities, spirits, ghosts, and ancestors can be pleased or displeased by any number of human actions, thoughts, or sentiments and moved to act in some way toward a person whose actions have impinged upon them, wittingly or unwittingly. Daily human life in most traditional societies is understood to take place within a web of relationships, human and nonhuman.

Sickness is often seen in this context. It is the result of, or the fallout from, a disharmonious relationship between the sick person and some being. Disharmony often results from the patient having willfully or accidentally offended another person or spiritual being. A broken taboo, a sexual escapade, a rude gesture or remark, or a variety of other actions may anger another person or being to the point where he or she will seek to injure the offender. In many cases, this way of thinking frames illness within a moral context. Sickness is understood as the result of immoral, reckless, and offensive behavior on the part of the patient.

The exact kinds of personalized agents who might be responsible for sickness vary from culture to culture, but there are many types of beings that are important cross-culturally. Among these are:

1. Deities. In most traditional cultures, deities, or one supreme deity, are assumed to exist and to an take interest in human affairs. In many cultures it is affirmed that a god instituted human culture and laid down certain rules and regulations to guide human life and human interactions with each other and with the divine. Violations of this code (whether written or orally transmitted) are punished by the gods, often in the form of misfortune, sickness, or death. Sickness in this context is thus understood to result from or to be evidence of the sick person's violation of some norm established by a deity.

Needless to say, there is a great variety of theologies, and of behavioral or moral codes, from culture to culture. In some cultures, there is an overarching deity who enforces a basic code of conduct, while in other cultures there may be many deities, each associated with a certain area of custom, economy, or human relations. In Judaic and Islamic cultures, for example, one god dominates the scene, providing a detailed code of human conduct and supervising and implementing that code, primarily through a system of reward and punishment. Sickness is often used as a means of divine punishment. This view is also quite strong in certain Christian cultures. In other cultures, a host of deities may be involved in supervising human conduct. Some deities, for example, may be involved primarily with hunting. If a hunting taboo is broken, a mistress- or master-of-animals type of deity takes appropriate action. In some cases, specific diseases such as smallpox are associated with a particular deity (in Hinduism, the goddess Shitala is an example), and the appearance of that disease is interpreted as the result of an offense against that deity by human beings.

2. *Ancestors and ghosts.* In most traditional cultures the dead are believed to be very much concerned about the living. Ancestors in many societies are believed to exist in bodiless form and to retain a deep interest in human affairs, especially those of their descendents. They are particularly interested in both the fortunes of their descendents and the respect or reverence shown to them by their descendents. Getting out of harmony with your ancestors by treating your relatives or spouse badly, or by ignoring respectful behavior toward the ancestors themselves (for example, not providing them with sacrifices and offerings), can result in sickness, bad luck, or worse in many cultures. In these cultures you must act as if your ancestors were ever present.

Inimical ghosts and demons are also believed to be the cause of disease in many cultures. These are often unhappy spirits of the dead, who envy the living and take out their frustrations on them. In such cases, sickness may be interpreted primarily as bad luck for the patient. Usually, though, one attracts the attention of a demon because of some personal fault or action, which allows the illness to be placed in a moral framework.

3. *Other human beings.* Inconsiderate behavior toward other human beings also may precipitate a series of events that lead to illness. In many cultures, illness is held to be the result of, or evidence of, strained or hostile human relationships. By arousing another's enmity, a person can cause the other to take actions to harm him. The evil eye, *mal ojo*, is a typical example of this kind of understanding of the relationship between human relationships and sickness. If people flaunt their good fortune and brag about the beauty and success of their children, especially in the presence of a childless person, they invite the wrath and envy of that person. The idea seems to be that if someone feels strongly enough against others that person can bring calamity and sickness down on those people. Sometimes this human hatred is understood to act on its own, in direct cause-and-effect fashion. In other cases an intermediary is used. This person is usually a witch or sorcerer. In many cultures these powerful, malevolent human beings are said to be the cause of a wide range of misfortune, especially serious illness. They are human beings who have mastered techniques (rituals and charms, for example) that enable them to harm and even kill their enemies or the enemies of clients.

THEORIES OF DISEASE CAUSATION

Although concepts of disease vary from culture to culture, there are some fairly common ideas in traditional societies about what actually makes a person sick. I spoke above about the theological and moral frameworks within which illness is often understood. Those frameworks provide what might be considered the ultimate causes of sickness. Here I would like to mention the immediate causes of sickness. These ideas relate more to the actual mechanics of the illness process. They are attempts to explain in fairly concrete terms what is making a person sick. Among the most common theories concerning the immediate causes of illness are:

1. Soul loss. In many cultures illness is understood to be caused by soul loss or the weakening of the soul. It is assumed that the body depends upon the soul and that if the soul leaves the body a person will weaken and die. Sickness is understood to be a reflection of the state of the soul. Healing becomes the process of finding the lost soul and restoring it to the body or of revitalizing a weakened soul. In our culture the tendency is to think of the body as primary and the soul (ego, personality, mind) as dependent upon the body, without which it would not exist. Even in our culture, however, we seem to be familiar with this idea when we speak of people who have "lost their will to live."

2. Object intrusion. In most societies the immediate cause of sickness is attributed to the intrusion or invasion of the person by a foreign object. The object is often understood to have been shot into the victim by an enemy, a witch, or a hostile spirit. The object itself then makes the person ill or kills the person if not removed. The art of sorcery in many cultures includes the ability to shoot people with objects. Although this idea is not found in our culture, many people do think of disease as an invasion of the body by hostile or foreign entities called germs or viruses.

3. Spirit intrusion. Many cultures believe that the immediate cause of illness is the result of an invasion or intrusion of a spirit. Particularly in the case of what we term *mental illness,* the cause is often said to be spirit possession. Such spirits are often said to be ancestral ghosts who have returned for one reason or another to trouble the sick person. Although our culture is extremely skeptical about the existence of spirits, the idea of spirit intrusion is suggested when we say such things as: "I wonder what got into him?" "She's not herself anymore." "I wonder what possessed him to do that?"

4. Disease sorcery. In some cases, the immediate cause of illness is the same as the ultimate cause. This is the case in disease sorcery. Here it is believed that the personal agent (usually a sorcerer or witch) who has become angry inflicts the disease directly upon the victim either through willpower (psychic energy) or through rituals or charms. Disease in this case is understood to be almost the tangible presence of the sorcerer's power, anger, or will, which is magically transferred to the victim.

5. Breach of taboo. This is the violation, intentional or unintentional, of a ritual rule or moral law. As in disease sorcery, the ultimate and immediate causes of disease are only weakly distinguished. In many cases, breach of taboo may be the immediate cause of sickness (or some other misfortune). It is the act itself that precipitates the illness, not a deity or some other being who has been angered. There is a direct cause-and-effect relation between moral or ritual transgression and sickness.

These theories about disease are not mutually exclusive; all five ways of thinking about illness may be found simultaneously in many cultures. It is easy to see how these theories might interact with or reinforce each other. Breach of taboo, for example, might weaken a person's general health to the point where she becomes susceptible to disease sorcery or where a spirit would find it easier to invade her system. Similarly, if a person is suffering from soul loss, this may be considered a symptom of having been shot with a foreign object.

In most traditional cultures, human beings are believed to be more or less susceptible to disease for a variety of reasons. In some cultures, for example, women are believed to be more susceptible than men, children more susceptible than adults, and menstruating women more susceptible than nonmenstruating women. Age, sex, and moral rectitude are just some of the factors that are related to who gets sick.

TYPES OF HEALERS

Given the existence of these ideas and theories about sickness in traditional cultures, it should be obvious that the diagnostic and therapeutic processes involve healers who are expert in understanding interpersonal relations, tribal customs, spiritual techniques, and religious knowledge. If, for example, a person's sickness is caused by a spiritual agent, only a healer who understands the dynamics of the spiritual world can be of help. If a person falls ill because of soul loss, the only healer who can help restore the soul is one who can travel in the spiritual realms where souls wander. If a person is ill because of having been bewitched, the diagnostician must be able to figure out who the witch is and how that witch has stricken the patient in order to bring about healing.

It is true that many healers in traditional cultures are bonesetters and herbalists with no special knowledge of the spirit world or spiritual techniques. For many kinds of sickness, however, a healer must possess special knowledge of, or insight into, spiritual aspects of the human condition. In many cases the priest and the physician are identical. Healers are religious specialists. In short, if it is assumed that the cause of disease is spiritual or moral, the patient must seek out someone knowledgeable in spiritual or moral matters. Among the most common types of healers in traditional cultures are the following:

1. Shaman. One of the most archaic and common types of healers is the shaman, who can be male or female. The shaman is the master of the soul. He has the ability to undertake soul travel, to roam the spirit world, where lost souls often travel. He is an expert in the soul, understanding its dynamics and having mastered the techniques of soul travel. He can see the soul and its condition, whereas normal people cannot. The shaman has direct access to the spirit world. He can go there, can communicate directly with spirits, and often has acquired a helping spirit or ally that lends him healing powers. In some respects the shaman is a seer or mystic, able

Massett shamans, Northwest Coast of Canada. Photograph by Dosseter. Courtesy Department of Library Services, American Museum of Natural History (Neg. 32960).

to experience the divine directly, while in other respects he is like a priest, performing elaborate rituals as part of healing ceremonies.

2. Spirit medium. Another common type of healer is the spirit medium, again male or female, through whom spirits appear, give advice, and bring about healing. The spirit medium has the ability to summon spirits, as does the shaman, and then empty herself to allow the spirit to appear and act in the world. In this process the medium is often completely passive, often remembering nothing of what the spirit said or did. The emphasis in this type of healer is on the power of the spirit that "replaces" or "possesses" her. It is the spirit that heals, not the medium. She is primarily a passive instrument. It is precisely when the medium is possessed and not herself that she exhibits healing power or is able to give healing advice. Skeptics have argued, however, that the medium is often far from passive and that the trance state is actually a condition in which she maintains considerable consciousness and control.

3. Priest or ritualist. The priest, priestess, or ritualist is also a very common type of healer. In cases where illness is understood to be the result of angering or offending a spirit or deity, the healing process may involve appeasing the spirit with ritual offerings and prayers. Priests are often understood to be servants of the gods and as such to know the proper rituals and prayers to supplicate the deities. In many cases, therapy involves primarily a ritual offering or supplication to a god or ancestor, which only a trained ritualist can perform.

4. Holy person. Some healers are believed to be effective primarily because of their innate or acquired sacredness, piety, or goodness. In many cultures, holy people (saints, ascetics, mystics) are sought out by sick people in the belief that they can influence their health. The touch or sight of such a person is believed to have healing effects. In some cases holy people attribute their powers to a god or spirit who works through them; in other cases both the healer and the people seeking help believe that the person has innate healing powers. Sometimes powerful political figures such as queens and kings are believed to have healing power.

5. Prescriptionist. Another type of healer found in many places is the specialist in preparing medicines—the prescriptionist. Often the prescriptionist may be an herbalist, a specialist in plants. Almost always, though, herbalist prescriptionists not only are experts in the natural properties of plants, they are also religious specialists who have achieved special rapport with plant spirits and who know the proper ceremonies and invocations to use in gathering and preparing plant-based medicines. Rarely are the ingredients of such medicines gathered without observing taboos and performing rites and prayers, and rarely are the medicines prepared without accompanying ceremonies. Some prescriptionists know little or nothing about plants and use primarily minerals or sacred substances or objects, such as verses from scriptures, in making their medicines. In these cases also, rituals and prayers are almost always essential in preparing effective medicine. The medicines themselves may be inhaled, imbibed, or worn as protective charms. In most cases, the recipient of the medicine is instructed to observe or perform appropriate rituals and prayers.

Chapter 2
Shamanic Healing

One of the most archaic types of religious figures is the shaman, and one of the shaman's most important functions is healing. Shamanic figures are prominent in the religious life of many technologically primitive cultures throughout the world—in Australia, Siberia, the Arctic, the Americas, and Africa. Such cultures may represent the most ancient styles of human existence. Even in more technologically advanced cultures, the shaman continues to be an important figure, while what we might term *shamanic features* characterize other types of healers throughout the world to the present day.

MASTERY OF ECSTATIC TECHNIQUES

As healers, shamans may be expert in a variety of medicines, especially plant-based medicines. They also may know about bonesetting, bleeding, massage, and other therapies, as well as elaborate rituals and how to make potent charms. That is, shamans may be characterized by skills and knowledge usually associated with other healers of the kinds mentioned in Chapter 1. From the shamans' point of view, however, healing power does not rest primarily on these skills. Shamanic healing power is dependent on mastery of spiritual techniques and the consequent ability to know and communicate directly with, even to travel in, the spirit world.

Foremost among these techniques is the shamanic mastery of ecstasy, the ability to enter a condition or state of consciousness in which the shaman is "beside herself" or "outside herself."[1] In most cases this ecstatic state is accompanied by a trance during which the shaman's soul (or living essence or inmost identity) transcends her physical body. Freed from the physical body, the shaman's soul can sojourn in

Kingiuna, Agiamiut shaman, Copper Eskimo, Canada. Photograph by Leo Hansen. Courtesy of the National Museum of Denmark, Department of Ethnology (Neg. 2019).

the spirit world. It can travel to heaven to converse with the gods. It can go to the land of the dead to communicate with the ancestors and spirits of the dead. In ecstatic trance, the shaman can see, converse with, do combat with, cajole, and otherwise influence the many spirits and forces that dwell in the spirit world or in the land of the living and influence the lives of human beings. The shaman can see and understand the actions and motivations of other spiritual masters (such as other shamans and sorcerers) who may be plotting against people or who may be actually undertaking spiritual attacks on people. In ecstatic trance, the shaman can also see into people—not only their true condition, their spiritual status, but also spiritual objects that may have been shot into them and are causing illness. The shaman, then, is an expert in ecstasy, which enables her at will to temporarily enter the spirit world and to understand and influence events there.

Cultures in which shamans are important affirm that spirits impinge upon the world of the living. Events in the world of human beings are influenced by spirit beings. The spirits in question may be deities, demons, ghosts, animal spirits, plant spirits, or ancestors. They also may be human beings with highly developed spiritual powers such as other shamans or sorcerers, either from within one's own culture or from outside cultures. The world that typifies the cultures of shamans is a world alive with beings whose presence is not always obvious but whose actions often directly affect the lives of human beings for better or worse.

Sickness (and health also, by extension) is often understood in these cultures to stem from spiritual causes or spirit beings. An angry god or spirit, a lonely ancestor or deceased loved one who is still hovering around the dwellings of the living, a jealous neighbor applying sorcery, or an animal spirit who is angry because of a broken hunting taboo are possible causes of illness. Often these beings make people sick by weakening or stealing their souls. If the soul is not recovered, if the malicious spirit is not stopped, the victim may wither and die. But how does one find a soul that has been lost, and how does one determine who has taken it and why? Only the shaman can answer these questions and act effectively because she can enter the spirit realms, converse directly with the spirits, see souls, and find souls that are lost.

INITIATION BY ILLNESS

Shamans are also the masters and knowers of illness. In many cases they acquire their powers by means of an initiatory ordeal. During this ordeal, shamans may undergo symbolic death and rebirth. This symbolic death and rebirth is often experienced personally and directly, in dream or trance, for example, or it may be experienced ritually and ceremonially. A shaman's rebirth marks him as a special being, one who has died to many human limitations and been reborn with special, superhuman powers.

It is quite common for shamanic initiatory ordeals to take place during serious illness. Put another way, it is often a very serious illness that functions as the initiatory ordeal in the life of a shaman. The case of the Ogalalla Sioux holy man Black Elk illustrates this. When he was nine years old he became extremely sick and had to be carried on a pony drag when his family moved camp. His arms and legs swelled badly, and his faced puffed up. Black Elk himself describes what happened after they had made camp that evening:

> When we had camped again, I was lying in our tepee and my mother and father were sitting beside me. I could see out through the opening, and there two men were coming down from the clouds, headfirst like arrows slanting down, and I knew they were the same that I had seen before. Each now carried a long spear, and from the points of these a jagged lightning flashed. They came clear down to the ground this time and stood a little way off and looked at me and said: "Hurry! Come! Your Grandfathers are calling you!"

> Then they turned and left the ground like arrows slanting upward from the bow. When I got up to follow, my legs did not hurt me any more and I was very light. I went outside the tepee, and yonder where the men with flaming spears were going, a little cloud was coming very fast. It came and stooped and took me and turned back to where it came from, flying fast.[2]

Black Elk. Photography by Joseph Epes Brown. Courtesy of the National Anthropological Archives, Smithsonian Institution.

Black Elk was taken on a tour of the cosmos. He met the powers of the four directions, the thunder beings, and other powerful sacred beings. From each of them he received a special object that would enable him to heal. From the Grandfather of the North, for example, he received the "herb of power" with which he was told he would be able to cure people of sickness. From another Grandfather he received a special pipe and was told that with it he would be able to make people well no matter what sickness afflicted them. Yet another Grandfather gave Black Elk the power to fly, that is, to travel outside his body. After this dramatic and extended tour of the spirit world, after having met the different divine powers and received their blessings, Black Elk returned to his family's tepee. As he approached, he saw himself lying there deathly ill. His mother and father were huddled close to him weeping. He entered his body, and from that moment on he became better and soon regained his health.

A similar initiatory experience occurred in the case of a Siberian Samoyed shaman. The future shaman became sick with smallpox and was unconscious for several days. He was so near death that funeral preparations were made for him. It was during this time that he underwent his initiation into shamanism. He was taken by a spirit guide to the middle of an ocean, and there his illness, the spirit of smallpox, spoke to him, saying that he would receive the power to shamanize. He was taken to different parts of the cosmos and given blessings by various deities. Of particular significance was his journey to the underworld, where he met the spirits of the dead, many of whom had died of illness. They tore out his heart and threw it in a pot. They took him to several tents, each of which housed the deity of a certain sickness, such as madness and syphilis. In these encounters the shaman-to-be learned about the diseases that afflict human beings.[3]

The story of the initiation of a woman from southern Africa is similar. The woman, named Dorcas, resisted the call to become a shaman and during this period was several times visited by spirits. She resisted for good reason, because in order to become a shaman in her culture one had to suffer serious illness. Dorcas herself said: "No one becomes a sangoma [healer with a powerful spirit] without first getting sick. Everyone who is called by the spirits gets the sickenss, a bad sickness. No one can become a sangoma who does not get this."[4] So she refused, but one day the spirit who would eventually become her helping spirit forced the issue. She herself describes the experience:

> When my spirit came I was sick—Oh! I was so sick! I lay in bed for three years—I could not eat or drink or even walk. I just lay there day after day and at night dreams would come! At night I would leave my body and my spirit would go far, far away to other places that my body never sees. My spirit would see so many things in the night. And then in the morning, before the sun comes up, my spirit would return to my body, and I would [lie] in bed another day.[5]

In these examples, which are typical of shamanic initiatory experiences, healers become qualified to heal because they have experienced serious illness deeply and completely and have overcome it, survived it, learned from it, and been transformed by it. In dealing with people who are sick, shamans can help because they have experienced what the patient is suffering and have mastered it.

SHAMANIC THERAPY: THE SEANCE

Shamanic healing often takes place in the context of a seance. The seance is used both as a means of diagnosing illness and as therapy. In both diagnosis and treatment, shamanic trance is central. In ecstatic trance, whether induced by drumming, dancing, and chanting, as in North America and Siberia, or by drugs, as in Central and South

America, shamans can often "see" inside patients and detect objects that have been shot into them. In trance, shamans also can determine what deity, spirit, or person has caused an illness and combat that being in order to heal the patient. Such confrontation or battle may be supplemented by massage or by sucking an object from the patient's body.

The seance is often dramatic and usually takes place in the patient's own dwelling, often at the patient's bedside. It may be attended by many people, especially relatives and friends of the patient. These people are often carefully incorporated into the healing rituals. Sometimes several shamans will be involved in a seance. It is usual for seances to be held at night. Most last several hours, many last all night, and some may take several days to complete. Shamanic healing seances are as much religious dramas as they are healing rituals.

Healing seances as they were practiced by the Paviotso, a North American tribe, illustrate many of these themes.[6] After agreeing to undertake a cure, the shaman interviews the patient (if he is conscious) concerning his recent actions. These may contain important hints concerning the nature of the illness, which is often related to morality and breach of taboo. At this point, the shaman also sets up a specially prepared stick with an eagle feather attached to the top. This marks the patient's dwelling as a sacred place and provides a signal to the spirits that a seance will take place at which their presence may be requested.

The shaman arrives, often with assistants, about nine o'clock in the evening. One of his assistants is a "translator," who repeats everything the shaman says. The shaman often mumbles quietly, and it is necessary to have such an assistant so the audience can understand what is being said. The shaman also may have a female dancer to accompany him in his own dancing or to dance by herself at certain points in the ceremony. Family members and friends may also attend. Preliminary rituals include walking around the fire, smoking a pipe that is passed around for everyone to enjoy, and chanting songs, which are "translated" and then repeated by the audience. These rituals are aimed at summoning the shaman's helping spirits and making contact with the spirit world.

At a certain point the shaman enters a trance. In some cases the aim of the trance is to find the patient's lost soul. If the patient is unconscious, it is almost certain that his soul has been lost and must be recovered for healing to take place. In other cases, the aim of the trance is to determine the cause and nature of the illness. While the shaman is in trance, the audience continues to chant, smoke, and pray. When the shaman returns from his trance, he relates in detail what he experienced. This may include a battle with a malevolent spirit that had stolen the patient's soul, or it may involve primarily an interpretation of certain images or symbols the shaman saw in trance that give clues to the patient's sickness.

Many seances include sucking an object from the patient with much ceremony and drama. Members of the audience sing songs and smoke a pipe, and the shaman and the dancer dance around the fire at intervals between suckings. At one point, the shaman produces an object (a pebble, insect, or worm) from his mouth and buries it. This is identified with the sickness-causing object in the patient. After the

Igjugarjuk, an Inuit shaman. Photography by Knud Rasmussen, 1922. Courtesy of the National Museum of Denmark, Department of Ethnography.

seance is complete, usually not until dawn, the shaman prescribes certain dietary restrictions for the patient and indicates what kind of decorative designs should be painted on his body to avert future illness.[7]

A central theme in shamanic seance is combat with forces that are afflicting the patient. Battles with hostile spirits often are dramatically described by the shaman while he is in a trance state, that is, while the battle is actually happening. Dialogue with the spirit being confronted is sometimes part of this performance, as are sound effects. In other cases the battle is recalled after the shaman has returned to normal consciousness. In some cases the shaman will rush out of the dwelling in which the seance is taking place and return later with dramatic tales to tell. The Danish explorer Knud Rasmussen described such a healing drama among the Iglulik Inuit. A shaman named Anarqaq was conducting a seance in which he was seeking to heal a young boy. At a certain point, Anarqaq lept up and ran from the dwelling. He continued to run until he was out of sight. He returned sometime later, after dark. His clothing was torn and his hands bloody. He gasped for breath and seemed completely exhausted. He fell down on the floor unconscious and gradually recovered his strength. Everyone gaped at him without speaking. When he regained consciousness he said that he had been attacked by the spirit afflicting the sick child and that he had defeated the spirit in a fierce battle.[8]

HALLUCINOGENIC DRUGS AND TRANCE

An important part of shamanic seances in many cultures is the use of hallucinogenic substances as a means of communicating with the spirit world. The use of mind-altering or mind-expanding drugs is especially common among South American shamans. These drugs are usually gathered, prepared, and imbibed in a ritual atmosphere and are treated as sacred substances. Indeed, the plants from which they are taken are often regarded as powerful spirits with whom the shaman has established an alliance or spiritual rapport. The plants are considered guides who help the shaman enter and travel in the spirit world.

Among the Tukano people of eastern Columbia, illness is cured by establishing communication with the spirit world, "with the forces that 'know' the remedies and solutions."[9] Taking certain drugs is the key to gaining access to the spiritual world, where these things are known or where one communicates with the spiritual beings who know these things. Although anyone can take these drugs, only the shamanic specialist can interpret the signs and comments of the spirit beings and arrive at the correct diagnosis and therapy for healing patients.

The Tukano attribute most illness to tensions and hostilities between people. In the context of interpersonal rivalry, people may employ their guardian spirits to make others ill. The shaman's task is to determine which spirits (and by implication, which people) are involved in illness and to combat the afflicting spirit. The shaman does this by entering the spirit world through a drug-induced trance. In trance, the shaman consults the powerful being Viho-mahse, who lives in the Milky Way, where he observes all the actions of humankind. He is the spirit of the hallucinogenic drug that the shaman imbibes. With the help of Viho-mahse, who communicates in images and mystical language that only shamans can properly understand, the shaman arrives at a diagnosis and cure for the sick person. He learns the correct formulas to invoke, which gems to use in treating the patient, and whether the patient should also imbibe some of the trance-inducing drug.

The healing seance takes place outside the patient's house during the day. Treatments include a variety of therapies: washing the patient with warm water infused with herbs, blowing tobacco smoke on the afflicted part of the body, invoking incantations to various spirits, and sucking out sickness-causing objects from the patient's body. Tukano shamans also employ gems in their treatments. Particular stones are believed to have certain healing qualities and are employed according to the nature of the sickness involved. Yellow chert (a flint-like rock), if properly manipulated by the shaman, is believed to invest the patient with vitality and fertility. Another kind of stone, if expertly moved over and around the patient's body, is sensitive to the presence of sickness-causing objects inside the patient. Properly manipulated, this stone tells the shaman where to suck the patient to extract pathogenic substances.[10] In some cases the shaman also encourages the patient to take hallucinogenic drugs and while in trance to talk about his sexual and social relationships. The shaman tries to relate the patient's illness to these relationships and will often give the patient what we would term moral or personal advice.[11]

CONCLUSION

The most distinctive feature of shamanic curing is the shaman's ability to gain direct access to the spirit world. Because illness so often is related to the spirit realm, the shaman is able to treat illness effectively because he or she is able to act in that world. The specific power or knowledge that enables the shaman to heal is often represented by a spirit guardian with whom the shaman has a special relationship. It is often through the spirit that the shaman diagnoses and treats illness. The central point is that the shaman heals because of the ability to bring to bear powers and knowledge of the spirit world. The shaman is the expert in contacting and understanding the dynamics of the spirit world.

The actual therapeutic methods of the shaman are certainly important for healing—purification, emetics, herbal treatment, massage, sucking, confession, moral instruction, and other techniques. In short, shamanic curing involves a variety of therapies and practices. A modern medical point of view probably would look to these therapies to explain any positive effects of shamanic healing. For shamanic cultures, however, it is not the therapies that are central to healing but the power to gain access to the spirit world and summon powers that reside there. The shaman's healing power resides in his or her spiritual or psychic rapport with spirits and their world. The focus is on the charisma of the healer, not on technical skills. The shaman heals because of expanded, developed spiritual powers.

ENDNOTES

[1]See Mircea Eliade, *Shamanism: Archaic Techniques of Ecstasy*, trans. Willard R. Trask (New York: Pantheon Books, 1964), pp. 13–32.

[2]Joan Halifax, *Shamanic Voices: A Survey of Visionary Narratives* (New York: E. P. Dutton, 1979), pp. 96–97.

[3]Eliade, pp. 38–39.

[4]Cited in John A. Sanford, *Healing and Wholeness* (New York: Paulist Press, 1977), pp. 67–68.

[5]Cited in ibid., p. 68.

[6]See Willard Z. Park, "Paviotso Shamanism," *American Anthropologist*, n.s., 36, no. 1 (January-March 1934): 98–113; summarized in Eliade, pp. 302–5.

[7]Eliade, pp. 302–4.

[8]Knud Rasmussen, *Intellectual Culture of the Hudson Bay Eskimos*, trans. W. E. Calvert, Report of the Fifth Thule Expedition, 1921–1924, vol. 7 (Copenhagen: Gyldendal, 1952), p. 43.

[9]Gerardo Reichel-Dolmatoff, *The Shaman and the Jaguar* (Philadelphia: Temple University Press, 1975), p. 103.

[10]Ibid., pp. 89–90.

[11]Ibid., p. 91.

Chapter 3
Individual Healers

EDUARDO CALDERON PALOMINO, "WIZARD OF THE FOUR WINDS"

A *curandero* is a traditional folk healer native to Central and South America. *Curanderos* combine several abilities and techniques in bringing about healing: the classic shamanic techniques of soul travel and contacting spirits, mastery of herbs, divination, elaborate rituals, manipulation of sacred symbols, and colorful drama. They often make use of power objects, some with clear Christian meanings, which are carefully arranged and displayed on an altar, or *mesa*. The kinds of problems *curanderos* deal with are serious illnesses, as well as cases of bad luck (financial ruin, for example), romantic problems, and family troubles (disrespectful children, for example). Illness, bad luck, and soured social relations are often believed to be caused by spirits or sorcerers, and the *curandero* is a specialist in dealing with such forces.

Eduardo Calderon Palomino is a *curandero* from Peru. He was born in 1930 and from an early age sought employment to help out his parents.[1] Between the ages of eight and fifteen he worked for his father making shoes. Then he worked in a slaughterhouse, as a cargo loader in a market, as a bricklayer, as a fisherman, and at several other jobs. He always showed an interest in both ancient ruins and art and for many years was employed at Chan-Chan, an archeological site, where he worked at restoring the damaged buildings and carvings. He also attended theological seminary at one point with a view to becoming a Catholic priest. Over the years he has become an accomplished artist, working with clay to make figures that are often inspired by ancient Peruvian traditions. He also is a skilled wood carver and potter. Eduardo is married and has a large family with whom he lives in the city of Trujillo on the coast.

An important part of Eduardo's success as a *curandero* probably derives from the fact that he is much more than a healer. He is a man of many talents, great experience, and considerable artistic ability. Healing is only one of his many interests. He is an important man in his neighborhood, very much honored and liked. In his role as healer he thus brings with him an aura of importance and respect. He is a charismatic figure whose presence dominates social and ritual affairs, whose views are listened to carefully, and who is consulted on important matters by neighbors and friends. Even as a child, Eduardo had dreams and other experiences that in retrospect indicated his affinity for becoming a *curandero*. In his dreams he sometimes would leave his body and travel about the universe, a common shamanic experience.

It was in the context of a serious illness, however, that Eduardo began to seriously consider becoming a healer. During a period of his life as a young man, when he was heavily abusing alcohol and seemed to lack any serious purpose in life, he became very ill. His body was covered from head to toe with eruptions that oozed pus. He lost all energy and interest in life and thought he was dying. Both of his grandparents were *curanderos*, and they decided to call in a woman who was expert in sickness caused by witchcraft. She was a great herbalist and prescribed a brew that quickly brought about Eduardo's recovery. Shortly after this dramatic recovery, Eduardo attended a healing ceremony conducted by a *brujo*, a sorcerer, aimed at freeing a man from a love spell. During the proceedings, a voice from the healer's *mesa* (a kind of altar) spoke to Eduardo, "calling" him to become a healer.[2] Eduardo identified the voice as Christ's. Subsequently he took a vow to serve all suffering people, whoever they might be, whatever their circumstances, without thought of gain.[3]

While much of Eduardo's healing is done through the prescription of herbs and by giving sensible advice to people, many patients are treated during seances that involve elaborate rituals and almost always take place at night. The seance is often preceded by a divination ceremony in which a guinea pig is killed and inspected for signs of the patient's problems. If the divination indicates the possibility of witchcraft, a seance may be in order to combat it. In these seances, Eduardo's *mesa* is set up, and he and the participants imbibe hallucinogenic drugs to induce a state of consciousness in which contact with the spirit world is possible. (The use of such drugs is common in much of Central and South American shamanism.)

The acquisition and preparation of the appropriate ingredients for the hallucinogenic beverage may involve elaborate rituals on the part of the healer. Eduardo's preferred plant is the San Pedro cactus (*trichocereus pachanoi*).[4] This and other plants used by *curanderos* are collected during pilgrimages to sacred places in Peru (often mountains). The plants are believed to contain, or actually to be, powerful spirits who must be propitiated and treated with respect before their powers can be released and utilized.[5] During a seance, the healer and the participants, in communication with the plant spirits, are able to "see" realities that are ordinarily hidden, to understand spiritual dynamics at work in their lives, or to perceive secret enemies who are hostile toward them. The San Pedro cactus and other plants, according to Eduardo, are able to expand one's consciousness and understanding and to put one in touch with what is traditionally referred to as the spirit world. The San Pedro plant is a night-blooming cactus, and by imbibing it at night during a seance, according to Eduardo, the recipient's consciousness also blooms, expanding and flowering, experiencing its full potential and receptivity.[6] Eduardo prepares the San Pedro beverage himself prior to seances.

Eduardo's *mesa*, which is also central in healing seances, is a symbolic microcosm in which the different spiritual zones and cardinal directions are represented. The *mesa*, which functions as a kind of altar, contains a variety of objects, each of which has its particular potency and symbolism. Bones, stones, swords, statues of saints, and many other objects adorn Eduardo's *mesa*. At the center is a crucifix. Each *curandero*'s *mesa* is unique, and each object has its special history, or "account," which relates the object in a particular way to the healer. Eduardo uses the analogy of a radio receiver in explaining the role of the *mesa* in the seance. By means of the healer's innate magnetism, which is believed to be greatly concentrated in powerful healers, he or she can establish direct contact with all areas and dimensions of the cosmos through the *mesa,* which incorporates the entire cosmos. The San Pedro beverage heightens the healer's magnetism and state of consciousness so that he can "play" the *mesa* and "tune in" to the inner rhythms of the cosmos. Through his ability to utilize the *mesa*, and with the blessing of the San Pedro spirit, the healer can contact the spirit world directly, see into it, converse with it, and manipulate it for the purpose of healing patients.[7]

In some cases, the healer makes contact with hostile spirits, often the spirit of a sorcerer who is abusing the patient and trying to disrupt the seance. In one such case, Eduardo grasped a sword from the altar, cut the air viciously with it several times while making swift, agile movements that formed the shape of a cross, and then explained that he had banished the spirit of the sorcerer who had been afflicting the young woman he was seeking to heal.[8] For Eduardo and his patients, healing involves spiritual struggle. His patients have been overwhelmed by malevolent forces that they refer to as spirits or sorcerers (and that we might refer to as economic misery, social malaise, interpersonal rivalries, or envy). Eduardo, astute in the ways of hostile beings (and of demoralizing and despiriting social, economic, and personal forces), brings his own powerful positive force to bear for the good of the patient, reenergizing that person, helping his consciousness bloom again, putting the patient in touch with healing forces.

"BABA," THE PIR OF PATTESHAH

In a small room within the compound of a mosque in a neighborhood of Delhi known as Patteshah, a very old man, known simply as Baba (father) to his patients, practices his healing profession.[9] In Muslim circles Baba is known as a *pir*, a wise elder. The room itself is cluttered with pots, jars, remnants of amulets, and other paraphernalia of Baba's profession. The furniture is minimal and includes a string cot, on which Baba himself usually sits, and an old couch, on which patients and members of their family sit. The room is dimly lit by a single electric bulb hanging from the ceiling. Baba himself is quite poor, and most of the patients he treats are also poor. Most of his patients are diagnosed as suffering from demon possession. Baba is an expert in treating such ailments and has a fairly widespread reputation in the city as an effective healer.

At a young age Baba began his apprenticeship with his master, whom he also refers to as Baba. He attributes his abilities to his master, and although his master died some years ago, Baba is still guided by him in dreams or special states of consciousness. His master began as the manager of a pharmacy but eventually took up healing full time. For many years Baba served his master, looking after his needs and learning his healing art and techniques. Having given over his life to the healing profession, Baba says, he decided not to get married. Baba stresses that both his family and professional lineages are special. His ancestors (who later fell on hard times), he claims, are descended from the seventeenth-century Moghul emperor Shah Jahan. His professional lineage (the line of his master and his master's master and so on) goes back to a famous *pir* who lived in Baghdad five hundred years ago.[10] Despite his modest surroundings and unimpressive demeanor, then, Baba claims to have inherited special characteristics that make him an effective healer.

A belief in the existence of malevolent spirits and their involvement in human affairs is a central part of the view of reality shared by Baba and his patients. In Muslim tradition, belief in spirit beings can be traced back to the Koran, which attests to the existence of *farishta* (angels), *shaitans* (satanic beings), and *jinn* (demons or spirits).[11] It is the *jinn*, whom Baba refers to as *balas*, who are his primary antagonists in his healing work. According to Baba, these mischievous, malign spirits are made of fire. They usually enter their victim's body hidden in food or drink, and once inside they drink the victim's blood and eat his flesh until the person dies. They also provoke their victim to antisocial acts such as illicit sex.

Baba says that *balas* attack individuals for two reasons. First, they may have been coerced or bribed to do so by a sorcerer; sorcerers are believed to enslave *balas*, who then must obey their every command. Second, a *bala* may attack a person out of sheer caprice, simply because it fancies that person as a victim. In neither case is the victim primarily responsible for his or her affliction. In the healing process this is important in disassociating the patient from the affliction, which is often mental ("this antisocial behavior is not really me"). On the other hand, it is also the case that being a good Muslim, which clearly has ethical and moral overtones, tends to be a good defense against attacks by *balas*. That is, while *bala*-inflicted ailments are not the fault of the patient, proper Muslim behavior, leading an upright, pious life, is good protection against *balas*.

Baba's primary diagnostic technique is the interpretation of patients' dreams. Like a Western psychoanalyst, he finds in dreams indications of his patients' problems. For Baba, dreams are one of the primary means by which human beings experience contact with the spirit world. If he diagnoses affliction by a demon, as he often

does, his therapy almost always involves invoking Allah's names and preparing medicines using sacred substances, such as verses from the Koran. Baba knows which of
the ninety-nine names of Allah are effective in healing particular maladies and which
Koranic verses are appropriate to use in preparing medicines or amulets for different
maladies. The name Al-Qadri, "lord of power," for example, protects against anxiety, while the name Al-Muhyi, "the quickener," is particularly effective in warding off
spirits.[12] These names, along with Koranic verses, are written down by Baba in special mystical diagrams that make use of the twelve signs of the zodiac, the twenty-
eight letters of the Arabic alphabet, and geometric patterns that have sacred power.
Baba then decides on the basis of his special knowledge of demons the most effective way for the medicine to be taken by or applied to the patient. In many cases the
patient wears the diagram around the neck as an amulet. In other cases the diagram
is burned and the patient fumigated with the smoke. The diagram may be dissolved
in water and drunk by the patient, or it may be bound up with a piece of cotton, soaked
in perfume, and then burned as a wick in a lamp.[13]

Baba's healing knowledge is only a small part of a much larger body of curative, healing wisdom known as *ilm-i-ruhani*, "soul knowledge," which is based on the
mystical practices of the Sufis, Muslim mystics. *Ilm-i-ruhani* consists of philosoph-
ical and religious answers to the basic human mysteries, such as birth, death, and suffering, as well as techniques that enable one to gain direct access to and control
over the spirit world.[14] This knowledge is usually passed on from one healer to
another, from a master to an apprentice. That is, it is knowledge that is best learned
from an experienced practitioner in actual healing contexts.

Familiarity with soul knowledge alone, however, is not enough to create an effective healer. Baba, and other healers in the same tradition, insist that this body of knowledge is ineffective apart from the healer's *ruhani-takat*, his "soul force." Baba
describes soul force in two differing, but complementary, ways: (1) as something the
healer himself cultivates and (2) as a gift or blessing from Allah, a kind of divine infusion. In speaking of this special quality as something healers acquire through self-
cultivation, Baba says: "Soul force requires many years of internal preparation. I have
already told you about the necessary service to teacher and devotion to God. Together with these you need purity, truthfulness and to develop selflessness and detach-
ment."[15] As a gift from Allah, Baba insists that soul force is not the possession of the
healer himself, but something Allah bestows upon him. He says: "Once a man
receives the soul force he starts running toward Allah and Allah too starts pulling him
toward him. Once their connection gets established then he only needs to concentrate
to get the soul force flowing through him."[16]

In his description of himself as a healer, Baba stresses the power of Allah and
minimizes his own abilities. He says, for example, that he only knocks on Allah's door
on behalf of his patients. It is then up to Allah to decide what to do. "My job is to
carry your voice to Allah. If he hears you then that is *your* good fortune. . . . I just
play the notes. Whether Alah will make music out of my efforts, only he knows."[17]
In this vein, Baba sees himself as a devotee of Allah, one who has cultivated his piety
over a lifetime and who petitions Allah on behalf of others.

KAU DWA AND WA NA, "COMPLETELY LEARNED" KUNG HEALERS

Among the Kalahari Kung of Southern Africa, every individual has the potential to develop healing powers.[18] To learn to heal is a normal part of Kung socialization. Indeed, a very great number of Kung do become healers. According to the Kung, healing power resides in the form of latent energy within most individuals. When this power or energy, which the Kung call *num*, is agitated and in their imagery begins to boil, it can lead to an altered state of consciousness called *kia*. It is in this state of consciousness that Kung healers are able to "see" sickness and to pull it out of individual sick people. It is also in the state of *kia* that healers have direct access to the spirit world. They see spirits, they see events at great distances, and sometimes they visit the abode of the gods.

Although Kung healers do not form a professional class and do not undertake healing as an alternative to the normal economic activities of hunting and gathering, they do posses characteristics that set them somewhat apart from nonhealers. They tend to be more emotional, more open. In Kung terminology, they are more *xga ku tsiu*, their hearts rise more, they are more passionate than others.[19] This is to be expected insofar as the arousal of *num* and entering *kia* are often described as involving an unwinding, unfolding, or untying of oneself. *Kia* involves the experience of *hxabe*, in which, as one Kung healer put it, "you spread apart your flesh. . . . It makes your heart sweet."[20]

Certain Kung healers are known as *geiha*, "completely learned," and the most powerful of all are called *geiha ama ama*, "absolutely completely learned," or "very powerfully completely learned."[21] The implication of this term is that accomplished healers have matured in some fashion, that they have come to understand very deeply certain human realities. Such healers are also sometimes referred to as lion healers. This is because they are believed to be able to transform themselves into lions or other beings. They are also believed to be able to travel directly to God's home in the sky. In this sense, they are characterized by shamanic qualities.

While Kung healers sometimes heal individuals in more or less private contexts, such as in their own families, healing is usually a public, community event in which the healer, having aroused his or her *num* and entered *kia*, will heal anyone or everyone who is present and requires it. Traditionally, no payment was given to healers, and it was (and still is, to a great extent) understood that the healer was a vehicle of healing energy that was meant to be given to the group as a whole. In the words of Kau Dwa: "The boiling num is painful and the work of healing is difficult. But that is what we have learned to do, and that is what we want to do. We drink num because we want to heal others of their sickness."[22] Kung healers cultivate their healing energy in what might be thought of as a kind of spiritual discipline. They do this not for their own benefit, however, but for the good of the group.

Two of the most powerful and respected Kung healers are Kau Dwa, an elder male, and Wa Na, an old woman, both of whom are completely blind. Kau Dwa says he was destined to be a healer from birth, that he began to develop his *num* while still

Kau Dwa, Kung healer. Courtesy of Richard Katz, *Boiling Energy: Community Healing among the Kalahari:Kung*, Harvard University Press.

an infant. "I was small and at the breast. . . . I was about three or four years old. I would cry and cry and cry. My mother would sing to me, and I would cry and suck the breast and cry. I just sat in my mother's lap and danced. I was afraid of num. Num was hot and it hurt."[23] Kung healers almost always comment on how painful it is to arouse *num* and how frightening it is to enter the state of *kia*. Kau Dwa also says that he received *num* from his father and that after this his father became weak and died.[24] The implication here is that healing power can be transferred from one person to another and that it may be hereditary. There is the implication also that loss of *num* means loss of personal health and vitality for the healer. Although Kau Dwa speaks of possessing *num*, and of having had *num* since he was a small child, he also speaks of it as something given by God, as something he asks for when he is healing. "I ask god for num. . . . I say to god, 'Here's my child, give me some num so I may put it into him.'"[25] Healing power, it seems, is something that is both intrinsic to an effective healer and something that is independent of him or her. It is a force that the healer either is able either to awaken in him or herself or has learned how to summon from the spirit world.

Although Kau Dwa is completely blind, he is able to see during *kia*. Indeed, he is able to "see" things at distances far beyond normal sight, such as lions prowling in the bush far away, and to "see" things that have happened in the past or will take place in the future. That is, in *kia* Kau Dwa is blessed with mystical vision that transcends or intensifies normal sensory experience. According to Kau Dwa, God took his eyes, making him blind, and put them in a small bag that God wears on his belt. When Kau Dwa enters *kia*, God descends from heaven, takes his eyes out of his bag, and puts them back in place, restoring Kau Dwa's sight.[26] When the healing dance is over and Kau Dwa returns to normal consciousness, God takes back his eyes and goes up to heaven. This striking image of acquiring special sight during healing trance emphasizes the fact that healing involves special insight into the dynamics of the spirit world and the spiritual nature of human beings. Healing involves the awakening of the senses, or of the mystical sense, in which the true nature of sickness can be perceived and effectively treated.

Kau Dwa speaks of healing as a contest between himself and spirits, often ancestral spirits, and sometimes between himself and God. The spirits and God want to take the living to the spirit world, that is, they want to kill them. The healer's job is to protect the living from the attacks of spirits. This often requires combat, in which the healer defeats the spirits and restores the sick person's soul. Sometimes, of course, the healer loses this battle. Kau Dwa says that God is sometimes selfish and wants the person to live with him in heaven, and in such cases healers may be ineffective. "You might be sick some day, and I, a healer, might pull and pull and pull you. But in spite of this, god may be selfish and take you away, and you will die."[27] Indeed, Kau Dwa on several occasions has had patients die in his lap while trying to heal them.

In speaking of Wa Na, a very old woman who is usually acknowledged to be the most powerful of all Kung healers, Kau Dwa says: "She just got it. She's just got the num and she'll die with it."[28] Although frail and blind, Wa Na's healing power

Wa Na, Kung healer.
Courtesy of Richard Katz,
*Boiling Energy: Community
Healing among the Kalahari:
Kung,* Harvard University
Press.

does not diminish, and she is sought after by many for healing. She is also an important figure politically. She has extensive kinship ties, and her father is said to
have been the first resident at the Goshe water hole, where she lives, and so she is
said to be the "owner" of the place. Her great age also enhances her prestige in the
eyes of the Kung.

Like Kau Dwa, Wa Na says that she has had her *num* for a long time and that
it was given to her by her father and another strong healer.[29] Wa Na acknowledges
the claim that she is a powerful healer and says that women are stronger healers
than men.[30] For many years Wa Na has undertaken healing dances almost every day.
Four or five other women are her regular supporters and sing and clap for her during
healing dances. Although Wa Na speaks of having received her *num* from other
healers, she also says that it is necessary to observe certain habits, especially certain
dietary customs, in order to preserve and enhance *num*. For her, healing power must
be carefully protected and cultivated. Though Wa Na's physical strength has great-

ly diminished, she was still a striking presence when she was described by Richard Katz some years ago:

> I happen to look around the dance area. Two old women are sitting on the periphery of the dance circle. One is full-bodied, the other somewhat thin. They both sit very still, almost impassive, their knees drawn up close to their chests, a blanket wrapped around their shoulders, each holding on to a tall walking stick. They are like ancient but proud statues.
>
> The full-bodied one is studying the dance. Then she methodically and laboriously raises herself up with the walking stick. Approaching the dance, she begins to move about, slowly, gracefully, with great dignity. She is dancing, but all she shows with her body is the suggestion of a dance step, the mere fragment of a dance gesture. Her presence, though, is unmistakable. This old, almost heavy body is floating along the sand's fragile surface. After no more than two minutes, she is again sitting down, still and silent. Her dance has emerged from a statue and returned to a statue in one continuous rhythm. That is my first contact with Wa Na.[31]

ABBA WOLDE TENSAE, AN ETHIOPIAN HEALER

Abba Wolde Tensae for many years was known throughout Ethiopia as a powerful healer who specialized in curing people afflicted by *zar* spirits.[32] Patients came from all over the country to seek his help, and in the course of his career he probably treated over one hundred thousand patients. In one survey, only fourteen percent of his patients came from his own village or its vicinity, indicating the extent of his fame.[33] Most of his patients came from far away, and thus for them (and their families who accompanied them) their treatment was undertaken in the context of a pilgrimage, a sacred journey in quest of healing.

Abba Wolde Tensae initially learned healing from his father. His impressive healing power was further enhanced when he entered the priesthood and became ordained. His healing effectiveness can be thought of both as inherited (from his father) and as bequeathed to him through the offices of the Ethiopian Orthodox Church. In the village of Ghion, about an hour-and-a-half drive from Addis Ababa, where he lived for many years, Abbe Wolde Tensae was an important figure in the church and a large landowner. But it was his role as a healer that made him famous and made the village of Ghion a pilgrimage center for thousands of afflicted people.

Abba Wolde Tensae was a large, imposing figure weighing about two hundred pounds. He had a long, black beard, and when he undertook his healing rituals, he wore a black robe, white sash, white cap (clerical garb), and sometimes black sunglasses. His attitude toward patients was paternal and authoritarian. He evinced an intense concern for his patients and expected respect and obedience from them. He also displayed an air of absolute confidence in his own diagnostic and healing abilities. In almost all cases, not surprisingly, his patients were diagnosed as having spirit-inflicted diseases.

Abba Wolde Tensae's treatment of such afflictions was impressive and apparently effective (there were very few patients who returned for a second treatment). He held healing ceremonies in a large room furnished with benches for patients and a raised pulpit from which he read passages from the Bible. There were often two or three hundred people at these ceremonies. Along the walls were crutches and canes left behind by those who had been healed. There were also jars of worms said to represent spirits he had exorcised and gifts given to him by satisfied patients. These items naturally enhanced and reinforced Abba Wolde Tensae's reputation as a powerful healer.

The pulpit from which he read was decorated with scriptural verses, a picture of Jesus, colored lights, and even a telephone. The service began by Abba Wolde Tensae reading from the Bible. It was not long until this scriptural "medicine" struck a hostile *zar* spirit and a patient/pilgrim cried out and fell to the floor. The patient was then brought to the front and placed directly before Abba Wolde Tensae. Sometimes the patient, possessed by the *zar* spirit, struggled violently and shouted and had to be restrained by attendants. Abba Wolde Tensae slowly came down from the pulpit and engaged the spirit in a dialogue:

ABBA WOLDE TENSAE: What is your name?

SPIRIT SPEAKING THROUGH CLIENT: Buda.

ABBA: What kind of devil are you?

SPIRIT: *Zar* devil.

ABBA: When did you take possession of this woman?

SPIRIT: Three years ago near a river while she was washing clothes.

ABBA: Why?

SPIRIT: Because she did wrong. She did not care for her baby properly. She left it uncovered to the evil eye.

ABBA: I command you to leave this woman now.

SPIRIT: No.

ABBA: You will. Howl like a hyena and leave her.[34]

The woman then did, indeed, let out a howl and fell on the floor thrashing about. After a short time she became quiet and was taken away to recover in another room.

When Abba Wolde Tensae was confronting and conversing with these *zar* spirits, he held a large wooden cross in one hand and placed his other hand in a pail of holy water held by an assistant. When rebuking or commanding the spirit, he alternately struck the patient with the cross and splashed her with handfuls of water. Under this barrage the demon usually surrendered and left the patient.[35] This usually took only about ten minutes; in one service Abba Wolde Tensae might treat ten to twenty people in this way. Although some patients may have received extensive subsequent treatment from him in the form of confession and counseling concerning proper behavior to prevent spirit possession, the vast majority were treated in the public services, which seemed to be effective in most cases. According to his own records, Abba Wolde Tensae treated about five hundred people every month. Fewer than fifteen percent returned for further treatment.[36]

MARIA SABINA, A MAZATEC HEALER

When she was visited by an anthropologist in 1977, Maria Sabina was eighty-three years old but still retained a reputation as a powerful healer among her people, the Mazatecs of Mexico.[37] She lived near the village of Huautla de Jimenez, close to the Mountain of Adoration (Nindo Tocoxho), in a small adobe house with three rooms. In the house were a few pieces of simple furniture and an altar. She was described at the time as having a worn, strong, brown face and a slight bend to her small body and to be dressed in rags like the poorest of the Mazatecs.[38] Twenty-two years earlier, another scholar who visited her described her as a woman "without blemish, immaculate, one who has never dishonored her calling by using her powers for evil . . . [a woman of] rare moral and spiritual power, dedicated in her vocation, an artist in her mastery of the techniques of her vocation."[39]

In her own account of her life, Maria Sabina said that her father, grandfather, and great grandfather were shamans who partook of the sacred mushroom *teonanacatl*, which blesses certain people with great visions. That is, she was a woman born into a shamanic lineage and thus, perhaps, predisposed to a particularly strong rapport with the great spirits associated with this sacred plant. In her own words, "the mushroom was in my family as a parent, a protector, a friend."[40]

Maria Sabina remembered that it was shortly after her father died, when she was only four years old, that she first ate some of the sacred mushrooms while she was taking care of the family animals in the forest with her sister. The mushrooms, according to Maria Sabina, entered her body and penetrated her soul. She described her first trance experience this way:

> The goats were grazing on the mountains, and I was there sitting on the grass as though drunk. My soul was coming out of my body and was going toward the world that I did not know but of which I had only heard talk. It was a world like this one, full of sierras, of forests, of rivers. But there were also other things—beautiful homes, temples, golden palaces.[41]

The mushrooms themselves appeared as playful children who danced and sang and answered Maria Sabina's questions with words of assurance and promises that they would help and protect her in the future, whenever she should call upon them. They would be her guardian spirits, her allies in her future career as a healer. Shortly after this experience, Maria Sabina encouraged her mother to teach her all she knew of the sacred mushrooms.

When she was only eight years old, her uncle became very ill, and Maria Sabina remembered the promise of the mushroom spirits. She ingested several of them, and they took her to their world, explained what was wrong with her uncle, and said that a particular kind of herb was necessary to save him. They took her to a place where this special herb grew and pointed it out to her. After returning to a normal state of consciousness, Maria Sabina went to the area that she had been shown in her dream, collected the herb, and gave it to her uncle, who subsequently recovered.[42] Many other cures followed this. In some cases, both Maria Sabina and the patient would ingest mushrooms and seek help and medical advice from the spirit world.

Maria Sabina temporarily ceased her healing art after she married and had three children. She simply did not have time, she said, to spend on healing ceremonies. After her first husband died, she remained a widow for thirteen years and was busy working to feed her family. Her second husband was a *curandero* who used herbs for healing. Maria Sabina had nine children by him. He was a violent man, often drunk, and beat her and her children regularly. He discouraged her from doing healing ceremonies and was jealous of her superior powers. Eventually he was beaten to death by a jealous husband whose wife he had seduced.

Maria Sabina said that the sacred mushroom resonates with one's soul. It enhances or intensifies the inclinations of one's soul. It does not reveal its secrets to everyone, and what it does reveal depends upon the nature of the seeker. In the context of trying to heal her sister, Maria Sabina ingested many mushrooms and had a particularly vivid vision. Her soul drifted off to the land of the spirits, and she was taken deep inside that world. A spirit appeared to her and asked:

"But what do you wish to become, you, Maria Sabina?"

I answered him, without knowing, that I wished to become a saint. Then the spirit smiled, and immediately he had in his hands, something that he did not have before, and it was a big Book, with many written pages.

"Here," he said. "I am giving you this Book so that you can do your work better and help people who need help and know the secrets of the world where everything is known."

I thumbed through the leaves of the Book, many written pages, and I thought that unfortunately I did not know how to read. I had never learned, and therefore that would not have been of any use to me. Suddenly, I realized I was reading and understood all that was written in the Book and that I became as though richer, wiser, and that in one moment I learned millions of things. I learned and learned. . . . Millions of things I saw and I knew. I knew and saw God . . . , the spheres that go slowly around, and inside the stars, the earth, the entire universe, the day and the night, the cry and the smile, the happiness and the pain.[43]

The cult of the sacred mushroom no doubt predates Christianity in Mexico but has become suffused with Christian symbolism over the centuries. A central legend concerning the holiness of the mushroom says that the mushrooms initially sprouted where Jesus once walked and drops of his blood fell to the ground. To ingest the mushroom is be infused with sacrality, to perform a kind of Eucharist in which the celebrant partakes of Christ's blood and is transported to the spirit world.[44] During a ceremony undertaken to heal a young man in 1958, in which she had ingested the sacred mushroom, Maria Sabina intoned a long chant describing herself as a woman worthy to receive special healing knowledge from the spirits.

> Daughter of Mary am I,
> Humble woman am I,
> Poor woman am I,
> Humble woman am I,
> Clean woman am I,
> Woman of clean spirit am I,
> Woman of good spirit am I,
> Woman of the morning am I,
> Woman of the day am I,
>
> . . . .
>
> Woman of justice am I,
> Woman of law am I,
> God knows me,
> The saints know me,
> Woman of the Southern Cross am I,
> Woman of the first star am I,
> Woman of the Star of God am I,
> For I go up to the sky.[45]

DON PEDRO JARAMILLO, "BENEFACTOR OF HUMANITY"

In southern Texas during the late nineteenth and early twentieth centuries lived a very popular healer, Pedro Jaramillo (died 1907). At the height of his career, people traveled hundreds of miles to see him. He received many letters every day requesting his advice on treating every imaginable kind of illness and tirelessly traveled the sparsely populated countryside on horseback to treat the sick. He charged nothing for his services and often refused money or gifts from the poor. He lived in a modest house and grew his own vegetables on land donated to him by a grateful patient. He lived frugally and was of a pious nature. He became affectionately known as the Benefactor of Humanity.[46]

Don Pedro undertook his career as a healer as the result of a serious illness when he was a young man. While working as a laborer on a ranch in Mexico, he was stricken with an infected nose. One night, in great pain, he walked out into the woods. Coming upon a small pond, he got down and put his face in the mud at the edge of the water. He found relief and remained at the pool for three days until he was completely well. His nose, however, remained disfigured. Descriptions of him often mention his disfigured nose, and it is often associated directly with his healing powers. Like many healers, Don Pedro seemed to have discovered his healing powers during his own serious illness. In this respect, he is another example of the wounded healer, a person who deeply understood sickness because he himself experienced it and overcame it.

After his nose healed, Don Pedro returned home and slept. A voice awakened him and said that he had received the gift of healing from God. He was also told that his employer had become sick and that he had the power to cure him. Don Pedro went to him and prescribed the first thing that came into his head, a bath in warm water each day for three days. This first patient recovered by following Don Pedro's therapy, and his career as a healer began. Throughout his career, Don Pedro said that he prescribed the first therapy that came into his head whenever he saw a patient. His therapies often involved water, which had been central in the cure of his own affliction. Sometimes he only prescribed a glass of water as medicine, sometimes daily baths in water, and sometimes water infused with medicinal plants. Don Pedro seemed to be able to intuit what was wrong with people. He would see a patient for just a few minutes and understand completely the nature of the person's ailment. Although it is likely that Don Pedro knew some of the prescriptions and rituals of traditional Mexican-American medicine, *curanderismo*, apparently his presence or the faith people had in him and his healing powers were effective alone. He does not seem to have studied medicine with a teacher. His medicines and therapies were unique to him.

The following account is typical of how Don Pedro operated. A young man, Dionisio Rodriguez, developed headaches so severe that they incapacitated him and he could not work. Unable to find relief from local doctors, he made the long trip to Los Olmos Ranch, where Don Pedro lived.

> When I saluted the curandero and told him that I was seeking a remedy for the sickness from which I suffered, he took a glass of water and offered it to me. I started to take it with my right hand, but he told me to use the other one. Immediately after drinking the water I felt a relief through all my body." [47]

The next day, after the patient had slept well for the first time in months, Don Pedro told him to collect pieces of a particular plant on his way home, boil the leaves in water, strain the water, and then bathe in it. He was also given pills to take while bathing. He recovered completely.

Don Pedro is remembered as often claiming that he himself had no healing power. He told his patients: "I have no healing power. It is the power of God released through your faith which heals you."[48] He even credited God with inspiring him concerning which medicines and therapies to prescribe. He also said that he did not charge patients for his services because he believed that God might take his healing powers away from him if he employed them for his own profit. He understood himself to be a servant of God sent to relieve the sufferings of his fellow human beings. Many people regarded him as a saint, and his picture can still be found in a place of honor in Mexican–American homes in southern Texas. Don Pedro was the holy-person type of healer, whose pious, saintly reputation attracted people and seemed to have a healing effect on them. It may have seemed to people that Don Pedro's estimable character was an appropriate instrument through which

God dispensed healing power. Whatever his patients thought of him, Don Pedro took no credit for himself.

ENDNOTES

[1]See Douglas Sharon, *Wizard of the Four Winds: A Shaman's Story* (New York: Free Press, 1978). A film entitled *Eduardo the Healer* by the National Film Board of Canada also features this healer.

[2]Ibid., pp. 13–14.

[3]Ibid., pp. 13–16.

[4]Ibid., p. 39.

[5]Ibid., pp. 34–38.

[6]Ibid., p. 48.

[7]Ibid., pp. 49–72.

[8]Ibid., p. 18.

[9]The following description is based on Sudhir Kakar, *Shamans, Mystics and Doctors: A Psychological Inquiry into India and Its Healing Traditions* (New York: Alfred Knopf, 1982), chap. 2, pp. 15–52.

[10]Ibid., p. 19.

[11]Ibid., p. 24.

[12]Ibid., p. 34.

[13]Ibid., pp. 34–35.

[14]Ibid., p. 32.

[15]Ibid., p. 37.

[16]Ibid., p. 36.

[17]Ibid., p. 33.

[18]The following section is based on Richard Katz, *Boiling Energy: Community Healing among the Kalahari Kung* (Cambridge, Mass.: Harvard University Press, 1982).

[19]Ibid., p. 235.

[20]Ibid., p. 203.

[21]Ibid., p. 239.

[22]Ibid., p. 245.

[23]Ibid., pp. 212–13.

[24]Ibid., p. 215.

[25]Ibid., p. 213.

[26]Ibid., p. 216.

[27] bid., p. 219.

[28]Ibid., p. 223.

[29]Ibid., p. 226.

[30]Ibid., p. 227.

[31]Ibid., p. 224.

[32]The following description is based on E. Fuller Torrey, *Witchdoctors and Psychiatrists: The Common Roots of Psychotherapy and Its Future* (New York: Harper & Row, 1986).

[33]Ibid., p. 121.

[34]Ibid., pp. 120–21.

[35]Ibid., p. 121.

[36]Ibid.

[37]This description is based on Joan Halifax, *Shamanic Voices: A Survey of Visionary Narratives* (New York: E. P. Dutton, 1979).

[38]Ibid., p. 129.

[39]R. Gordon Wasson, *The Wondrous Mushroom* (forthcoming); cited in ibid.

[40]Halifax, p. 130.

[41]Ibid., p. 131.

[42]Ibid., pp. 131–32.

[43]Ibid., pp. 134–35.

[44]Ibid., p. 195.

[45]Ibid., pp. 196–97.

[46]For Pedro Jaramillo, see Ruth Dodson, "Don Pedro Jaramillo: The Curandero of Los Olmos," in Wilson M. Hudson (ed.), *The Healer of Los Olmos and Other Mexican Lore*, Publications of the Texas Folklore Society, no. 24 (Dallas: Southern Methodist University Press, 1966), pp. 9–70.

[47]Ibid., p. 19.

[48]Ibid., p. 17.

Chapter 4
Healing among
the Kalahari Kung

KUNG SOCIETY

The Kung people of the Dobe area of the Kalahari desert in Southern Africa are among the most archaic and technologically primitive peoples of the world.[1] They number about 4,500 and live in a dozen or so independent, economically self-sufficient camps. During the long dry season, the Kung gather around water holes, the larger ones supporting several camps. The Kung are hunter-gatherers pursuing an economy and style of life that probably reflects that of our ancestors for thousands of years before the invention of agriculture.

For the most part, males do the hunting and women the gathering. Hunting is often unsuccessful, producing little or no food. Compared to gathering, it is risky and probably supplies no more than twenty to forty percent of the Kung's caloric intake. The women supply most of the food for their people by gathering the nutritious mongongo nut. In general, the nutrition of the Kung who follow this traditional way of life is extremely high, and anthropologists have described them as a particularly healthy group of people. Their life is by no means easy. Both hunting and gathering are strenuous activities, water is always scarce, and during the dry season especially they sometimes go hungry.

An important aspect of Kung life is sharing, especially sharing of food. Any individual feels free to depend on others for help in times of shortage. Although there are rules and rituals concerning the sharing of some things, particularly meat, a basic assumption of Kung culture is that people are responsible for each other. The Kung are also an egalitarian people with very little social hierarchy and very few extremely rich or poor individuals. As the Kung are nomadic, they accumulate few possessions, so there is little of a material nature with which to express prestige and hierarchy. Such prestige and hierarchy that do exist accrue to people who play important social roles or who have earned the respect of others.

Although there are gender roles among the Kung (men do the hunting and women the gathering, for example), Kung culture is marked by egalitarianism between the sexes. Relations between women and men seem relaxed, neither being subordinated to the other. Both women and men become political leaders and important healers. Men sometimes even do the gathering and women take part in hunting. Children are indulged and rarely punished and are looked after by all the adults in the camp.

A traditional Kung camp is a physically unimpressive sight. One can see from one end of the camp to the other, dwellings are makeshift, and the walls usually can be seen through. There is very little privacy. Women, men, and children are permitted free access to all parts of the camp, and movement and interaction are free and open. During leisure time, people sit about in small groups chatting and sharing food and tobacco. The Kung believe in the existence of a spirit world that is dominated by a great god, Gao Na, who lives in the sky. The spirit world also contains lesser deities and the spirits of the ancestors. The gods, spirits, and ancestors take an active interest in the life of the Kung and often are said to be the sources of illness and bad luck. As we will see, Kung healing is often understood to represent a defense of the living community against these beings, who try to lure the living into the realm of the dead to keep them company.

KUNG HEALERS

Healing pervades Kung culture and is one of the most important ways in which Kung social solidarity is affirmed. A high percentage of the Kung have developed healing powers; there is no professional healing class. Healers take part in the routine aspects of Kung life, such as hunting or gathering, and traditionally are not paid for their services. While some of those who develop healing powers have parents, uncles, or aunts who are healers, heredity does not seem very important in determining who becomes a healer. The Kung believe that healing power, which they call *num*, resides in most people and can be cultivated by anyone who possesses it. About fifty percent of males eventually develop their healing powers and become healers, while about ten percent of women become healers.[2] Everyone is a potential healer.

Normally, a healer's *num* is latent and is only aroused in particular settings or situations, usually a healing dance. The Kung use the image of boiling to describe the awakening of a healer's *num*. In the context of a healing dance, or in other healing contexts, the individual healer is able to stir up his or her *num* and get it "boiling." Once healing energy is aroused, it can precipitate an altered state of consciousness, which the Kung call *kia*. Arousing *num* and entering *kia*, almost all Kung healers agree, is very painful and often frightening. Indeed, the most common image used to describe *kia* is death. To enter *kia* is like dying. To become charged with *kia* is also sometimes described as being shot with many arrows.[3] It is also described by some healers as hot. Kinachau, an older Kung healer, said: "You dance, dance, dance, dance.

Then num lifts you up in your belly and lifts you in your back, and you start to shiver. Num makes you tremble; it's hot."[4]

The state of *kia* seems similar to trance states that are common to shamanizing in many other cultures. In *kia* the Kung healer can see directly into the spirit world, and some healers say they travel to the home of God in the sky, or travel underground, or transform themselves into lions. In *kia* healers experience expanded or intensified perception that permits them to understand the spiritual forces that impinge on human society and often cause illness. They can see the ancestral spirits, who gather near the dance ground. Healers can perceive the spiritual or true condition of individuals. Kau Dwa, one of the most powerful Kung healers, said: "When you kia, you see things you must pull out, like the death things that god has put into people. You see people properly, just as they are. Your vision does not whirl."[5] The Kung healer Kinachau put it this way: "When we enter kia, we are different from when our num is not boiling and small. We can do different things."[6] Another healer said: "When I pick up num, it explodes and throws me up in the air, and I enter heaven and then fall down."[7]

It is in the state of *kia* that healing is actually undertaken. In this altered or enhanced state of consciousness, Kung healers say they can see the illness inside people and are able to extract it. The term used to refer to this art of extracting disease is *twe*, which means "to heal" or "to pull out." In *kia* Kung healers will approach someone they perceive to be ill and rub their hands over his or her body and then in dramatic gestures throw their arms and flick their hands as if throwing away a dangerous substance. Because healing takes place during *kia*, when the healer can see directly into the spirit world, it appears that illness for the Kung is understood as a spiritual matter. Illness is understood as something that is sent by spirits, that debilitates one's vitality, and that must be "seen" and dealt with in an altered state of consciousness that involves insight into the spirit world.

HEALING DANCES

The usual context in which Kung healers work is a healing dance. The most elaborate is the Giraffe dance. These dances are regular events but are most likely to take place during the dry season, when several groups are camped around a spring. Healing dances are not considered distinct from everyday life. Like hunting and gathering, the healing dances are part of the Kung's routine. The dances begin in the late afternoon and last all night, reaching a climax during the middle of the night. The main participants are the healers themselves, the singers, and those wishing to be healed. Everyone, however, is invited, and most people in the camp take part. Since the majority of Kung healers are males, the dance is usually dominated by men, usually in their forties or fifties, when they are at their peak as healers. The singers are almost always women. Youngsters both sing and dance. Many young males take part to practice their dancing or cultivate their healing powers. The atmosphere is convivial, young people take the opportunity to flirt, and many people make jokes.

Kalahari Kung healing dance. Courtesy of Richard Katz, *Boiling Energy:*
Community Healing among the Kalahari:Kung, Harvard University Press.

    While many healing dances are small affairs, involving perhaps only the heal-
er, a patient, and a few friends or relatives, the Giraffe dance often includes fifty to
eighty people. Everybody attends, including infants and the very elderly. As many
as thirty women may participate as singers. Sometimes a Giraffe dance may be held
for a special occasion: to heal a very sick person or to welcome a visitor. Usually, however, the dance is considered part of normal Kung social life and is undertaken for no
particular reason. During dances, the healers employ a minimum of medical technology. They do use plants that are believed to contain *num*, the same healing power
that resides in healers. These plants are ground up, mixed with other ingredients, and
put in a turtle shell. The healer then puts a hot coal in the mixture and waves it over
sick people.[8] With the exception of this herbal incense, Kung healers rely on their own
internal healing powers to help the sick.
    The overall structure of the Giraffe dance is simple. No special preparations are
made to mark off a sacred space. The dance takes place right in camp. In the center of the dance ground, the women sit in a circle with their legs linked together to
form a human chain. Throughout the dance they provide the singing and clapping that
energizes those who dance. Around these women move the dancers, who include the
principal healers as well as those just learning to dance and adolescents showing off.
The principal healers often have distinctive steps and mannerisms indicating a certain
creativity and individuality associated with healing among the Kung.

Kau Dwa healing a Heroro woman. Courtesy of Richard Katz, *Boiling Energy: Community Healing among the Kalahari:Kung,* Harvard University Press.

It takes some time for the atmosphere to intensify. Usually around midnight, the first healers will begin to stagger about, shudder, and sometimes fall to the ground as their *num* boils up and they enter the state of *kia*. They then begin to go to individuals whom they discern to be sick (or they are guided to these people by others if they are not entirely steady, which is sometimes the case with healers in *kia*). They place their hands on the individual, usually one hand on the person's chest and the other on his or her back. Or they may move their hands all over the person in a kind of fluttering manner to "pull" sickness from the person. Often this "pulling" is painful to healers, and they howl or shriek in pain. It may take several hours for a healer to completely treat a person.[9] This healing treatment places a premium on physical contact. In addition to placing his hands on the body of the person being healed, the healer often sits behind the person and wraps his arms and legs around the patient. Sometimes the healer lies down on top of the person being healed or cradles the patient in his arms. The Kung say that the healer's *num* appears in the form of his perspiration. When *num* boils up it oozes out through the pores of the healer. The healer transmits this healing energy to the person being treated by bodily contact.[10] In the healing process a double transference takes place. The healer pulls the sickness out of the sick person and shakes it off and then infuses the patient with his healing energy.

During *kia* the healers say they see the spirits of the ancestors watching the dance just outside the dance ground. The ancestors are said to inflict sickness on the living because they want the living to keep them company in the spirit world. During *kia* the healer may address these spirits directly, telling them to leave the living alone, to go away and mind their own business.

Eventually the intensity of the dance subsides, the singing becomes softer, the healers gradually return to normal consciousness. Around dawn the dance ends.

AFFIRMATION OF LIFE

A healer often concentrates on one particular person in the healing dance, focusing his attention on that person for a long time. It is also the case that in smaller "dances" a healer may become preoccupied with healing the same person (perhaps a spouse or a child) over and over, perhaps daily over a period of time. In these cases Kung healing takes on a somewhat individual, healer-client character. In general, though, healing is undertaken not so much to heal a certain sick person as to heal the incipient sickness that resides in all people at all times. Healing dances are understood to be beneficial for everyone involved, including the healers themselves. The health of the group as a whole is implicated in the Kung emphasis on healing. Healing dances are not just undertaken in the event of serious illness or because a particular healer or sick person requests one, although this might be the case on occasion. The dance is a natural, routine way in which the Kung prevent incipient illness from maturing into serious illness.

The Kung say that illness is often caused by ancestors who want the living to join them in the spirit world. They exert constant pressure, or a constant pull, on the living. These spirits are actually seen by the healers when they are in *kia*, and healers often recognize individual ancestors and know which member of the living community they are attacking with illness. The experienced healer Kaha told of the following encounter with such an ancestral spirit:

> I cured Tankau. He had a strained back. Tankau's father, who was dead, appeared to me as a spirit and said to me, "My son must stop digging the well." Tankau had been digging a well. His father, the spirit, had made him strain his back. Then Tankau said, "How can I quit that job of digging the well. We need the well." Then I said to the spirit, "How can you chase this man from his work?" and I refused the spirit and took out the pieces of metal embedded in Tankau's back. I pulled the pieces of iron out and gave them to his father, the spirit, and said, "Take these pieces of metal away! Are you stupid? You worked in your day, and now your son follows you. You can't take someone from his work. Go away! Go away!"[11]

In another case, a woman performed healing night after night on her husband, who was diagnosed by a visiting Western doctor as having cancer. According to the woman, her husband's father was seeking to bring about his death. Her message to her husband was this: "Your dead father is trying to take you away. Those who are still alive have been mean to you. Your dead father is going to deprive them of you. You've been good all your life. I begged your dead father to give those who are still alive another chance to be good to you. Your dead father agreed, and spared you tonight."[12] Here, the pull of the ancestors is related to the behavior of the living. The message to the relatives and friends of the sick man is that they should join the healer, the man's wife, in supporting him in his illness and affirm how they appreciate and respect him. This will give the patient support, kindle his will to live, and lessen the power of the spirit of the sick man's father, who seeks to pull him into the land of the dead.

For the Kung, then, healing wards off the pull of death, which is constantly exerted by the ancestors and affirms the vitality of the group. Healers exert themselves for the good of the entire community, even when they are focusing their healing powers on a particular individual. Traditionally, the healer's services are not for sale, and healing is not undertaken as a profession by means of which one can earn prestige and opt out of normal economic activities. Healing is something that often involves pain and suffering on the part of healers (all Kung healers emphasize this). This suffering is undertaken on behalf of the group as a whole. Although healing powers can be narrowly focused on one individual, it is also clear that healing power is diffuse and radiates, as it were, in such a way that all participants are enhanced and empowered by it. For the Kung, healing dances are affirmations of life on the part of the community, testimonies to the vitality and vigor of the group, and a collective refusal to give in to the debilitating forces of illness and death. For the Kung, healing is a dance of life.

ENDNOTES

[1]The following description of the Kung and their healing dances is based primarily on Richard Katz, *Boiling Energy: Community Healing among the Kalahari Kung* (Cambridge, Mass.: Harvard University Press, 1982). Their way of life was undergoing "wrenching" changes even as he recorded it.

[2]Ibid., p. 35.

[3]Ibid., p. 99.

[4]Ibid., p. 42.

[5]Ibid.

[6]Ibid.

[7]Ibid., p. 44.

[8]Ibid., p. 39.

[9]Ibid., pp. 40–41.

[10]Ibid., p. 107.

[11]Ibid., p. 112.

[12]Ibid., p. 50.

Chapter 5
Healing Ceremonies among the Navaho

THE BEAUTYWAY CHANT

The Navaho are the largest group of native Americans in the United States, numbering around one hundred thousand. They live in the Southwest in an eroded plateau country in northwestern New Mexico and northeastern Arizona. They have lived in this area for nearly a thousand years. Initially, they lived by hunting and food gathering, but eventually they adapted to agriculture and animal husbandry. In recent years their economy has been supplemented by work off the reservation and by small industries on the reservation.

Despite increasing accommodation to white culture, the Navahos have preserved to the present day a traditional way of life in which healing ceremonies remain central. These ceremonies, usually referred to as chantways, are among the most impressive expressions of traditional Navaho religion and culture. They incorporate Navaho mythology and symbolism and are almost always concerned with restoring harmony that has been lost as a result of sickness. They are usually undertaken at the request of and for the benefit of an individual Navaho "patient." In this sense, we can think of traditional Navaho culture as having a dominant concern for sickness, health, and healing.

According to the Navaho, illness arises for several reasons. It may be caused by bad dreams containing inauspicious omens such as death, fire, or snakebite. It may arise because of excess in some activity, such as too much sex, hoarding food, wealth, or property, or preoccupation with one thing or person. It may result from ignorance of and transgression against ritual rules. It may come about because of contact with the dead or with something connected with the dead, even dead animals. If a person comes in contact with a place where an animal was recently killed, for example, he may become ill. The most feared source of sickness (and one of the most common) is witchcraft. The universe of the Navaho contains many things that are harmful. Contact with them can cause disharmony and sickness. Ghosts, certain animals or weather conditions, and even the gods themselves are dangerous in some circumstances and can cause bad luck, illness, or death if the proper rituals, taboos, or ceremonies are not observed or undertaken.[1]

Illness is an indication of imbalance; healing is the restoration of harmony in the sick person. Nearly every danger can be protected against or attenuated with the proper ceremonies, which have been given to human beings by the gods, the Holy People, for just such restorations of harmony. The rituals aim at restoring harmony on a grand, cosmic scale and in the process are effective means for restoring an individual's health. The rituals must be performed correctly in every detail as a precondition for their effectiveness, but if so performed they are understood to be extremely powerful means for reestablishing health and well-being.[2]

Before engaging a Navaho singer to perform a chantway, the sick person or his or her family must determine the cause and nature of the illness to determine if a chantway is called for and, if so, which chantway is most appropriate. The cause of illness is usually determined by divination. The diviner often asks many questions about the patient's (and the family's) recent activities to find out if misconduct or breach of taboo is involved. The diviner will then perform a divination ritual for a clue to the cause of the disease. Certain images, symbols, or omens indicate the particular cause of illness and imply which chantway is the most appropriate cure.[3]

Navaho chantways are extremely complex and may take as many as nine days to perform, so chanters only know one or two. Although as many as forty-three names of different chantways have been recorded from Navaho informants, only about ten are well known and performed today.[4] The Navaho chanter is a master of ritual and must have a prodigious memory to learn a chantway. Doing so has been compared to the task of memorizing a complete opera of Wagner, including the part for each instrument, every vocal part, the staging, and the costuming.[5] Increasingly, it is difficult to find chanters who know the chantways, and most competent chanters are now quite old. Having determined the appropriate chantway to be performed for the particular patient, and having found a chanter who knows and is willing to perform it, the stage is set for an ancient and dramatic Navaho religious event.

The healing ceremony takes place at the patient's own hogan. The chanter may have assistants, and in addition to the patient and his or her family the ceremony as a public event may attract and involve hundreds of people, who will join in the singing and chanting at certain points in the ceremony. Navaho chantways are sometimes divided into Holyway and Evilway types of ceremonies. The theme of attracting goodness and holiness is dominant in the former type of chantway, and exorcising evil dominates the latter type of ceremony. Both themes, attracting good and expelling evil, however, are evident in nearly all Navaho chantways. As representative of a Holyway chant, let us look at the main ceremonies that constitute the performance of the Beautyway chant.

Much of the performance is done at night and may take as many as nine nights to complete. The priest-singer who organizes and performs the Beautyway chant begins by sacralizing the patient's hogan. He (most of the singers are males) does this by placing cornmeal and sprigs of oak on the roof beams to mark the four quarters. Thus the patient's home is marked off as an appropriate place for the Holy People to visit and bring about healing. The home becomes an altar, as it were, where sacred ceremonies will be performed, where divine presences will appear, and where mythological events will be reenacted.

The patient is also purified so that the Holy People will be attracted to the place. The Holy People dislike impurity and will not respond to the priest-chanter's summons if participants have not been purified. The patient is purified by sweat and emetic rituals and on the last day by a yucca-root suds bath. The sweat and emetic rituals are done every day of the ceremony to keep the patient (and sometimes other participants) in a state of high purity. These rituals take an hour or two to complete. According to the Navaho, one can expel impurity, which is strongly associated with illness, by sweating or vomiting it out. A huge fire is kindled with a fire stick (denoting archaic purity) and the patient bundled in heavy blankets to induce sweating. At the same time he or she is given an emetic to induce vomiting. After these rituals, the priest-chanter sprinkles the patient with a fragrant lotion.

At an early point in the performance, the priest-singer unravels his sacred bundle, which contains the necessary ritual objects, and sets up prayer sticks, which are decorated in colorful fashion. This signals to the Holy People that a healing ceremony is about to begin and that their presence is desired. In setting out his holy objects, the singer also begins the construction of a sacred microcosm that will contain the essential components and powers of the cosmos at large. Divine powers will be concentrated within this potent area for the benefit of the patient. In some of the longer ceremonies, an elaborate sand painting is constructed later on to enhance and intensify the theme of constructing sacred space.

From an early point in the performance, the priest-singer (sometimes accompanied by his assistants and others present) chants hymns, prayers, and excerpts from Navaho mythology. This continues throughout the ceremony more or less nonstop. These chants are often aimed at visualizing certain Navaho gods. By describing and invoking these deities in detailed, repetitive chants, the singer gradually identifies himself with the deity and thereby makes the deity present. An example of an excerpt from such a chant is as follows:

O Male God!
With your moccasins of dark cloud, come to us.
With your leggings of dark cloud, come to us,
With your shirt of dark cloud, come to us,
With your head-dress of dark cloud, come to us.
With your mind enveloped in dark cloud, come to us.
With the dark thunder above you, come to us soaring.
With the shaped cloud at your feet, come to us soaring.

With the far darkness made of the dark cloud over your head, come to
   us soaring.
With the far darkness made of the he-rain over your head, come to us
   soaring.
With the far darkness made of the dark mist over your head, come to
   us soaring.
With the far darkness made of the she-rain over your head, come to us
   soaring.
With the zigzag lightning flung out on high over your head, come to us
   soaring.
With the rainbow hanging high over your head, come to us soaring.

With the far darkness made of the dark cloud on the ends of your
   wings, come to us soaring.
With the far darkness made of the he-rain on the ends of your wings,
   come to us soaring.
With the far darkness made of the dark mist on the ends of your wings,
   come to us soaring.
With the far darkness made of the she-rain on the ends of your wings,
   come to us soaring.

With the zigzag lightning flung out on high on the ends of your wings,
   come to us soaring.
With the rainbow hanging high on the ends of your wings, come to us
   soaring.
With the near darkness made of the dark cloud, of the he-rain, of the
   dark mist, and of the she-rain, come to us.
With the darkness on the earth, come to us.[6]

Offerings are also made to the Holy People throughout the chant in order to
please and attract them. The usual offerings are tobacco, cornmeal, and prayer sticks.
These are set out at various places around the hogan.
       Throughout the long Beautyway chant, nearly every action is accompanied by
singing. The priest-chanter leads these songs by shaking a rattle, and anyone who knows
the songs is invited to join in, which many do (usually men). The Beautyway chant
requires the priest to know hundreds of songs. At certain points in the chant, the participants eat small amounts of corn pollen and inhale smoke made by putting herbs on
a fire. Medicines are also taken from special, ritual cups made of abalone or tortoise
shell. Sometimes a bullroarer is swung around to make the noise of thunder.[7]
       Perhaps the most dramatic part of the Beautyway chant takes place when the
patient is placed on the elaborate, delicate sandpainting, which depicts an appropriate Navaho deity or some event in Navaho mythology. This "painting" is made with
pinches of colored sand by the priest-chanter or an assistant. As it is highly perish-
able, it is mostly obliterated when the patient is placed upon it. At this point in the

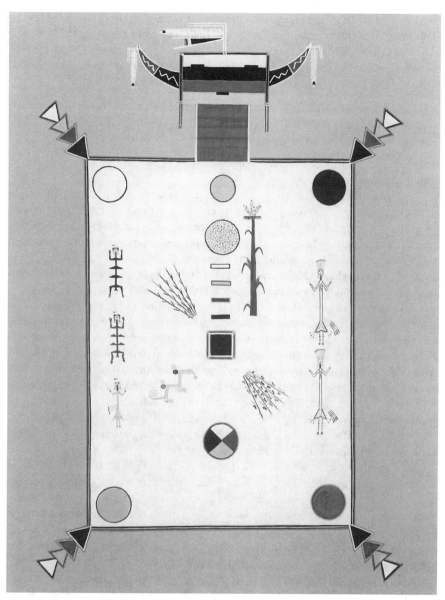

Blessingway, the White Spirit Land. Sandpainting. Courtesy of the Wheelwright Museum of the American Indian, P1. 17.

chant, however, the aim is to identify the patient with the sacred figures depicted in the painting. As the figures in the painting are obliterated, they are transferred to the patient.

Accessory rites may be incorporated into the Beautyway chant (or any other chant) at the request of the patient. An example is the Shock rite. This involves the ritual eating of cornmeal mush or a meat and herb stew. The rite is intended to lend the patient stability in the presence of powerful, supernatural things that are made present in every chantway or with which the patient may have come in contact prior to the chant. The rite is supposed to give the patient confidence.

CENTRAL THEMES

Two themes central to healing in traditional cultures are clearly expressed in the Navaho chantways.

1. An important preoccupation in these ceremonies is purification. The sweat and emetic rituals are done daily, and a more elaborate bath is undertaken near the end of the chant. A main aim of the ceremony seems to be achieving cleanliness or purity. The emphasis on bathing reiterates Navaho mythology. When the first human beings emerged from the earth, the Holy People required them to bathe to rid themselves of offensive odors. Odors offensive to the Holy People are associated with impurity, the profane, and ugliness and are assiduously combated in Navaho chantways.

The Navaho also believe that illness is caused when sorcerers shoot arrows into the victim's flesh. These arrows are impure and polluting. They can be removed be means of sweating. Fasting is also employed as a way of preparing oneself to be visited by the Holy People or purifying oneself to receive their healing power. Sometimes these fasts last twenty-four hours and include total abstention from food. Sexual abstinence may also be observed. In general, the restraint of normal bodily functions is part of a process that aims at purifying the individual and making him or her receptive to divine healing power. Before the gods will bestow this power, the patient must first become a clean, pure, holy vessel. For the Navaho, healing involves the expulsion of dirt and the ingestion of purity.

2. Another important theme, suggested in the emphasis on purification, is attracting the holy and identifying with the gods. Attracting the holy is partly accomplished by re-creating the world during the ceremonies. The long, detailed Navaho creation myth tells of the gradual creation of the world. To restore harmony, beauty, and health, this myth is reiterated in the ceremony, and the world is ritually re-created—fresh, harmonious, beautiful, without flaw. As part of the re-creation, the patient is restored also. Particularly in the Holyway chants, there is also a strong emphasis on summoning the gods to the ceremony to infuse their healing powers into all involved, especially the patient. The priest-chanters themselves identify with the gods by invoking them in their repetitive chants and reiterating their deeds in Navaho mythology. The theme of identifying the patient with the gods is concretely dramatized in the part of the ceremony employing the sandpainting. In deliberate, detailed ritual gestures the patient is identified with the deity depicted in the painting. The priest-chanter, for example, takes pinches of sand from the limbs of the painted deity and applies the sand to the corresponding parts of the patient's body. When the ritual is complete, the painting has been transferred to the patient. The patient has

become the painting; the painting has become the patient. The patient has entered the sphere of the Holy People, has entered the spirit world, and has there found harmony and healing.

The overall aim of Navaho chantways is to restore harmony, typically referred to as beauty, to a particular person. This person may be suffering from a severe illness, but not necessarily. It is common, for example, for a person who has been away from the Navaho traditional territory for a long time to undertake such a chantway to restore her balance. A person who has committed violent deeds or distasteful actions might feel that he has lost his inner, essential harmony. When young Navaho men return from United States military service, for example, they often undergo a chantway to restore their inner harmony. Sickness is interpreted as a symptom of a deeper malaise, being in disharmony with the cosmic and moral order. An important part of a Navaho chantway involves the patients themselves affirming that this harmony has been restored. As in most other cultures, it is important for the patient to affirm for him- or herself that health has been restored, that he or she is "feeling better." At the conclusion of the Navaho chantways, then, the patient testifies that things are better, that beauty has, indeed, been restored. The following is an example of such an affirmation:

> In the house of long life, there I wander.
> In the house of happiness, there I wander.
> Beauty before me, with it I wander.
> Beauty behind me, with it I wander.
> Beauty below me, with it I wander.
> Beauty above me, with it I wander.
> Beauty all around me, with it I wander.
> In old age traveling, with it I wander.
> I am on the beautiful trail, with it I wander.[8]

ENDNOTES

[1]Gladys Reichard, *Navaho Religion: A Study of Symbolism* (Princeton, N.J.: Princeton University Press, 1950), p. 82.

[2]Bernard Haile, Maud Oakes, Laura A. Armer, Franc J. Newcomb, and Leland C. Wyman, *Beautyway: A Navaho Ceremonial* (New York: Pantheon Books, 1957), p. 6.

[3]Reichard, p. 99.

[4]Haile et al., p. 13.

[5]Bert Kaplan and Dale Johnson, "The Social Meaning of Navaho Psychopathology and Psychotherapy," in Ari Kiev (ed.), *Magic, Faith, and Healing: Studies in Primitive Psychiatry Today* (New York: Free Press, 1964), p. 223.

[6]Donald Sandner, *Navaho Symbols of Healing: A Jungian Exploration of Ritual, Image, and Medicine* (Rochester, Vt.: Healing Arts Press, 1979), pp. 89–90.

[7]Haile et al., pp. 9–10.

[8]Sandner, pp. 64–65.

Chapter 6

Healers and Healing Rituals among the Zinacanteco

The Zinacanteco are a group of Mexican Indians, numbering about 7,600, who live in the township of Zinacantan in the State of Chiapas in southwest Mexico.[1] Linguistically and culturally they are related to Mayan traditions. They live in the highlands in small communities and support themselves primarily by cultivating maize. They have a distinctive culture and dress and have limited contact with Spanish-speaking lowland peoples, whom they refer to as Ladinos. A typical Zinacanteco household may include more than one related family and forms the basic unit of their society. Such a household is called a *sitio* and usually consists of an extended patrilineal family. Clusters of such households form a hamlet, which may number from about 120 to 1,300 people.[2]

The Zinacanteco are nominal Catholics, but their religion is a mixture of Roman Catholic and Mayan elements in which the latter dominate. In Zinacanteco cosmology the world has three layers: the underworld, where live powerful beings called earth owners, who are like Ladinos in appearance and can afflict the living with illness; the middle layer, the realm of the living; and heaven, which is above the realm of the living and where live two principal deities, the sun (male) and the moon (female). Mountains represent an intermediary zone between the realm of the living and heaven and are inhabited by powerful, subsidiary, ancestral deities who are the immediate objects of many Zinacanteco rituals and petitions, especially healing rituals. A host of spirits visit, impinge upon, or dwell permanently in the realm of the living. Many of these beings take an active interest in human beings and interact with them on a regular basis. Among the most important of these beings are the spirits of the ancestors, who usually are implicated in negative influences, and the saints, who usually are petitioned for help and protection. Sorcerers are also implicated in causing illness.

Zinacanteco healers are called *hilol* and may be men or women. Generally, they become healers because they have been chosen by the gods. Healers describe being summoned by the gods to their abodes in the mountains and told that they must become healers or sicken and die. The candidate is often instructed in healing knowledge and techniques during dreams. The *hilol*, then, is divinely elected to his profession. The *hilol* certainly learns healing techniques, the most important of which is "pulsing," but his healing power is understood to be primarily something that is bestowed as a gift from the gods. The *hilol* is initiated in his healing career by direct contact with the spirit world, contact that remains central in Zinacanteco healing. In this sense the *hilol* has shamanic characteristics. The *hilol* also must master elaborate rituals and by doing so takes on a priestly role as healer. Both as shaman and as priest, the *hilol* is clearly and primarily a religious specialist more than a medical technician (although individual healers may know much about herbal remedies and bonesetting).

The immediate cause of illness among the Zinacanteco is usually explained in terms of soul loss or weakening of the soul. Why the soul of the sick person is stolen or weakened, and who (or what) has caused the soul's loss or weakening, is almost always related to the behavior of the patient. For the Zinacanteco, a basic assumption is that one's physical condition, one's health or lack of it, reflects the condition of one's relationship with other human beings and the spirits of the Zinacanteco cosmos. One's physical condition reflects how well or badly one is getting along in society at large (which includes human and nonhuman dimensions). Each individual is involved in relationships with other human beings and with spirits. When sickness arises, it is assumed that one of these relationships is under stress, has become hostile, or has completely broken down. The assumption often is that the sick person has offended, insulted, or harmed some person, spirit, or deity and is being chastened because of this. Sickness is prima facie evidence that the sufferer's relationships, human or nonhuman, are in disarray.[3] Sickness, then, is only part of a much larger picture; it is a visible symptom of a complex, dynamic social process that is an ongoing drama. Ideally, this drama tends toward harmony and health, but it can be disrupted because of human malice, envy, or ignorance. Understood in this general framework, it is clear that illness for a Zinacanteco is an occasion for reflecting on his or her relationships with other human beings and the gods. The healer often plays the role of guide in helping the sick person to undertake this reflection.

A sick person consults a healer when she determines that the illness has evil portents. Naturally, an important factor in this determination is one's physiological condition. One normally seeks a healer only if one is physically sick. But the primary concern seems to be to determine who or what has "sent" the illness. The healer urges the sick person to pay particular attention to dreams, in which messages from the gods and spirits may be sent. Then the healer carefully queries her about dreams. In the vast majority of cases, the healer whom the patient contacts for help is a relative, friend, or at least an acquaintance who lives within a few hundred yards of the patient's own house.[4] It is highly likely, then, that the healer will be extremely well informed about the patient and her social relationships and recent behavior.

Zinacanteco healers depend on a technique called pulsing to determine both the nature and cause of an illness and the proper therapy for treating it. Pulsing involves "listening to the blood" by taking a person's pulse. Illness is something that enters the blood and influences its strength and flow. By means of heightened sensitivity to pulses, healers claim to be able to feel or hear divine messages concerning the patient's illness. The blood tells the healer not only what has caused the disease but what kind of treatment is necessary, for example, how many candles should be burned and whether shrines or sacred mountains should be included in a pilgrimage.[5] It is as if the blood represents the patient's spiritual or inner voice, which communicates its condition to a healer conversant with its "language."

If spirits are implicated in the cause of the illness and rituals are necessary for a cure, which is often the case, the healer assembles the necessary materials and arranges for the patient's family members or relatives to assist in the healing drama that will take place. The healing drama may last for many days, and from beginnig to end the patient is the center of attention and is treated with great concern and deference. The patient is believed to be in great danger, as she has already been attacked by spirits and is in a weakened, vulnerable state. The patient is greatly restricted in her movement and must be guarded and served by assistants throughout the ceremonies. She is not allowed outside of her house, is instructed to talk very little and in a soft voice, and is never left alone in the dark. The healing process underlines the centrality of family and community solidarity in combating illness among the Zinacanteco.[6]

Much of the healing drama takes place in the patient's own house. The healer sets up an altar that includes candles, flowers, and a censer and places plants and flowers around the patient's bed and an arch of pine boughs over it. The healer thus marks off the patient's house as a sacred place within which rituals dealing with supernatual power can be performed. The patient undergoes purification rituals from the start. She is bathed with water from sacred wells and infused with healing herbs and is dressed in clothes freshly washed and censed by members of the family. The aim of these rituals is to refresh and renew the patient by washing away physical and moral "dirt."

In the early stages of the healing ceremony, a chicken of the same sex as the patient is selected. It is bathed and censed in the same manner as the patient. Then its throat is nicked and some of its blood applied to the patient. Later in the ceremony the chicken is released as an offering at a sacred shrine. Near the end of the ceremony another chicken is sacrificed to the gods. Throughout the ceremony the chickens are identified with the patient in such a way that the patient receives their health and vitality while they receive the patient's sickness. They are presented to the gods as substitute sacrifices for the patient. A double transference is apparent here, whereby the illness is transfered to the chickens and the health of the chickens transferred to the patient.

Throughout the ceremony the healer shares toasts of rum with members of the family and sometimes the patient. These toasts are performed with ritualized bowing and ceremonial verbal exchanges in rapid speech in which each member of the family helping in the healing drama exchanges toasts with the others. The ritualized toasting aims at conciliating any quarrels there may be between family members.[7] Rum is an important medium of exchange in Zinacanteco culture and an important means of establishing communication between people and between people and the gods. Offering rum to a person or a deity is a form of showing respect. During the ceremony, all the rum that is drunk is understood to be an offering to the gods. Rum is also thought to enable healers to "see" better, helping them in their divination. The term for rum, *posh*, also means "medicine" and is believed to have healing effects.[8] In short, the periodic drinking of rum in ritualized fashion throughout the ceremony is understood to facilitate respectful communication among all the parties concerned and to have a healing effect on family relationships, which may be implicated in the illness of the patient.

A central feature of the healing drama often includes a pilgrimage to a sacred place, such as wells, mountains, or churches. The type of pilrimage depends on the illness. A particularly common and powerful pilgrimage is the one undertaken to the town of Hteklum, the center of the Zinacanteco cosmos, where visits are made to its churches and the nearby mountains, which are believed to be the abodes of important deities. If at all possible, the patient makes the journey along with the healer and family members. The healer leads the sacred procession, and the other participants form a ceremonial order, with older males given priority. During the pilgrimage, the patient and her family members undertake a shared quest in search of healing. Their efforts are galvanized around a common goal, which can restore strained or broken relationships that may have been an important part of the patient's illness in the first place.

A typical healing pilgrimage to Hteklum involves visiting four sacred mountains and three churches. Arriving at the sacred mountains, the healer and members of the party (including the patient if she is well enough to be with the group) kneel before large, permanent crosses that have been erected as part of the pilgrimage circuit. The crosses are six feet tall and embedded in concrete. Flowers are tied to the crosses, candles offered and burned in special niches made for this purpose, and the crosses sprinkled with pine needles and decorated with pine boughs. Food, liquor, and incense are also offered. The crosses, in addition to being Christian symbols, are considered the doorways to the abodes of the gods who dwell in or on top of the mountains. In front of the crosses, the healer prays to the gods to accept the offerings and to restore the patient's health if they are pleased. Just prior to leaving a cross and proceeding to the next site on the circuit, the healer and patient pray, and every member of the party drinks a shot of rum, bowing to each other and crossing themselves as they do so. At one of the crosses, the chicken that earlier was identified with the patient is released as an offering.

Upon arriving at the churches in Hteklum, each member of the party salutes the large wooden crosses placed in front of the church. This involves touching the base of the cross, touching the hand to the face, and crossing oneself. Everyone assembles at the door of the church in ceremonial order, and drinks of rum are exchanged. Once inside the church, everyone kneels facing the altar and prays. The healer and the patient kneel and pray at several points in the church while the other members of

the party decorate the altar and the images of the saints with pine boughs and flowers, cense the images, and burn candles to them. Before leaving the church, the
entire party moves around the church in ceremonial order, bowing respectfully to each
image.[9] Several mountains and churches and many crosses may be visited on such
a pilgrimage, which may take all day to complete.

After the party returns to the home village, the healer washes the patient with
special herbal water prepared at the beginning of the ceremony. The patient is then
put to bed. The healer censes the patient and invokes the gods to guard her during
her recovery. A chicken is sacrificed to the gods on behalf of the patient.[10] This ends
the formal healing drama.

The family members and the patient, however, are instructed in rules and procedures that are needed to bring about a complete cure. Two women are designated
to watch over the patient twenty-four hours a day. One of them must be awake at all
times. The women's job is to protect the patient, who is in a weakened state, from
further attacks by spirits. The two "watchers" are instructed to desist from all other
work and devote their entire attention to the patient. Everyone in the house must
observe dietary restrictions. The entire household, that is, continues to invest its
energies in bringing about a cure of the patient. At first the movements of the patient
are greatly restricted. Gradually these restrictions are eased. First she is allowed to
sit by the fire for a short while. Then she is allowed a short walk outside in the company of her "watchers." The patient is not allowed outside the house alone until she
takes several sweat baths. In these sweat baths, she is accompanied by her husband
or by her mother, if she is unmarried. Her first outing alone should be on a bright,
sunny morning when the sun can give her strength. Eventually the cure is considered
complete. Sometimes these healing dramas are undertaken after, or in addition to, treatment by Ladino (Western) doctors to insure a total healing.

Zinacanteco healing ceremonies are particularly impressive in two respects. First,
they place a premium on enlisting total family support in the healing process. This
emphasis aims at restoring, refreshing, and healing personal relationships, which
almost always are associated with illness. Second, the ceremonies emphasize the healing power of a sacred journey. The pilgrimage, to Hteklum or another sacred site,
actively engages the patient and her family in a collaborative search for a cure and thus
raises their expectations. The sacred journey insures that the patient does not remain
passive in the healing process and probably is a factor in arousing her own healing
powers. An implicit theme in the healing pilgrimage is that healing cannot be expected unless it is actively sought.

ENDNOTES

[1]The following description of the Zinacanteco is based on Horacio Fabrega, Jr., and Daniel
B. Silver, *Illness and Shamanistic Curing in Zinacantan: An Ethnological Analysis* (Stanford,
Calif.: Stanford University Press, 1973).

[2]Ibid., pp. 21–22.

[3]Ibid., p. 89.
[4]Ibid., p. 149.
[5]Ibid., p. 152.
[6]Ibid., p. 174.
[7]Ibid., p. 177.
[8]Ibid., p. 264.
[9]Ibid., p. 183.
[10]Ibid., p. 185.

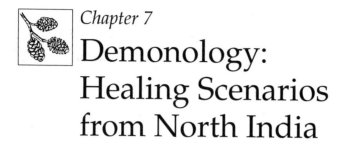

Chapter 7

Demonology: Healing Scenarios from North India

The belief that many human problems are caused by demons has existed throughout human history and throughout the world. Illnesses of all kinds, physical and mental, are often attributed to demons who attack, molest, or possess people. A study surveying 488 different societies found that belief in demons was present in 388 of them.[1] In most parts of the world, belief in demons as the cause of illness is the dominant disease etiology.

Belief that demon attacks and possession cause a wide range of human troubles—physical illness, bad luck, outrageous behavior—is widespread in India, and in villages it is the most common explanation for the cause of illness. Both Hindus and Muslims in India have a healing tradition that we might refer to as demonology. In every village there are local healers who specialize in curing sickness caused by demons. Throughout India, furthermore, there are major and minor healing centers, usually temples (in the case of Hindus) or mosques and shrines associated with holy people (in the case of Muslims), to which family members or local healers take the more serious cases of those afflicted by demons.

LOCAL DEMONOLOGICAL HEALERS IN HINDU NORTH INDIA

In North India there is a large class of healers called *ojas* and *shokas* who specialize in treating problems caused by spirits or demons. Hindus in this area assume that many human problems, including many illnesses, are caued by spirits called *prets* and *bhuts* (there is very little difference between the two). These spirits are actually ghosts of the dead who, for various reasons, still dwell in the land of the living and cause trouble. Many *prets* and *bhuts* died in tragic circumstances with strong, unfulfilled desires. Women who die in childbirth often become *prets* because they refuse to leave their newborn child and go to the land of the ancestors. They feel cheated and want to linger in the land of the living to enjoy their child. A barren woman who feels unful-filled also may become a *pret* and afflict other women with barrenness in a spirit of revenge. Other spirits become *prets* or *bhuts* because the proper funeral ceremonies (*shraddha*) were not performed for them. These ceremonies translate the spirits of the recently dead to the land of the ancestors (*pitri lok*), where they are honored and nourished by their descendents. If these ceremonies are not done, the spirit becomes stuck between worlds, where it does not receive offerings to satisfy its needs. Whether *prets* and *bhuts* themselves have decided to linger in the world of the living or have been forced to by the lack of proper rituals, they are stuck between the world of the living and the world of the ancestors. They are troublesome, frightening, unpre-dictable, and uncontrollable except by those who have special powers and knowledge, namely, the *ojas* and *shokas*.

Some *prets* and *bhuts* are more powerful than others. The ghosts of former Brah-mans, for example, are believed to be particularly strong. This reflects the Hindu view of social and human hierarchy according to which human beings are born with innate spiritual qualities that make them superior or inferior to other beings. Brahmans are the highest kind of human being and have superior spiritual and moral qualities. The ghosts of Muslims are also greatly feared and difficult to deal with. This prob-ably reflects the Hindu fear of Muslims as aggressive and violent, foreign and dan-gerous. Conversely, Muslims are particularly afraid of Hindu ghosts.

Bhuts and *prets* are said to afflict people for certain reasons. First of all, these troublesome spirits are always hungry and thirsty, because they are not in the realm of the ancestors where they would receive the routine offerings given by the living. *Bhuts* and *prets* are often depicted as having tiny mouths, indicating their inability to satisfy their desires. In their attempts to satisfy their desires, the *bhuts* and *prets* lit-erally feed off the living. When they afflict people, these spirits actually enter the vic-tim's body. Once inside, they eat human flesh and drink human blood, consuming their victim from within and causing that person to sicken or die.

Second, spirits may seek to fulfill desires that were frustrated during their life-times. In such cases, *bhuts* and *prets* often possess a person's mind, personality, and will. The person experiences bad luck, becomes barren, or behaves in unacceptable, outrageous ways (what we might call mental illness). The spirit of someone who has died sexually frustrated, for example, may take over a living person and force that per-son to indulge in promiscuous or illicit sex. Someone who has died poor and become a *pret* may seek to satisfy his discontent by making others poor, while a barren woman who becomes a *pret* may take out her anger by forcing other women to be barren.

Third, *bhuts* and *prets* also afflict the living in order to settle grudges against them or to chasten them for offensive behavior. Since *bhuts* and *prets* are invisible, it is not uncommon for people to anger them inadvertently by spitting or urinating on them, for example.

The powers of the *ojas* and *shokas* are not innate but must be learned and acquired. This is done by studying under a guru, a master already accomplished in the healing arts. The apprenticeship of the would-be healer may last several years. During this time the student learns how to diagnose disease, deal with *prets* and *bhuts*, and establish and maintain contact with a helping spirit. An essential aspect of the healer's apprenticeship is establishing rapport with a spirit that will empower and assist him or her in healing patients. The spirit may be either a benevolent spirit or a deity. Many healers in the Varanasi area, with which I am most familiar, establish a relationship with local goddesses or heroes (*birs*), who are village protectors. It is common for healers in that area annually to renew their healing powers, which stem from their helping spirits, during the large autumn festival to the goddess Durga (who herself often plays the role of a helping spirit). During this time, healers make a pilgrimage to a goddess or *bir* temple or shrine, where they make special offerings to their helping spirit (blood sacrifice and liquor are sometimes given in addition to the more common flowers, sweets, and incense). Many healers also undertake rigorous fasting during this period and abstain from any healing rituals. It is a time of renewal for them.

Apprentice healers also learn to distinguish between problems caused by *prets* and *bhuts* and other kinds of problems. Healers, for example, learn to recognize "sorrow sent by God," a sickness they cannot cure. Apprentice healers also learn to see *bhuts* and *prets*, usually by going into a trance. Like shamans, they learn techniques for communicating with or even entering the spirit world at will.

When the healers actually undertake healing, they enter a trance state of controlled possession in which their helping spirit or deity comes to them. In this state, the healer and his or her spirit "play" with the *bhut* or *pret* who is afflicting the patient. In this "play," which often takes the form of verbal give-and-take, the healer tries to determine the identify of the demon. This happens when the demon takes over the victim's consciousness and speaks out loud through the victim. An assumption in the healing process is that the demon cannot be controlled and defeated until it reveals its identity, which it can be forced to do by certain rituals or by a superior spirit. Once the spirit has been identified, the healer applies two tactics in exorcising it. First, he may coerce it by transferring it into an object, usually a lime, clove, ball of rice, or piece of the victim's clothing, and then destroying or incapacitating this object. Second, he may placate the demon by offering it worship (*puja*) in which it is given liquor, marijuana, clothing, or food. At some point in the ritual, usually near the end, the demon is given over to the healer's helping spirit, who imprisons the demon, preventing it from harming the victim in the future.

Healers' power over spirits is partly due to their own spiritual strength and partly to their alliance with a spirit or deity who helps them. Some healers emphasize that all of their healing power comes from a deity and that they simply play the role of a devotee who petitions the deity on behalf of patients or through whom the deity works. This was the case with a well-known healer, Mithai Lal, whom I met in Varanasi some years ago. He saw patients in his home, diagnosed their problem, and then advised them to go to the Durga temple on Tuesday evenings, where he would lead them in an appropriate ritual to appeal to the goddess Durga, his chosen deity, on their behalf. When I questioned Mithai Lal about his powers, he said that he was only a devotee and attributed all healing to Durga. At the temple, he made offerings on behalf of patients into a fire pit. In a state of controlled trance he also brushed his hands over each patient and then shook his hands into the fire pit as if ridding himself of the person's illness. Having made offerings to the goddess and having cleansed the patient of illness, Mithai Lal then invoked the goddess to protect the patient from further demon-caused troubles.

PISACH MOCHAN

It sometimes happens that *ojas* and *shokas* are unable to dispel the demon afflicting a patient. When this happens, the healer may take the patient to a special place to enlist the help of stronger spiritual forces. Many such healing centers exist throughout North India. A particularly powerful center at which spirits are exorcised is in the holy city of Varanasi. Healers take patients there when they have been unable to cure them in their home villages. The place is called Pisach Mochan, which means "the place where demons get liberated," or "the place where one gets release from demons." The power and prestige of Pisach Mochan is said to have originated from an event in the mythological past when the god Shiva freed a demon from bondage at this very place. Shiva freed him from bondage to his demonic condition and enabled him to become a *pitri* (literally, "father"), an ancestral being. Since that time Pisach Mochan has been under the control of that former demon, who in gratitude for being liberated by Shiva now liberates other demons, especially those who are afflicting human beings.

Pisach Mochan consists of a large pond or tank with six temples on its east bank. Each temple is owned by a Brahman family. The priests in these temples work in conjunction with the village healers to free patients from their illnesses caused by *prets* and *bhuts*. Patients who come here suffer from a variety of troubles: barrenness, leprosy, financial problems, mental illness, bad dreams, etc. What they have in common is that they have been diagnosed as suffering from demon affliction.

After arriving at Pisach Mochan with their local healer and often with family members, patients prepare themselves by bathing in the tank—something the original demon did in the process of gaining his freedom. At the temples the power of the *ojas* and *shokas* is enhanced and supplemented by Brahman priests, who employ Sanskrit mantras and Vedic rituals in their treatment of patients. The powers of village healers' guardian deities are also supplemented by the power of the presiding deity at Pisach Mochan, who, it is said, has power over all *bhuts* and *prets*. In the image used by the priests at the temples, the offending spirits are arrested by the local healers and brought to court, that is, to Pisach Mochan. At the court, the demons are either jailed or "settled." A demon usually is settled by satisfying it with offerings or converting it into a friendly, harmless ancestral spirit by means of Vedic rituals.

Patients and healers at Pisach Mochan. David Kinsley.

The healing rituals usually involve three main actors—the healer, the patient, and a Brahman priest from one of the temples—and take place in the temples in front of the images of the gods. Members of the patient's family or friends of the patient also may be present. The *bhut* or *pret* is often represented by a clove, coin, or rice ball into which the healer has "trapped" it for purposes of transporting it to Pisach Mochan. The ritual performed by the priest is a modified *shraddha* ceremony, the ceremony performed at funerals and thereafter to insure the translation of the spirit of the dead person from the land of the living to the land of the dead, from wandering spirit to ancestor. This ritual is accompanied by Sanskrit invocations and prayers and carries immense prestige and power in Hindu culture because it is an ancient Vedic rite. If properly performed, *shraddha* transforms the spirit of a dead person into an ancestral spirit. The *pret* or *bhut* is provided with a new body and is safely transported to the land of the ancestors. In effect, the patient, with the help of the priest, performs a funeral ceremony for the demon who is afflicting him or her. By doing rituals that are associated with the departure of a spirit, the patient symbolically banishes the spirit that is causing trouble.

Sometimes during these temple rituals the healer and priest will "play" with the demon afflicting the patient. In many cases the village healer (the *oja* or *shoka*) has not been able to determine the identity of the demon. Under the great power of Sanskrit mantras and Vedic rituals, however, recalcitrant demons almost always are

Patients and healers at Pisach Mochan. David Kinsley.

forced to identify themselves and thus yield to the priests' and healers' control. This involves the patient going into trance, which signals that the demon has taken possession of his or her consciousness.

At one healing ritual I saw at Pisach Mochan, a goldsmith's wife, who was ordinarily quiet and modest, had come to be cured of a condition that periodically sent her into rages in which she would curse her husband and children and throw pots and pans about the house. She had been diagnosed as being afflicted by a demon, but the local healer had been unsuccesful in exorcising it. The woman had come to Pisach Mochan with her husband and two children for help. The temple priest forced her to enter a controlled trance, or rather forced the afflicting demon to speak through the patient. As the woman slowly went into trance, her body began to sway, and she moaned rhythmically. Prior to this she had been very quiet, speaking only in short sentences and soft tones. When the demon took over, she began to shout at her husband and, when pressed by the priest, identified herself as the spirit of the recently deceased wife of her husband's brother. The brother (the spirit's husband) had hired a magician to force the woman's spirit to afflict the patient in order to demoralize the patient's husband, who was involved in a bitter lawsuit over family property with the spirit's husband. The spirit was duly "settled," agreeing to accept some offerings and having a *shraddha* performed for it.

Before leaving Pisach Mochan many patients undergo another ritual. They take

Tree trunk at Pisach Mochan covered with bits of cloth nailed to the tree by patients. David Kinsley.

a piece of their own clothing and give it to the priest. The priest then invokes the demon who has caused the problem and by means of ritual gestures and invocations transfers the spirit into the cloth. The patient then nails the piece of cloth to an old, gnarled tree that grows in the center of one of the temples. The tree grows right through the roof of the temple, which was built around it, and the trunk is covered with nails and spikes and bits of cloth as high as one can reach. In other parts of India, locks of patients' hair are fastened to trees to symbolize the "jailing" of demonic spirits. Patients are also given certificates when they leave Pisach Mochan guaranteeing their cures. If there is a recurrence of the affliction, they are entitled to return for free treatment.

At Pisach Mochan, patients have the benefit of two different kinds of healers.

The *ojas* and *shokas* are shamanic-type healers who have direct access to the spirit world and are able to heal because of their rapport with spirits and helping deities. They know techniques whereby they can enter a trance state and communicate with the spirit world. The Brahmans at Pisach Mochan are priestly healers. They are ritual experts who know Sanskrit, a magically powerful, archaic language. In combination, the two types of healers seem to be very effective.

THE BALAJI TEMPLE NEAR BHARATPUR

Another famous healing shrine in North India is the Balaji temple near Bharatpur in Rajasthan.[2] Like the temples at Pisach Mochan, the Balaji temple is known as a place where people suffering from spirit-caused illnesses can find a cure. People with a great variety of ailments go there, but it is famous primarily as a place where the mentally ill are successfully treated, and the majority of patients who go there are so afflicted.

The presiding deity at the temple is the Hindu monkey god Hanuman, who is known there as Balaji, "the strong one." Balaji established this temple in the mythic past in order to help both the human beings who are afflicted by demons and the demons themselves. He felt compassion for the demons as well as the patients. At his temple, demons are settled as ancestral spirits or become guardian spirits of the human beings they afflict, while patients gain relief from the afflictions caused by the demons. Balaji invited other powerful gods to help him at his temple. Two in particular are significant. Preta-raja (lord of the *prets*) is king of the underworld (he is known as Yama in most Hindu texts). It is he who ultimately passes judgment on the demons who are brought to the temple. The other deity is Mahakal Bhairav, a form of the god Shiva, who is entrusted with administering punishments to the demons. The temple complex as a whole is described by the priests, staff, and patients as a court to which people come seeking justice. At Balaji's court, judgments are passed on the offending demons, and they are sentenced (for example, to become ancestors, guardian spirits, or prisoners of Balaji).

Every patient must be accompanied by a family member, and in many cases individuals who come to Balaji's temple are doing so as a last resort. They have tried other alternatives and have been unsuccessful. Sometimes they, or a family member, have had dreams in which they have been summoned to the temple by Balaji. For most who come to the temple, the excursion is a pilgrimage, a sacred journey in search of healing. Undoubtedly, expectations are high for many who arrive at the Balaji temple. Such expectations are heightened by the fact that many volunteers at the temple are former patients who have been cured by Balaji. These people often relate their tales to patients and magnify the miraculous powers of the temple.

An important element in the healing process is the point at which the patient enters a state of controlled trance called *peshi* during which the afflicting demon appears. Until and unless the spirit is made to appear and identify itself, it cannot be exorcised or "settled." The aim of the rituals and routines of the temple, especially in the intial parts of the healing process, is to precipitate *peshi*. Two kinds of rituals are particularly effective in inducing this state. At the very outset, an application for help is made by the patient or by a family member on behalf of the patient. Many patients, dominated in their actions by their afflicting demons, do not cooperate. We could say that they have a lot invested in their illness, which may be a means of coping with a very difficult family situation or some other problem. Offerings to Balaji accompany the petition, which is made every morning and evening. The offerings, usually of sweets, are taken by a priest, placed against the image's lips, and then returned to the patient. The patient then eats the sweets, which have been infused with the healing power of the god. Balaji's power is believed to be irresistible to demons.

While this daily routine infuses Balaji's healing power into the patient, the patient's family members are also put to work in bringing about a cure. The priests ask them to chant mantras or read aloud passages from scriptures in which Balaji's feats are told. They also may be told to transfer spoonfuls of water back and forth between pots while they do this. The mantras infuse the water with sacred power and create a potent medicine that will be drunk by the patient. The expectation that the patient will enter the state of *peshi* builds. This is enhanced by the fact that many other patients are already entering this state. The pressures on the patient (that is, the demon) are tremendous.

The start of the *peshi* state is marked by the patient swaying rhythmically and shaking his head this way and that. It is also marked by self-punishment, which indicates his desire to afflict and exorcise the demon. Patients may beat the floor with their hands, hit their backs against the wall, or ask to have heavy stones placed on their backs when they lie down. In *peshi* the patient (or the demon possessing the patient) carries on a conversation with people who are present. The patient often does not remember the conversation later. In the early stages of *peshi,* the demon (or the patient, depending on one's point of view) is often defiant, refusing to admit that it can be defeated by Balaji or that it can be forced to leave its chosen victim. The audience, which usually includes family members, will often jeer at the demon, make fun of it, and call on Balaji to teach it a lesson. The torrent of abusive language and hatred that comes from the mouths of ordinarly demure young women patients in such cases is impressive and is convincing proof of how much pent-up emotion and resentment must exist in them. Intense shouting matches between patients and their families are common and undoubtedly offer both parties the opportunity to vent their emotions and resentments toward each other in an acceptable ritual setting.

At some point the demon almost always submits to the superior power of Balaji and agrees to obey him. The patient stops abusing himself, and the demon asks for forgiveness. The demon identifies itself and promises to leave the patient alone, throwing itself on the mercy of the divine court. In some cases, Balaji provides the patient with a reformed, benign spirit called a *duta* to protect the patient from demons in the future. The coming of the *duta* is the occasion for another trance state, during which the patient prostrates himself to the deity in gratitude.

The overall aim at the Balaji temple is to exorcise the demon afflicting a patient and to reintegrate the person into the community. The task of reintegration is brought about by convincing the patient that socially unacceptable behavior is not an expression of the patient's true self. By emphasizing the theme of demonic possession, the hope is that the patient will disassociate himself from behavior deemed mad by Hindu society. In addition to the rituals discussed above that aim at exorcising the demon, other strategies are used to encourage the patient to resist indulging his demonic tantrums and to affirm his acceptable social identity.

Mental illness in India is often spoken of as analogous to moral pollution. The victim is thought to have a kind of psychological leprosy. At the Balaji temple, patients must observe strict prohibitions. Sexual abstinence is observed. Dietary restrictions prohibit the use of spices, onion, garlic, and any other foods that are considered in the least impure. Patients must take daily baths and wear fresh clothes every time they enter the temple grounds. These rules seem aimed at involving patients in routines that will help purify their impure state. They also prepare patients for meeting the pure, healing power of the deities. They actively engage patients in an attempt to rid themselves of their dirty condition, a condition that repulses members of their families and society in general.

In the context of dormitory life on the grounds of the Balaji temple, patients and their families openly discuss details of the patients' afflictions. In many cases these have been mentioned only in hushed, embarrassed whispers, but now they are discussed publicly in great detail. Patients and family members are free to compare notes with others in a community of fellow sufferers. Patients typically ask each other: "How is your *sankat* (affliction) doing?" They will tell each other what their afflicting demon "made them do." At some point, when it is clear that the patient is beginning to disassociate herself from the illness, she will speak almost affectionately about her demon by using the diminutive *bhutra*. She will talk about what pranks it did, how it tried to embarass her by making her make obscene gestures or speak insultingly to her mother-in-law, and so on. At this point, it is clear that the patient's attitude is changing and that the demon is now something that is endured instead of a force that has complete control over the patient. The illness is seen as something distinct from the patient, something she would like to be rid of. The patient is gaining some control over the illness.[3]

The family's presence and involvement in the cure, finally, is crucial. If the patient is under great pressure to give up his illness and return to normal behavior, the family also is under pressure to admit and own up to the patient's illness, to accept it as something that is not his fault, and to lend support in every way it can. The alienation the patient has felt because of his disease may well be strongest and most painful in the family context, in which recrimination, embarrassment, and outrage are strongest. And clearly the patient's condition may directly implicate the family, or at least a member of the family. In restoring integration, the efforts of the family are crucial. Their active involvement in the healing process is an implicit admission that they may be involved in the illness. Together the patient and his family work to restore normality, to strengthen the true self of the patient, which longs to be rid of debilitating, polluting, and alienating behavior. It is not, after all, the patient's fault. In the healing context of the Balaji temple, it is an alien presence that has afflicted the suffering patient. Together, the patient and his family, with the help of the gods, can be rid of the demon and bring about reintegration and healing.

ENDNOTES

[1]Erika Bourguignon, "Spirit Possession Belief and Social Structure," in Agehananda Bharati (ed.), *The Realm of the Extra-Human: Ideas and Actions* (The Hague: Mouton Publishers, 1976), p. 19.

[2]The following description of the Balaji temple is from Sudhir Kakar, *Shamans, Mystics, and Doctors: A Psychological Inquiry into India and Its Healing Traditions* (New York: Alfred Knopf, 1982).

[3]Ibid., pp. 85–86.

Chapter 8

Central Themes
in Traditional Healing

In many of the scenarios and individuals we have looked at in traditional cultures, certain themes seem to be common cross-culturally. A closer look at some of these themes will serve as a summary of healing in traditional cultures.

CONFESSION

Most traditional cultures take for granted a relationship between morality and illness. If a person gets sick, it is assumed that he deserved it. Illness is understood to be the direct or indirect result of infringing moral codes or violating taboos. In many cases, the sick person must confess his moral transgressions; it is frequently assumed that unless such actions are confessed, often publicly, healing cannot take place. Secretly harboring immoral or antisocial deeds enhances their power to make one sick. Confession makes these thoughts and deeds amenable to treatment that renders them harmless or at least less powerful. Confession is a way of getting them outside the patient, where they can be dealt with by the healer or the community.

The Aurohuaca Indians of Columbia believe that sickness is related to sin and that sin can be rendered harmless only if it is confessed to a healer. If a patient's sins are confessed, the healer can transfer them to pieces of shell or stone. Objectified in these objects, this "sin matter" can then be exposed to the rays of the sun, which destroys it.[1] Confession was also important in the Yucatan, where illness was related to immorality. The patient was encouraged to confess her sins to a priest, parent, or spouse. In some cases the person hearing the confession (priest, parent, or spouse) would urge the patient on if she hesitated, in order to bring about a complete and detailed confession.[2]

Among the Ndembu of Zimbabwe, sickness sometimes is related to the anger and aggression of male ancestors. If a person breaks a law or customary rule, a male ancestor may become upset and cause illness by biting that person. What the Ndembu call *ihamba* illness is clearly related to morality and tribal custom and often requires confession as part of therapy. *Ihamba* is the upper central incisor of a dead hunter and is said to contain the power to kill animals. Part of the healing rites aimed at removing the *ihamba* involve the healer summoning the kin of the patient to an improvised shrine where the rites take place. At the shrine, the kin are instructed to confess their sins, grudges, and grievances. It is said that the *ihamba* will not come out, or allow itself to be extracted by the healer, unless the patient's kin have confessed all their wrongdoings. The patient also must confess his grudges and complaints against others if he is to become free of the ancestral bite. In the case of the Ndembu it is assumed that illness is an indication that something is wrong in the social body, that illness is a symptom of social strife, tension, or malaise. This is what is really being treated in the *ihamba* rites. The hostilities of the patient and the village are made apparent by means of the confession of the patient and his kin and friends. The patient, ideally, becomes reconciled to his friends and they to him through confession.[3]

The centrality of confession is also clear in a healing ceremony among the Iglulik Inuit that was recorded in 1920 by Knud Rasmussen. The ceremony was being held to heal a woman who was so sick that she could barely sit upright. She was placed on a bench inside a hut, and everyone in the village was invited to attend. The shaman then began to summon his spirits and to ask them what the woman might have done to have caused her illness; he was making the very common assumption that illness is related to morality. As he put questions to his spirit helpers, he paced up and down, swung his arms about, and breathed heavily. He asked if the sickness was the fault of the woman herself or whether someone else had caused it. Perhaps it was his, the shaman's, own fault, or the fault of his wife? Perhaps the illness was caused by the patient's own misdeeds? At this point the woman answered: "The sickness is due to my own fault. I have but ill fulfilled my duties. My thoughts have been bad and my actions evil."[4] The shaman then said that he saw something polluting inside her body, the concrete result of her misdeeds. The patient then confessed a series of misdeeds, taboos she had broken, and envious thoughts. Her confession was punctuated throughout by the pleas of those in attendance, her family, friends and neighbors, that the woman should be forgiven her shortcomings. In chorus they said: "It is such a slight offence, and means so little, when her life is at stake. Let her be released from this burden, from this cause, from this source."[5] In the course of the healing ceremony the woman remembered her past life and mentioned all those deeds and thoughts that had troubled her. In the presence of the shaman and her friends, neighbors, and kin, she begged the spirits for forgiveness. After each confession the shaman peered into her body to search for remaining pollution and several times said that she was not yet completely free from her illness and that she should confess further, which the woman did. After a long period, the shaman finally declared the patient free of sickness, free of unconfessed faults, and fit and well.[6]

An underlying assumption in most of these examples is that misdeeds, improper behavior, bad thoughts, sin, or immorality can become transformed into illness or into bits of dangerous matter that may cause illness in a person's body. Restoration of health involves getting rid of what we might call karmic residue. This is done by confession. Another assumption in these examples is that harboring misdeeds and ugly thoughts can cause illness. Being secretive, especially about one's improper actions and thoughts, is unhealthy and dangerous. In these examples there is an unburdening of the patient through confession that is held to be curative, or at least purifying and preparatory to the healing process. There is also probably a catharsis involved on the part of the patient in telling people what he really thinks of them, or once thought of them. Finally, all of this—the linking of sickness with morality and curing with confession (often public confession)—has a strong effect on social control and everyday moral behavior and thought. Using confession for diagnosis and therapy is a powerful means of social control, especially in small tribes or groups.

TRANSFERENCE AND OBJECTIFICATION OF ILLNESS

In the treatment of sickness in many cultures we find that an important part of the healing process involves transferring the illness from the patient to some object or other being, sometimes to the healer herself. Ritually, symbolically, or psychologcally the sickness is removed from the patient and identified with some object (or being). It is then condensed, objectified, and bound by the healer or the ritual; finally, the sickness is dramatically, ritually, or symbolically destroyed or banished.

Transference is a central theme in a discharge ceremony for mental patients among the Yoruba of Nigeria. Treatment takes place in a special center adjacent to the healer's own house and may last for days or weeks. When the healer deems the patient fit to return to normal society, an elaborate discharge ceremony is performed. The rituals are done at a river in a deserted place. The patient first takes off her old clothes and puts on a new white dress. Next her head is shaved and small cuts made in her scalp. The healer, her assistant, and the patient wade into the stream waist deep. The healer then takes one of three doves to be used in the ceremony and uses it as a kind of sponge, wetting it and rubbing it over the patient's body, drawing out her illness, transf ering it to the dove. This dove is then drowned and its body thrown downstream, along with the patient's disease, which it has absorbed. The second dove is then killed and its blood smeared over the patient's head and upper body. The vitality and calmness of the dove is thus transferred to the patient. The patient is washed and her bloodstained dress thrown downstream with the body of the second dove. Back on shore the patient is rubbed with medicines, and another dove is killed and its blood splashed over her body and then washed off. The patient then stands on the body of the dove, and an incantation is invoked. The body of the last dove is then thrown downstream with the declaration that the dead bird carries the patient's sickness with it and that, just as water never flows upstream, so the patient's sickness will never return.[7]

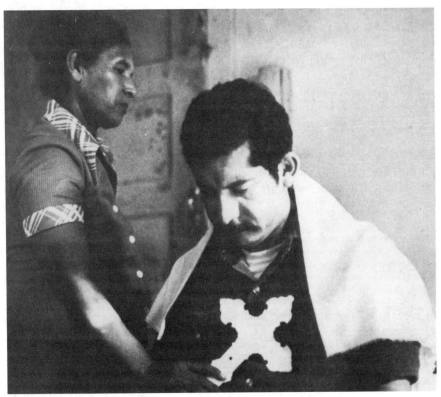

Patient being treated with a cross by a *curandera*. From Robert Trotter and Juan Chavira, *Curanderismo* (Athens: University of Georgia Press, 1981).

In *curanderismo*, the traditional healing practices of Mexican-Americans in the American Southwest, a very common ritual practice is "sweeping" a patient's body. The *curandera* does this by holding an egg in her hand and moving it all over the patient's body, especially the place where the disease seems to be localized. This process is believed to extract the sickness from the patient and transfer it into the egg. While sweeping the patient, the healer appeals to God, the saints, and other spirits to heal the person. After the sweeping ritual the egg is burned, thus destroying the disease, which has been transferred to and objectified in the egg.[8]

Another ritual that employs transference and objectification in *curanderismo* is a ceremony called *sortilegio* that heals patients of afflictions caused by sorcery. These afflictions often include infidelity of a spouse, rebellious children, unemployment, and excessive drinking by a family member, in addition to illness. A series of different-colored ribbons is set out on the floor, each color representing a kind of affliction or magical power that has been used against the patient. The patient then walks forward and backward over the line of ribbons three times. While he is doing this, the patient and healer together make invocations, such as the following:

> In the name of the Holy Trinity, God the Father, God the Son, and God the Holy Spirit, I conjure and I reject the red works, the black works; I conjure them to the seven red seas, the seven black seas. In the name of God, I conjure and reject all the evil that has been done to me. I conjure my enemies in the flesh and without the flesh. In the name of God I lock up my enemies here.[9]

The patient then ties knots in the ribbons while he and the healer continue to pray as follows:

> In the name of God, here I lock up my enemies. I ask for my happiness, good luck, health and money. By all the dominating spirits, may the evil doings depart to the seven red seas and the seven black seas. By all the dominating beings, I here lock up my enemies. I here tie and conjure all my enemies in the flesh and without the flesh. In the name of all powerful God.[10]

The knotted ribbons are then put in an empty jar. As the patient screws on the lid he is instructed to say: "Now I here lock my enemies, and they will leave me in peace." Then the jar is buried along with the patient's problems or illness.[11]

Transference of disease from a patient to an object (which is then destroyed) also occurs in the very common practice of extracting illness from a patient by sucking or bleeding. The healer typically produces a hair, feather, insect, or string that she has sucked or extracted from the patient. The disease is identified with this object and then destroyed.

Transference of illness often takes the form of the healer taking on the disease of the patient. In cases like this, the healer cures by taking on the illness herself and overcoming it with superior vitality, energy, or spiritual force. Among the Kalahari Kung (discussed in Chapter 4), healing often involves the healer assuming the patient's sickness. One Kung healer said: "When I lay my hands on a person, I take sickness into my hands. Then I shiver from the sickness, and then I throw it away."[12] The close physical contact that takes place between healer and patient in the Kung healing dances encourages or allows transference to take place. A kind of osmosis takes place in which the positive, healing energy of the healer, which is objectified in her sweat, spreads into the body of the sick person, restoring health and wholeness. At the same time, the sickness of the patient leaks out and enters the body of the healer, who then expels it with violent gestures and shouts. For the healer this is exhausting and often painful work.

When the cause of sickness is said to be an afflicting spirit, ghost, or demon, which is a very common idea in traditional cultures, transference often takes the form of exorcism. Among the Balahis of Central India, elaborate rituals are done to exorcise demons. At the conclusion of the ceremony the healer forces a sandal into the patient's mouth. This is considered extremely insulting and offensive to the possessing demon and is believed to force it to leave the patient. The patient is then taken to a nearby tree. The sandal is taken from the patient's mouth and fastened to the tree, and a lock of the patient's hair is nailed to the tree and then cut off. The demon, who has been transferred to the sandal and the hair, is thus fixed permanently to the tree.[13] Similar rituals are practiced at the healing shrine of Pisach Mochan (discussed in Chap-

ter 7), where exorcised demons are transferred to cloves or rice balls and then banished or destroyed. Sometimes the demon is transferrred to or objectified in a scrap
of the patient's clothing, which is then nailed to a tree growing through the center of
the temple. In transference by exorcism, the healer, by means of rituals or superior
spiritual force (which may involve a spirit ally), forces the offending demon to leave
the patient and render itself controllable by entering an object that can be manipulated
or destroyed.

SACRED SPACE, PILGRIMAGE, AND HEALING CONTEXTS

In many healing scenarios in traditional cultures, sacred space and sacred places are
central to the healing process. Although we tend to separate medical space from sacred
space in our own culture, thinking it necessary, for example, to demarcate a chapel
from the rest of a hospital, in most cultures curing and medical practice often take place
within specially marked-off sacred space. In Navaho chantways (discussed in Chapter 5) special care is taken to purify the hogan and mark it with sacred objects before
the main ceremony begins. In this way the normal secular dwelling is transformed
into a sanctuary fit for the invited gods. The sandpaintings in Navaho ceremonies also
illustrate the theme of sacred space. The paintings depict aspects of the Navaho
cosmos and portray sacred beings. At a certain point in the chantway, the patient is
placed directly on the painting. That is, the patient physically enters intensified
sacred space represented by the painting and is identified with that space when the
painting is "destroyed" and poured over his body. To a great extent, patients are healed,
restored to wholeness, in Navaho chantways by being infused with sacred power, which
can only take place within sacred space.

In Sri Lanka, there is an elaborate ritual tradition aimed at healing illness
caused by demon affliction. These dramatic exorcisms are conducted in the courtyard
of the patient's house. The house is purified, and then several altars are erected to
demarcate the place within which the combat between the healer and the demons will
take place. A large structure called the "palace of the demons" (*yak vidiya*) is built
and features prominently in the drama. Indeed, this structure represents the spirit world,
which the healer enters and where the struggle against the demons takes place. The
healing ceremony from beginning to end is a religious drama that takes place in
sacred space: medical space is religious space in these ceremonies.[14]

Among the Zinacanteco (discussed in Chapter 6) healing ceremonies take place
in the patient's home. The patient's bed is transformed into sacred space when the
healer decorates it with flowers and pine boughs and sprinkles the patient and the bed
with special water. The healer also sets up an altar in the patient's house that becomes
the center for many of the healing rituals performed.

Many *curanderos* make use of an elaborate altar in their curing rituals. This altar,
which is called a *mesa*, is usually rectangular in shape and represents a microcosm
of the spiritual universe. Most *mesas* contain a crucifix, images of Catholic saints, and
objects that are special to the particular healer. The different spiritual zones are rep-

resented (heaven, earth, and the underworld), and medicines to be used in the rituals are often set out on the *mesa*. The *curandero* employs the *mesa* as a sacred center where communication with spirits may be established.[15]

In most cases, sacred space is established temporarily for healing rituals and ceremonies. When the rituals are completed, the sacred space is disestablished or reverts to normal, profane space. In some cases, though, healing rituals take place in permanently sacred places such as shrines, churches, or temples. The Balaji temple in Rajasthan and the Pisach Mochan shrine in Varanasi are only two examples of thousands of healing centers that dot the Indian subcontinent. Permanent healing shrines are also found throughout Christendom. Lourdes in southern France, Fatima in Portugal, and Saint Anne de Beaupré in Quebec are famous examples of such healing centers. Among the Zinacanteco, the town of Hteklum, with its churches and shrines, is a much more modest, local shrine and is typical of thousands of such healing centers in traditional cultures. At all of these shrines, divine power is believed to exist in concentrated form, and pilgrim-patients are given access to it with the help of ritual specialists. Spirits, deities, saints, or ancestors are believed to dwell permanently at these healing centers and to be available for healing by means of special rituals or petition. However, just being present at the shrine is sometimes held to be efficacious.

In cases where healing involves traveling to a permanent sacred place, the process of a healing journey or pilgrimage becomes central and features in the healing process. Preparations for the journey and the journey itself may be as important, or more important, to the healing process than the actual rituals and therapies undergone at the sacred shrine itself. In the case of a healing journey, the assumption is that to make contact with the healing powers of the gods (saints, spirits, or ancestors) one must undertake a pilgrimage to their dwelling place. The sacred and healing power of the gods and spirits is concentrated at certain points; to be at those points is to benefit from that power. In the healing rituals of the Zinacantecos, the centrality of pilgrimage is clear. The healer, patient, and the patient's family undertake a pilgrimage to the sacred centers of their culture in order to gain the healing blessings of the gods and saints.

We know the positive effects pilgrimage has on many patients. The considerable effort involved in undertaking a journey to a place like Lourdes, for example, the great expectation aroused during the journey itself, the special atmosphere of the place, and the great reputation of the sacred center have a powerful effect on many patients-pilgrims. Pilgrimage often is a powerful "liminal" experience. One steps out of the normal world of daily routine and undertakes an often difficult and perhaps dangerous journey with a group of like-minded people who form a tight, warm community with a specific goal in mind. In such circumstances, personal transformations can take place, even if physical transformations do not.

Pilgrimage also suggests another important part of many healing scenarios, namely, the importance of directly involving the patient in her own cure. In most healing rituals the patient is the center of attention and has a clear part to play. She will be asked to confess her sins, sing, chant, dance, or perform some ritual gestures. In very few cases does the patient remain entirely passive. It seems to be understood in most cultures that to mobilize a person's healing powers, the patient herself must be physically or mentally engaged. Participation in a pilgrimage is a very effective way of mobilizing the whole being in the healing process. It is an active, energetic quest for healing by the patient herself.

EFFECTIVE HEALERS: PRESTIGE, CONFIDENCE, AND EMPATHY

An important characteristic of effective healers is their prestige. Across cultures, it is clear that the healer is an imposing figure with an impressive reputation and is often sought out by patients from far away. It is also the case in many cultures that the healer plays powerful and prestigious religious, social, or economic roles in addition to being a healer. Healing is often something that healers only do incidentally. They also may have power over the weather, be able to communicate with gods and spirits, and be community leaders. Shamans, for example, usually not only are healers but are extraordinary in ways that make them leaders of their groups, communities, or tribes.

Healers often have impressive titles and credentials. Among the Lebou of Senegal, for example, healers are called *baroom xam-xam*, "masters of knowledge." In many cultures, healers have undergone long and arduous training. Among the Yoruba, most healers can trace their healing ancestry back many generations, and in many cases they have learned medicine from their parents. They also claim that they learn about healing from their ancestors through their dreams. This lends Yoruba healers an aura of prestige connected to the wisdom and power of the ancestors.[16] The credentials of a traditional Muslim healer from Southeast Asia are impressive and generate respect, even awe, in patients:

> Salaam aleikum salaam: I studied with my father, my father studied with my grandfather, my grandfather studied with a childless ancestral doctor, the childless ancestral doctor studied with Doctor Bado, Doctor Bado studied with Doctor Tembukan, Doctor Tembukan studied with Doctor Muning Bueun, Bueun studied with Muning Mas, Muning Mas studied with Setangai Remas, Setangai Remas studied with Radjo Makombumai, Radjo Makobumai studied with Setangai Renyang. That is the pedigree of my learning, which derived ultimately from the Holy First Being. The Holy First Being knew how to approach the Lord of Omnipotence. The Lord of Omnipotence communicated with knowledge to Archangel Gabriel. This is the pedigree of my learning. The Holy First Being knew how to approach the Lord of Omnipotence and the Seven Deities, the Nine Custodians, the people who guard the Hall of Mists, the Abode of Winds, the men who guard the gold mines, the Four Gods who guard the village community and watch over it. The Holy First Being had the power to grant wishes, for he knew how to address the Creator, and the Ancestral Spirits.[17]

Healers sometimes proclaim or boast about their powers and past successes as a way of underlining their prestige. Apache shamans, for example, boasted of past successful healings in order to instill respect in their patients.[18] Closely related to healers' tendency to impress patients by proclaiming or boasting of their healing powers is the confidence with which healers present themselves. Effective healers are often portrayed as exuding confidence, especially in front of patients. They announce their diagnosis with assurance and perform therapies in a mood of complete confidence that what they are doing will heal the patient. A striking example of this is the demeanor of Abba Wolde Tensae of Ethiopia, discussed in Chapter 3. His manner, bearing, examination of patients, and ritual healings all bespeak a healer who has total confidence in his ability to heal his patients. It is understandable that the mere presence of the healer can have a dramatic healing effect on patients.

Healers sometimes are characterized by intimate, intense knowledge of illness based on their own experience. Shamanic initiation sometimes takes the form of a person being transformed by the experience of enduring and overcoming serious illness. In many cultures the most powerful healers are physically impaired or psychologically unusual in some way. Western observers have sometimes commented on shamans' being mad or socially abnormal,[19] and physically impaired healers are quite common. The two most powerful healers among the Kalahari Kung, for example, are both blind (see Chapter 3). This suggests the theme of the wounded healer, the person who deeply understands illness because she herself has suffered deeply through illness or is impaired in some way.[20] The wounded healer can deal effectively with illness in others because she herself understands it and has overcome it. The wounded healer has empathy, the ability to put herself in the place or condition of her patients and to understand illness from that person's perspective. In the case of the Iban of Borneo, the quality of empathy is symbolically transmitted to healers during their initiation. During this ceremony the prospective healer is given medicine to protect his skin, gold dust is sprinkled on his eyes to enable him to see spirits, a fishhook is embedded in one of his fingertips to help him combat demons, "and lastly they pierce his heart with an arrow [symbolically] to make him tender-hearted and full of sympathy for the sick and suffering."[21]

ASSIGNING MEANING TO ILLNESS

One of the most important roles healers play is to assign meaning to illness. In many cases this means relating a patient's illness to some aspect of his life. As we have seen already, a very common assumption in many cultures is that illness is related to morality. Antisocial actions, thoughts, or feelings, breach of taboo, and immorality are often viewed as the direct or indirect causes of sickness. The healer's task in such cases is to determine what the patient has done wrong, what deity, spirit, or ancestor has been offended, and what must be done to appease the offended party to allow healing to take place. The healer's job is to clarify the connection between the patient's illness and his behavior. The centrality of confession on the part of the patient must be understood in this context. The healer needs to know whom the patient has offended before she can diagnose the illness and prescribe an effective therapy. In many cases, healing is the process whereby the healer guides or helps patients reform their lives in ways that do not create illness. This often means restoring social relations, community harmony, and mutual respect within families. Among the Zinacanteco, the involvement of family members in healing ceremonies is important, as is the repeated ritual demonstration of mutual respect and forgiveness between all participants.

Framing illness in a meaningful context may involve little more on the part of the healer than naming the illness. In describing the role of a healer in rural India, a Western psychiatrist said: "What was expected from the healer was reassurance. So long as the illness was nameless, patients felt desperately afraid, but once its magic origin had been defined and appropriate measures taken, they could face the outcome calmly."[22] Naming an illness puts painful symptoms, fears, and feelings of disorientation of patients in a context that is manageable by healers in their cultural contexts. After all, it is unlikely that healers will name a disease with which they are totally unfamiliar. It is far more likely they will diagnose a condition they are familiar with and can treat effectively. Illness that is felt by the patient to be totally mysterious and overwhelming becomes far less threatening when named by the healer, who is confident she can effectively treat the illness. The very naming of an illness by itself has powerful healing effects. It puts what is unknown and frightening within the known and familiar.

In assigning meaning, it is obvious that the healer and patient must share the same view of reality, the same worldview. The healer must be able to diagnose and treat illness in a way that is meaningful to the patient. A Western psychiatrist, for example, would probably get blank stares if she told an African tribal person that his problems were caused by childhood experiences. Conversely, a Western person would simply shrug in disbelief if told his problem was caused by an ancestral spirit. A Mexican-American woman put it this way in explaining why she stopped going to see an Anglo-American psychotherapist: "I couldn't talk to him. All he ever did was ask me about things in the past. My problem was in the present. I couldn't talk to him at all."[23]

CULTURE-SPECIFIC NATURE OF ILLNESS

Closely related to framing sickness in meaningful ways is the culture-specific nature of many illnesses. To a great extent, illness is culturally defined. The etiology, symptoms, likely outcome, and treatment of specific illnesses often are distinctive from one culture to another and may reflect peculiar beliefs, customs, or tensions that are prominent in that culture. Not surprisingly, there are almost always qualified healers in these cultures who can treat these maladies effectively. In the case of culture-specific illnesses, the importance of patient and healer sharing the same worldview, or the same "assumptive world,"[24] is clear. The healer, in diagnosing and treating the illness, plays the important role of culture-bearer and interpreter, who defines, affirms, and manipulates cultural constructs for people undergoing personal or social crises. The healer resorts to culture-specific illness as a way of thinking about and dealing with common problems that beset his particular society. By defining these problems as illnesses, native healers can treat them, often effectively.

In Chinese culture, *koro* is an illness that afflicts older males. The primary symptom is the gradual shrinking of the penis. If untreated, the penis is believed to disappear up into the body, resulting in the death of the patient. This condition is caused by the overactivity of the *yin* (female) part of the brain and is treated by the administration of medicines aimed at calming the *yin* and stimulating the *yang* (male) energy of the patient.[25] Not surprisingly, Chinese healers are able to treat *koro* successfully.

Among Mexicans and Latin Americans a very common illness, especially among children, is *susto*, the "fright disease." Like *koro* among the Chinese, *susto* is peculiar to one culture. *Susto* is caused by a traumatic experience, either of a natural or supernatural kind, in which the patient's soul becomes lost from the body. Fatigue, loss of appetite and interest in one's surroundings, sadness, and withdrawal are symptoms of *susto*. *Curanderos*, Mexican-American folk healers, successfully treat *susto* with prayers, herbal medicines, and techniques such as "sweeping" the patient with a branch.[26]

Culture-specific illnesses suggest quite clearly that healers in traditional cultures are often accomplished in symbolic healing. By means of images and rituals, they define and describe a condition and prescribe appropriate rituals (therapies) for effectively dealing with that condition. While such activity is not always religious, it is often the case that healers involved in symbolic healing (which includes most healing rituals) are religious specialists (or at least learned in religious symbols).

GROUP SOLIDARITY IN HEALING

In several of the healing scenarios presented above, the presence of people or participants in addition to the healer and the patient is notable. Many healing procedures and rituals include, or even require, the presence of community members, family members, or friends.

Among the Kalahari Kung, most healing dances are public affairs in which every member of the community is invited to take part. While the most dramatic healings may take place between one healer and one patient during a public healing dance, the support of the wider community is obviously held to be important. Indeed, the community healing dances of the Kung might be understood as a group affirmation of life and vitality vis-à-vis the ancestors who represent death and malaise. It is the vitality of the group as a whole that supports the individual healers in their exertions on behalf of individual sick members of the group. The dances represent a circle of life against which the ancestors have difficulty exerting their powers. Illness is something that the Kung understand to be endemic to every individual. Their healing dances restore vigor to each member of the group and to the group as a corporate body. Individual health is dependent on the health of the whole community.

Participation of community and family members is also important in Navaho chantways. While the ceremonies aim at restoring the health of a particular individual and are conducted primarily by a healer knowledgeable in the rituals being performed, family and community members are encouraged to attend and take part in the rituals. Although the patient may have arranged for the healer to perform the ceremony, and may have a specific ailment that she wishes to have healed, the setting of the chantways is open and public and often takes on the air of an important social event. Members of the community sing songs, invoke prayers, and sometimes undergo purification rituals along with the patient. One of the aims of the chantways is to restore balance, harmony, and beauty in the cosmos and by extension to restore health to the individual. In many cases, illness may be related to stresses and strains in the social fabric. Imbalance may have expressed itself in witchcraft. In attending and participating in the chantway, people reaffirm the harmony of the family and community. Their presence assures the patient that the community is concerned for her and anxious to help restore her health by participating in the rituals on her behalf.

The situation is similar among the Zinacanteco. The healer recruits members of the patient's family to take part in the healing ceremonies. Family members prepare medicines for the patient, bathe him, accompany him on a sacred journey, and guard him throughout his convalescence. During the ceremonies, furthermore, ritual exchanges of rum between participants aim at restoring harmony to family relationships, which are often implicated in the cause of illness.

The importance of confession, often public, also implicates the wider community as important in the healing process. It is clear in many cases that illness is directly related to interpersonal relationships and that the healing process must include confession and forgiveness among members of a community. In this role, many traditional healers play the role of confessor, priest, and counselor. They act to restore group solidarity and harmony. As healers, their main role often is to facilitate rapprochement between alienated members of a family or community.

ENDNOTES

[1]Weston La Barre, "Confession as Cathartic Therapy in American Indian Tribes," in Ari Kiev (ed.), *Magic, Faith, and Healing: Studies in Primitive Psychiatry Today* (New York: Free Press, 1964), p. 38.

[2]Ibid., p. 39.

[3]Victor W. Turner, "An Ndembu Doctor in Practice," in Kiev (ed.), pp. 258–60.

[4]Knud Rasmussen, *Intellectual Culture of the Hudson Bay Eskimos*, trans. W. E. Calvert, Report of the Fifth Thule Expedition, 1921–1924, vol. 7 (Copenhagen: Gyldendal, 1952), p. 133.

[5]Ibid.

[6]Ibid., pp. 133–34.

[7]Raymond Prince, "Indigenous Yoruba Psychiatry," in Kiev (ed.), pp. 101–2.

[8]Robert T. Trotter II and Juan Antonio Chavira, *Curanderismo: Mexican American Folk Healing* (Athens: University of Georgia Press, 1981), p. 82.

[9]Ibid., p. 87.

[10]Ibid.

[11]Ibid., pp. 87–88.

[12]Richard Katz, *Boiling Energy: Community Healing among the Kalahari Kung* (Cambridge, Mass.: Harvard University Press, 1982), p. 107.

[13]Stephen Fuchs, "Magic Healing Techniques among the Balahis in Central India," in Kiev (ed.), pp. 136–37.

[14]See Bruce Kapferer, *A Celebration of Demons: Exorcism and the Aesthetics of Healing in Sri Lanka* (Bloomington: Indiana University Press, 1983), pp. 131–37.

[15]See Douglas Sharon, *Wizard of the Four Winds: A Shaman's Story* (New York: Free Press, 1978), pp. 73–100.

[16]Raymond Prince, "Indigenous Yoruba Psychiatry," in Kiev (ed.), p. 94.

[17]Peter Worsley, "Non-Western Medical Systems," *Annual Review of Anthropology*, 11 (1982): 336.

[18]Ari Kiev, "The Study of Folk Psychiatry," in Kiev (ed.), p. 25.

[19]See Mircea Eliade, *Shamanism: Archaic Techniques of Ecstasy* (New York: Pantheon Books, 1964), pp. 23–26.

[20]See John A. Sanford, *Healing and Wholeness* (New York: Paulist Press, 1977), pp. 47, 65, 80–81.

[21]J. Perham, "Manangism in Borneo," *Journal of the Straits Branch of the Royal Asiatic Society* (Singapore, 1887), p. 101; cited in E. Fuller Torrey, *Witchdoctors and Psychiatrists: The Common Roots of Psychotherapy and Its Future* (New York: Harper & Row, 1986), p. 125.

[22]Torrey, p. 19.

[23]Ibid., p. 140.

[24]The term is used by Jerome D. Frank and Julia B. Frank, *Persuasion and Healing: A Comparative Study of Psychotherapy*, 3d ed. (Baltimore: Johns Hopkins University Press, 1991), pp. 24–29.

[25]See H. Rin, "A Study of the Aetiology of Koro in Respect to the Chinese Concept of Illness," *International Journal of Social Psychology*, 11, no. 1 (1965): 7–13. *Koro* is also referred to in Torrey, p. 30.

[26]A. J. Rubel, "The Epidemiology of a Folk Illness: Susto in Hispanic America," *Ethnology* 3 (1964): 268–83. *Susto* is also discussed in Torrey, pp. 144–45.

PART TWO
Christianity

INTRODUCTION

As in most religious traditions, healing is a prominent concern in Christianity. There are famous healers throughout the history of Christianity, many rituals for healing, many religious centers specializing in healing, and some Christian denominaions or sects that focus primarily on healing. There is nothing exceptional in this. Sickness and healing are such basic human experiences that it would be extraordinary if a major religious tradition, such as Christianity, remained indifferent to them. Because they touch the existential roots of people, sickness and healing relate directly to religious concerns.

The following section surveys the Christian tradition's diverse ways of thinking about and dealing with illness and healing. There are several striking similarities with the materials we covered in Part One. This certainly should come as no surprise. Indeed, some of the examples we dealt with in Part One were Christian, such as Eduardo Calderon Palomino, Don Pedro Yaramillo, Alba Wolde Tensae, *curanderismo*, and the Zinacanteco. Until very recently, Christianity has existed in traditional, nonscientific, or prescientific cultures. Views of sickness, theories of disease, and types of healers in Christianity therefore overlap or are identical to views, theories, and types of healers in traditional, nonscientific, or prescientific societies such as the kinds dealt with in Part One. One of the principal aims of Part Two is to show that the views of illness, strategies for healing, and types of healers we find in Christianity are very much like those we looked at in Part One.

Beginning with Jesus himself, Chapter 9 tries to show that in his healing practices Jesus has certain characteristics of a shamanic healer. This should not be surprising. The shaman is preeminently a spiritual healer, one who knows the spirit world and its dynamics, one who knows the nature and habits of the soul, that is, one who knows the spiritual nature of people. This type of healer, who draws upon the powers of the spirit world, or the powers of God, as they are usually referred to in Christianity, remains common throughout the history of Christianity. Those whom we might term *charismatic healers* (those having spiritual gifts) remain prominent in contemporary Christianity. So-called faith healers illustrate this type of healer in a flamboyant way (Chapter 12), while many others express it more discreetly in small church-related prayer or healing groups (Chapters 10 and 13).

Certain theories of illness are prominent in Christianity and indicate that there is a pervasive effort to frame illness in a meaningful context, something we saw to be central in the traditional materials we covered in Part One. As in many traditional societies, so in the Christian context illness is often thought about in terms of morality. Sin and sickness are closely related in many Christian materials. Sickness is a punishment for, or the result of, transgressing divine law or straying from spiritually wholesome habits of life. The direct or immediate cause of illness, as is the case in many of the examples we looked at in Part One, is a spirit. In this sense, as is very common throughout the world, Christian theories of disease tend toward externalizing and objectifying disease. It is something inflicted from outside. The inflicting spirit is often identified with Satan or a spirit under the control of the Devil. Again, this is very similar to theories of disease causation in many traditional cultures. Conversely, the spirit may be identified with God himself, who directly punishes sinners—again a very common theory of disease causation in traditional societies.

We also discuss the importance in Christianity of a sacred journey to one of Christendom's many sacred healing centers (Chapter 11). Such centers as Lourdes are often associated with the appearance and healing presence of a saint, which is an ancient tradition in Christianity. This type of center bears similarities to healing cults and beliefs in traditional cultures of the type we discussed in Part One. Like the Hindu god Balaji and his temple at Bharatpur, there are Christian spirits who specialize in healing and who may be approached at certain sacred centers, such as Lourdes. In both cases, healing is directly related to a pilgrimage undertaken by the sick person, often with his family or "support group."

In dealing with the Christian materials, then, I have taken pains to try to relate ideas of sickness and healing practices to materials in Part One. However, I have also tried to convey the distinctive nature of the Christian materials. Jesus as a healer is in many ways unique; he is not simply another shamanic healer. The saints as healing spirits are quite unlike healing spirits in other religions or cultures we looked at in Part One and are often said to be directly subordinate to God in terms of dispensing healing powers. Indeed, there is a strong emphasis in Christian materials on the ultimate power or position of God, without whom no healing whatsoever can take place. The Christian healer, while he or she may share remarkable similarities with healers in non-Christian traditional cultures, is almost always understood to be primarily a conduit for God's healing powers. Similarly, Christian healing rituals are almost always understood to be sacramental in the sense of being means by which God's grace or power is channeled. The ritualist is instrumental in the healing process but not essential to it.

Christians sometimes insist that Christian healers and healing rituals are totally different in kind from whatever powers are operating in non-Christian cultures. Christians sometimes contrast Christian healers and rituals with non-Christian ones in terms of truth and falsity. That is, Christian healing is said to derive from God's power, while non-Christian healing does not. One aim of Part Two is to suggest that such a dichotomy between Christian and non-Christian is not very helpful in understanding the dynamics of healing. There are so many similarities between Christian and non-Christian healilng materials that it is more likely that the healing dynamics in both cases are grounded in common truths about human existence, about how the human organism heals itself, and about how human society galvanizes itself to help people get better. In this sense, I have tried to deemphasize Christian healing as uniquely miraculous or supernatural and to place it in a more rational context by showing how Christians, like people in many non-Christian cultures, are trying to achieve similar results in similar ways based on similar views of illness.

Chapter 9
Jesus as a Healer

One of Jesus' main roles, perhaps his central role, in the Christian Gospels, was that of healer. Almost one-fifth of the Gospels are concerned with Jesus' healing and discussions or consequences arising from his healings.[1] In the Gospels we find Jesus performing healings everywhere he went, and it is also clear that people were often attracted to Jesus because of his reputation as a healer. There are forty-one different cases of healing in the Gospels,[2] but obviously there were many more, as several accounts of Jesus' healing mention that he healed many people at one time but do not describe or enumerate these cases.[3] For example, in Mark 6:56 we read: "And wherever he came, in villages, cities, or country, they laid the sick in the market places, and besought him that they might touch even the fringe of his garment; and as many as touched it were made well."[4] It is likely that Jesus healed hundreds, perhaps thousands, of people during his life.

SHAMANIC THEMES

As a healer, Jesus was a complex figure about whom it is difficult to generalize. He healed a variety of illnesses, used a variety of techniques, and healed in several different contexts. Nevertheless, in terms of healers and healing scenarios looked at previously, Jesus reveals certain shamanistic characteristics in his biography and his healing.[5]

First, Jesus experienced a period in the wilderness that is reminiscent of a shamanic initiatory ordeal. In the biographies of many shamans, the shaman-to-be undergoes severe testing in preparation for assuming a spiritual career. The forty days that Jesus spent in the wilderness, during which he fasted and was tested by spirits, serve a similar function in his biography. Enduring the test, he proved himself worthy of a spiritual vocation.

Second, Jesus undertook spirit or soul journeys that are reminiscent of shamanic soul travel and spiritual flight. During his forty days in the wilderness, for example, he traveled with the devil to the pinnacle of the temple, the sacred center of the universe in Judaism. He was also taken to a high mountain and shown the kingdoms of the world (Matt. 4:5–9). On another occasion, he went with three of his disciples to a mountain top and was transfigured. His face and garments shone brightly and became dazzling white. Moses and Elijah appeared next to him (Matt. 17:1–3). According to Christian tradition, after his death Jesus descended into hell and ascended into heaven. These events are similar to shamanic spirit journeys or soul travel in which the shaman demonstrates access to the spirit worlds: the shaman travels to heaven to converse with the gods or to hell to communicate with the spirits of the dead. Like a shaman, Jesus was able to have direct contact with spiritual dimensions of reality. Like a shaman, he was at home in the spirit world. Like a shaman, he had mastery over his spirit nature.

Third, Jesus was tended by, communicated directly with, and cultivated a special relationship with spirits, particularly God, whom he sometimes referred to as Father. In the wilderness, "angels ministered to him" (Mark 1:13; see also Matt. 4:11). After he was baptized by John in the Jordan River, Jesus had a dramatic encounter with a spirit. In the Gospel of Mark we read: "And when he came up out of the water, immediately he saw the heavens opened and the Spirit descending upon him like a dove; and a voice came from heaven, 'Thou are my beloved Son; with you I am well pleased'" (1:9–11). We are also told that the same spirit that "descended upon him" then "drove him out into the wilderness" (Mark 1:12). That is, the spirit that associated itself with him or adopted him then tested him, or was responsible for having him tested. A similar scene took place on the mountain where Jesus was transfigured. As he spoke to his disciples there, a bright cloud overshadowed them, and a voice from the cloud said: "This is my beloved Son with whom I am well pleased; listen to him" (Matt. 17:6). Like a shaman, that is, Jesus established a special rapport or relationship with a powerful spirit by whom, or in whose name, he did marvelous acts, such as healing.

Fourth, Jesus healed by means of, or in reference to, spiritual power or spiritual authority. He often confronted spirits directly. This is particularly clear when he healed illness caused by demon possession. In Mark we are told about a man possessed by an unclean spirit who approached Jesus in the synagogue. The spirit said to Jesus: "'What have you to do with us, Jesus of Nazareth? Have you come to destroy us? I know who you are, the Holy One of God.' But Jesus rebuked him saying, 'Be silent, and come out of him!'" The spirit then cried out loudly and convulsed the man and left him (Mark 1:21–26). A similar healing scene features a man who lived naked in a cemetery. Formerly the man had been bound in chains and fetters, but the powerful spirits who possessed him had broken them and driven him into the desert, where Jesus and his disciples came upon him. When the man (or the demons within the man) saw Jesus coming, he shouted and fell down in front of Jesus and said: "What have you to do with me Jesus, Son of the Most High God? I beseech you, do

Rembrandt Harmensz, "Christ Healing the Sick." The Hundred Guilder Print, 1649. Foto Marburg/Art Resource, NY.

not torment me." Jesus spoke to the demon, asked its name, and then exorcised all the demons that were troubling the man. He made them enter a herd of pigs, who then stampeded into a nearby lake and drowned. At that point the man returned to normality (Luke 8:26–33). In these and other cases, Jesus, like a shamanic healer, was able to communicate directly with spirits and they with him. He demonstrated his power to enter into the spirit realm and to dominate or control what happened there. In these cases of demon-caused illness, Jesus, like a shaman, healed by combating and defeating the spirits who caused the illness.

In several ways, then, it is clear that Jesus resembled the shamanic type of healer. This is not at all surprising when we realize that the worldview of first-century Judaism had much in common with cultures in which shamans were and are prominent and that healers in first-century Judaism used techniques that typify such cultures.

CHARISMA AND FAITH

Another characteristic of Jesus as a healer was his charismatic personality, presence, or power. He was not a medical technician, and very little emphasis was placed on his diagnostic or therapeutic skills. His healing techniques consisted primarily of touching the sick or saying something to them. His words were often in the form of a command for the person to be restored to health or wholeness. Sometimes Jesus touched the person with his saliva or with his saliva mixed with dirt (which may have been a common practice in his times). In a few cases people were healed simply by touching Jesus or his garments (for example, Matt. 9:20, Mark 5:25, and Luke 8:43).

It is very likely that people who were healed by touching Jesus' garments had great expectations from hearing stories of his powers. In Mark 6:56 we read: "Wherever he went . . . they laid down the sick in the open spaces, begging him to let them touch even the fringe of his cloak." It is likely that these people sought out Jesus and tried to touch him because they had heard of his reputation as a healer. In several cases the centrality of the sick person's attitude was underlined by Jesus himself, when he said that it was the person's faith that had brought about healing. Mark 5:34 tells of a woman suffering from chronic bleeding who touched Jesus' garment and was healed. Jesus said to her: "Your faith has made you well." Similarly, when he restored the sight of two blind men by touching their eyes, Jesus said to them: "According to your faith be it done to you" (Matt. 9:29).

In some of his healings, Jesus emphasized the faith of a third party, usually friends or relatives of a sick person. This was the case when a father brought his epileptic son to Jesus and Jesus cast out the demon that has been afflicting the boy. Before healing the boy, Jesus said to the man that "all things are possible to him who believes." This elicited from the father the declaration: "I believe; help my unbelief!" (Mark 9:23–24). Another case of this type occurred when several friends brought a paralytic to Jesus. They had to lower the stretcher through the roof because of the large crowd surrounding Jesus. Seeing the faith of the paralytic's friends, Jesus healed him (Mark 2:5).

There are some cases in which the faith of a third party is instrumental in healing a person who is not even present. In the Gospel of Matthew we read of a centurion who came to Jesus and asked him to help his paralyzed servant, who was at home. When Jesus offered to go to the centurion's house to heal the servant, the soldier said he was not worthy to have Jesus enter his home, but asked that Jesus heal the servant without moving from that place. Jesus marveled at the faith of the man and said: "Go: be it done for you as you have believed," and the servant was healed at that moment (Matt. 8:13). A similar story is told in the Gospel of John about a father who came to Jesus and asked him to help his dying son (4:47–54). Without seeing the boy, and impressed with the father's faith, Jesus healed the son.

FORGIVENESS OF SINS AND COMPASSION

In a few cases, forgiveness of sins was an important part of Jesus' healing. In the story of the paralytic who was lowered into Jesus' presence by his friends, Jesus was impressed by the faith of the friends and immediately said to the paralytic: "My son, your sins are forgiven" (Mark 2:5). Jesus then commanded the man to get up, take his stretcher with him, and go home. There was a direct relationship between the forgiveness of the man's sins and his dramatic healing.   A second healing involving forgiveness of sins concerned another paralytic at the pool of Bethzatha in Jerusalem as told in the Gospel of John.   The man had been ill for thirty-eight years.   After a brief exchange with him, Jesus commanded him to get up and walk, which he did.   Meeting the man later in the temple, Jesus said to him: "See, you are well!   Sin no more, that nothing worse befall you" (John 5:14).   In these two cases, but in very few others, Jesus seemed to relate illness to immorality and to relate ethical behavior to getting or staying well.   As we have seen above in Part One, this is an extremely common way of thinking about illness in traditional cultures.   It also became a common way of understanding illness in later Christianity (which we discuss in Chapters 10–12).   These two cases, however, were exceptional for Jesus and were not typical of his understanding of illness.

In the majority of cases, Jesus did not inquire into the moral conditon of people who were seeking healing.   That is, he did not seem to associate sin or immorality with sickness.   It was quite unusual for him to forgive people's sins before healing them or to inquire or comment about their faith.   Jesus usually did not restore health as a reward for something else, such as the confession of sins, moral uprightness, or repentence.   In the vast majority of cases, Jesus was not judgmental.   He did not heal in order to teach something else, although sometimes he did use a healing as the occasion for a religious discourse or lesson.

In the overwhelming majority of cases, Jesus is described as healing sponta-

Gabriel Max (1840–1915), "The Raising of Jarius' Daughter" (Mark 5), 1878.
Collection of the Montreal Museum of Fine Arts, Gift of Lord Atholstan. Photo Brian Merrett, MFA.

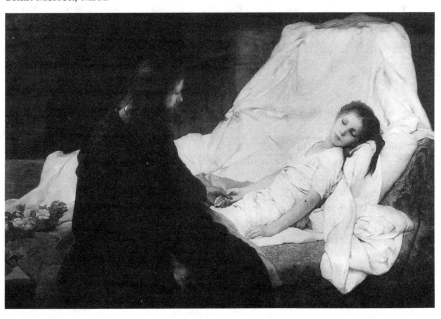

neously, with little or no preamble. He usually did not inquire about the person's past, or even about the nature of the illness, as many healers in traditional cultures would do. Such passages as this are common in the Gospels: "And when Jesus entered Peter's house, he saw his mother-in-law lying sick with a fever; he touched her hand, and the fever left her, and she rose and served him. That evening they brought to him many who were possessed wih demons; and he cast out the spirits with a word, and healed all who were sick" (Matt. 8:14–16).

In some cases Jesus is said to have healed out of compassion. At the gates of the city of Nain, Jesus and his disciples came across a funeral procession. The dead man was the only son of a widow who was accompanying his corpse to the cemetery. When Jesus saw her, "he had compassion on her" and told her not to weep. Then he touched the bier and told the young man to get up, which he did (Luke 7:7–11). At another point, Jesus came upon a large crowd, "and he had compassion on them, and healed their sick" (Matt. 14:14). Outside Jericho, in the midst of a crowd, Jesus came upon two blind men sitting by the road. They called out to him to have mercy on them. The crowd rebuked them, but Jesus stopped and asked what they wanted. They asked him to restore their sight. "And Jesus in pity touched their eyes, and immediately they received their sight and followed him" (Matt. 20:29–34). Elsewhere in the Gospels, a leper approached Jesus, knelt before him, and said, "If you will, you can make me clean." Moved with pity, Jesus stretched forth his hand and touched him, healing him (Mark 1:40).

COSMIC TENSION

In the Gospels, Jesus' healing is often placed within the context of a tension or struggle between opposing forces. This is particularly clear in those cases where Jesus exorcised demons. In some cases these demons challenged Jesus or expressed fear of him. In some cases Jesus rebuked the demon. In a synagogue at Capernaum, an unclean spirit possessing a man shouted angrily at Jesus. Jesus rebuked the spirit, saying: "Be silent, and come out of him!" The spirit gave a loud cry, shook the man he was possessing, and came out (Mark 1:23–27). Similarly, in the case of the man living in a cemetery who had been driven mad by a demon, the demon directly challenged Jesus, and Jesus exorcised it by saying: "Come out of the man, you unclean spirit!" (Mark 5:2–10). It seems clear in these cases that Jesus opposed sickness-causing demons, that he understood them as malevolent, that they offended his wish for human beings to be well. In this regard, he is like many healers in traditional cultures who are understood (or understand themselves) to be guardians of the moral and social order, which is threatened by malevolent spirits. The healer's role in many cases is defender of social harmony as reflected in the health and well-being of individuals.

Like most healers in traditional cultures, Jesus appears to have framed illness in a meaningful context, at least in certain cases. In the most general sense, the Gospel writers see Jesus' healings as aimed at overcoming the spirits of darkness, which opposed the kingdom of God. The Gospels portray Jesus as the agent by whom, or in whom, a new spiritual age was being brought about. They interpret his dramatic healings as signs of this new age. In some Gospel passages, Jesus' healings are regarded as proof of this cosmic transformation and of his spiritual mission. In response to an inquiry sent by John the Baptist through a messenger (John was in prison at the time) concerning whether Jesus was the Messiah, the figure in Jewish religion who was supposed to usher in a new spiritual age, Jesus replied: "Go and tell John what you hear and see: the blind receive their sight and the lame walk, lepers are cleansed and the deaf hear, and the dead are raised up, and the poor have good news preached to them" (Matt. 11:4–5).

Jesus' healing seems to have been an integral part of his ministry, which was to proclaim the advent of a new spiritual age. The Gospels see Jesus as an agent of God, or as God himself, who appeared in order to combat and overthrow forces that break and wound human beings. Sickness, both mental and physical, is seen as a symptom of brokenness and bondage, which Jesus, as the bringer of divine healing power, combated wherever he found it. Jesus' healing, furthermore, was unconditional. To my knowledge, there is not one example of Jesus' refusing to heal someone. His concern for people was not simply spiritual; he was more than a doctor of the soul. His preoccupation with physical and mental healing makes clear that for him (or at least for Jesus as understood by the Gospel writers) the physical and mental condition of human beings was inextricably bound up with their spiritual condition. Wholeness was not only spiritual but physical and mental, according to the Gospel writers' understanding of Jesus the healer.

ENDNOTES

[1]Morton T. Kelsey, *Healing and Christianity in Ancient Thought and Modern Times* (New York: Harper & Row, 1973), p. 54.

[2]Seventy-two accounts are given, but several are repeated in more than one of the four Gospels.

[3]Ibid.

[4]All quotations from the Bible are from the Revised Standard Version.

[5]For a discussion of Jesus' shamanic characteristics, see Aylward Shorter, *Jesus and the Witchdoctor: An Approach to Healing and Wholeness* (Maryknoll, N.Y.: Orbis Books, 1985), and Morton Smith, *Jesus the Magician* (New York: Harper & Row, 1978).

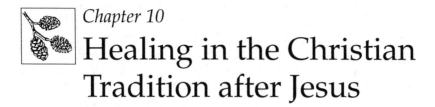

Chapter 10
Healing in the Christian Tradition after Jesus

HEALING TRADITIONS

There are three important and distinct healing traditions in the Christian tradition that we will discuss:

1. Charismatic healers. Throughout Christian history we find charismatic individuals who heal primarily by means of spiritual energy or power. This tradition of healing can be traced to Jesus himself. These healers are sometimes church officials, sometimes monks or ascetics, and sometimes laypersons. They usually heal without elaborate rituals, and their power seems to reside in their charismatic personalities. They often heal simply by touching a person or proclaiming a person healed. In this respect, they appear very similar to Jesus himself in their healing practices.

2. Healing rituals. Healing is also common in the Christian tradition (more so in some denominations than others) in what we might call a routine, ritual context. Healing rituals, sacraments, masses, and prayer groups (including pastoral or priestly counseling) are to be found in most periods of Christian history, and all of these "routine" types of Christian healing exist in contemporary Christianity.

3. Sacred healing centers. Healing is also associated throughout Christian history with sacred centers, shrines, or churches. Some churches associated with the healing powers of a particular saint have become the destination of healing journeys. Often a relic of the saint is enshrined in the church and is believed to have healing powers. Sometimes the shrine is associated with an apparition of Mary or another saint, as in the case of the most famous of all healing shrines, Lourdes, in southern France. The tradition of sacred centers is still vigorous in contemporary Christianity.

THEOLOGICAL INTERPRETATIONS

The theological frameworks within which sickness and healing are understood in Christianity differ from period to period and from one denomination to another. In general, however, there are two principal theological interpretations of sickness and healing:

1. Sickness is caused by forces, spirits, or beings opposed to God. The devil and malevolent spirits are believed to cause illness out of sheer perverseness or to thwart the divine plan for humankind; illness is not the fault of the sick person. This is the view that dominates the Gospels' picture of Jesus as a healer.

2. Sickness is caused by God for different purposes. It may be punishment for sin; in this view, sickness, as in most cultures, is directly related to morality. Or sickness may be sent by God to teach the person a lesson. Or it may be sent to test or temper a person so that the person will provide an example of faith for others, as in the case of Job in the Hebrew Bible (Old Testament).

Although these two theologies or interpretations of sickness and healing appear to be opposed to each other, they coexist in most periods of Christianity. Certainly this is the case in contemporary Christianity; even the same Christian community or an individual healer will refer to both views at different times. These two ways of coming to terms with understanding illness seem appropriate to the same individual in different circumstances. In the view that attributes illness to inimical, hostile, malevolent forces, the sick person is often viewed (or understands herself) as a hapless, innocent victim. Healing involves mustering divine powers to resist a demonic invasion or to defeat malevolent forces. In the view that attributes the origin of sickness to God, the sick person is usually understood, in some sense, to have earned the illness, to be responsible for it. The patient is being punished or tested by God. The aim of the sickness may be to change or moderate the nature of the person's life.[1]

CHARISMATIC HEALERS AFTER JESUS

In the Gospels, Jesus commissions his disciples to go forth to preach, teach, baptize, and heal. Indeed, they carry on his healing ministry in much the same way that he did. That is, they heal primarily by means of their individual healing power (or the power of God through them). They do not learn any sophisticated healing techniques or medical knowledge, nor do they employ elaborate rituals or take pains to create an appropriate healing setting. Like Jesus, they are primarily itinerant preachers, a part of whose ministry is healing. Usually they heal by touch or command or by their very presence, in much the same way that Jesus healed.

Several such examples of this type of healing are found in the Book of Acts. On the way to the temple, Jesus' disciples Peter and John were asked for alms by a lame man sitting by the gate of the temple. Peter asked the man to look at him and then said that he did not have any alms to give him, "but I give you what I have;

in the name of Jesus Christ of Nazareth, walk." He took the man by the hand and helped him up. The man's legs regained their strength, and he walked and then leaped about (Acts 3:2–8). On the island of Malta, where he had been shipwrecked, the apostle Paul visited the home of Publius, an important man there. Publius's father was very ill with fever and dysentery. Paul put his hands on the man and healed him, "and when this had taken place, the rest of the people on the island who had diseases also came and were cured" (Acts 28:7–10). Visiting the church at Lydda, Peter came upon a man named Aeneas who had been paralyzed for eight years. Peter said to him: "Aeneas, Jesus Christ heals you; rise up and make your bed." The man got up, healed (Acts 9:32–35). In one case, the sick were brought out to the street in their beds so that when Peter passed his shadow would fall on them and heal them (Acts 5:15–16).

The tradition in Christianity of individuals who heal by touch, word, or their mere presence includes some world renouncers who went to live ascetic lives in the desert, the so-called desert fathers, in the fourth through sixth centuries. The *Historia Lausiaca* by Palladius, written in the late fourth century, contains several descriptions of healings done by the ascetic Marcarius. The father of a very sick young boy brought him to Marcarius, deep in the desert where the ascetic was living. The boy was diagnosed as being possessed by a demon. Marcarius put his hands on the boy's head and over his heart. Then he prayed. The boy swelled up, his body became very hot, he cried out, and then his body cooled down and he assumed normal size. The ascetic gave the boy back to his father, cured.[2] The ascetic Hilarion, who also had retreated to the Egyptian desert, was renowned for his powers and attracted many people in search of his healing. He is described in Jerome's *Life of Saint Hilarion* as healing a woman of sterility, three boys sick with fever, and a man made rigid by a demon. In each case, Hilarion did little more than pray, make the sign of the cross, or touch the afflicted person.[3]

One of the most famous healers in the early history of the church was Martin of Tours (316–97), whose healings are described in Sulpitius Severus's (c. 360–420) *Life of Saint Martin*. Martin was a Roman soldier who converted to Christianity and eventually founded a monastery in France (Gaul). Many of his healings involved exorcising demons. A man possessed by a demon was brought to Martin. The man tried to bite anyone who came near him. Martin thrust his fingers into the man's mouth and challenged the demon to bite them. The man backed up as if frightened without biting Martin and from that moment was cured.[4] In some cases, Martin healed people by bodily contact. This is vividly illustrated in the case of his resuscitating a monk who had just died. Martin went into the monk's cell, closed the door, lay down full length on top of the corpse, and prayed. In less than two hours the monk slowly began to revive. Martin also used sustained physical contact to heal a paralyzed girl. In response to the touch of his body, she gradually regained movement.[5] In these cases, it is as if Martin were infusing his healing energy into the sick people in much the same fashion as the Kalahari Kung healers do in their healing dances.

The Venerable Bede (673–735) described healings performed by several church leaders in England in the late seventh century. John of Beverley, Bishop of York, healed many people by prescribing a bath in or sip of holy water. He healed others by touching and blessing them with such words as "May you soon recover." In the case of a mute boy, he had the boy extend his tongue, made the sign of the cross on it, and commanded him to say the world "yea," which the boy did.[6]

The following description of a healing done by Saint Cuthbert, also in seventh-century England, is typical of healings done by famous church leaders:

> There came some women bearing a certain youth who lay on a litter; they carried him to . . . the holy bishop . . . adjuring him in the name of our Lord Jesus Christ that he would bless him with holy relics and would utter a prayer for him to the Lord, beseeching God's pardon for the sins by which he was bound and on account of which he endured punishment. So the bishop . . . prayed . . . and blessing the boy, he drove away the disease and restored him to health.[7]

In some cases, the sick sought out famous Christian leaders who had achieved reputations as healers in order to simply touch their clothing, have a sight of them, or touch something with which the famous person had been in contact. Some people believed that food left over from Saint Anselm's (1034–1109) meals had healing power and that if one heard him bless the sacrament one would be healed.[8] Some people believed that bread consecrated for the Eucharist by Bernard of Clairvaux (1090–1153) cured illness. Saint Dominic (1170–1221) and Saint Francis (1182–1226) were believed to be able to cure illness by touch, gesture (usually the sign of the cross), or command.[9]

Saint Francis Xavier (1506–52), Saint Catherine of Siena (1347–80), John Wesley (1703–91) (the founder of Methodism), George Fox (1624–91) (the founder of the Quakers), and many others, both Catholic and Protestant, gained reputations for having healing power. In the nineteenth century, Prince Alexander of Hohenlohe, Dorothea Trudel, and Johann Christoph Blumhardt were all renowned healers in Germany and Switzerland. Blumhardt, a Protestant pastor, became the center of a healing cult when his fame attracted large numbers of people to his small church.[10]

All of these people knew little or nothing of medical science and did not practice elaborate therapy. Healing was accomplished by touch, prayer, command, or gesture.[11] Most of these people belong to the "holy person" category of healer. That is, they were individuals known for their piety, religious practice, or sometimes their religious office. Many were saints. Their healing power, at least in part, seems related to their pious, holy lives. It was not their medical knowledge, their therapeutic techniques, or the care they took in setting the proper context in which to heal that was effective. It was their reputation as holy, pious, and good that seems important. In most cases, healing was not their only or even their primary occupation. Healing was an incidental part of their lives, something they often did not encourage, that came to them as a surprise. It seems to have been a by-product of their religious lives or holy personalities.

GODFREY MOWATT AND AGNES SANFORD

The importance of individual charismatic healers in Christianity has persisted quite prominently into this century.[12] Two of the more restrained and subdued Christian healers of this century are Godfrey Mowatt (1874–1958) and Agnes Sanford (1897–1976).

Godfrey Mowatt was blinded in an accident when he was only seven years old.[13] His blindness did not prevent him from receiving an advanced education and becoming involved in a wide range of social and government agencies. He became particularly prominent in working for the blind in England and throughout the world. Another accident that greatly influenced the course of his life took place when he was forty-three years old. His glass eye was struck by a pellet from an air gun, and slivers of glass pierced deep into his eye socket. The recovery from this accident was long and painful and involved a lot of delicate surgery. It was during this period, when he described himself as feeling completely miserable, that his wife suggested he visit friends who were sick. This activity cheered him up, partly, he said, because it took his mind off himself. It was during these visits that people began to notice that, not only were they cheered by Mowatt's visits, they were becoming healed as well. On March 19, 1919, two years after the accident, Mowatt had a vision in which he heard the command: "Go forth and serve your fellow men." He said that he was given to understand that his own experiences with suffering had equipped him to understand, minister to, and alleviate the suffering of others.

It was not until 1936, however, that Mowatt decided to dedicate his life to healing. Before then, he had remained extremely active in public life. All through this period it had become increasingly clear that Mowatt had healing power, but his healing activities remained sporadic. In 1936 Mowatt visited the Guild of Health, a group dedicated to promoting divine healing. Soon Mowatt was heavily involved in the society and began to take part in regular healing services in a church in central London. By 1942 Mowatt's fame as a healer was widespread in England, and the Archbishop of Canterbury, William Temple, decided to commission Mowatt, who was now sixty-eight years old, as an official minister of healing. In the years that followed, Mowatt traveled throughout England and other countries bringing his healing touch to the sick.

The usual context in which Mowatt healed was a brief, simple service held in a parish church. Mowatt never asked for or received fees for healing. The services lacked the flamboyance and drama of many "faith healings" in North America. Mowatt usually would give a brief sermon explaining some feature of the church's healing ministry. For example, he often spoke on the theme of forgiving others before asking for healing from God. Then he would invite all who wished to do so to come forward and kneel at the altar rail, just as they might do to receive the Eucharist. Guided by the parish priest, he would then pass along the line of kneeling people and put his hands on their heads. He would always say this prayer when he did so: "May the mercy of God, which is present here with us now, enter into your soul, your mind, your body, and heal you from all that harms you."[14] After everyone had been blessed by Mowatt, there was a period of silent prayer, the saying of the Lord's Prayer, and then a final prayer of thanksgiving and blessing. The flood of letters that Mowatt received during his ministry indicates that many of those whom he touched and blessed found healing.

In general, the healings were not dramatic and instantaneous, of the type sometimes associated with the more colorful faith healers. People tended to report small but clearly noticeable improvements at Mowatt's touch, or immediately thereafter, and then steady improvement of their condition. Mowatt himself understood his power to heal in terms of the power of God that is constantly in and around us. He saw himself as someone who was able to put people in more direct touch with this power and attributed healing to this power, not to himself.[15] In Godfrey Mowatt we have a good example of the wounded healer, a person who has himself suffered deeply and seems able to understand intuitively the sufferings of others in such a way as to help them get well. Mowatt's tragic blinding when he was a boy and the later accident seemed to function as initiatory ordeals in which his perceptions were sharpened and intensified. During his convalescence after his glass eye was shattered, Mowatt discovered a purpose to his life. He awakened to the possibility of serving others in a healing ministry. Mowatt is also another good example of the holy-person type of healer, so common in Christianity, who seems to derive healing power from a pious life spent in serving others. His healing power did not reside in special medical knowledge or elaborate therapies. It consisted primarily of his presence, his touch, and his word.

Agnes Sanford (1897–1976) was born in China. Her parents were American missionaries there, and she lived in China until she was fifteen years old, when she went to the United States to attend Peace College in Raleigh, North Carolina. She returned to China with the idea of spending her life there as a teacher. She acquired a position in an Anglican school in Shanghai, married an American Anglican priest, and had her first child. Soon afterward she and her family left China for the United States, where her husband wished to acquire some further training. They were unable to return to China because of the civil war between the Communists and the Nationalists in the 1930s.

Her husband took a church in Moorestown, New Jersey, and it was there that Agnes Sanford spent much of her adult life. She became an active participant in the local church, leading Bible classes, and eventually became known as a writer and powerful healer.

Although Sanford had some inklings concerning her own ability as a spiritual healer at an early age and sensed that the established church should be exploiting its healing potential, it was an Anglican priest's healing of her child, Jack, and of Sanford herself shortly thereafter, that inspired her career as one of the most famous Christian healers in North America in recent times. When her youngest child was just a year-and-a-half old, he developed a serious ear infection and a high fever. When Sanford complained to a visiting Anglican priest about the child's condition, he answered that he would pray for the child and went upstairs and did so. He addressed the baby, saying: "Now shut your eyes and go to sleep. I'm going to ask God to come into your ears and make them well. And when you wake up, you'll be all right." Sanford's own account of this incident is as follows:

His prayer as I recall it was just as simple as were these opening remarks. He laid his hands upon the baby's ears and kept them there for several minutes. "Please, Lord Jesus," he said, "send your power right now into this baby's ears and take away all germs or infection and make them well. Thank You, Lord, for I believe that You are doing this, and I see these ears as You made them to be." The child shut his eyes, grew pale as the fever died out of his face, and went to sleep. And when he woke up, his temperature was normal and his ears were well.[16]

At this time, Sanford herself was suffering from severe depression and decided to seek help from the same priest. To her delight and surprise, she also was dramatically healed.

After a short time, the minister laid his hands on my head and prayed for the healing of my mental depression, quite as simply and naturally as he had prayed for the healing of Jack's ears. And it happened immediately! All heaven broke loose upon me and within me! Great waves of joy flooded my mind! I do not remember what I said or what Mr. Colwell said, but I sang and shouted at the top of my voice all the way home!"[17]

The nucleus for Sanford's healing career, especially in the early years, was the parish community in Moorestown. She was able to interest her husband in the importance of spiritual healing, and many of the people she first healed were members of the church. Healing services became a part of the regular church routine, and after a while she and her husband undertook what they termed *missions* at the invitation of other church groups. On these missions they would teach others what they knew about healing and perform healing rituals and services. After the publication of her book *The Healing Light* in 1947, Sanford became increasingly well-known and was soon in demand throughout North America.

In addition to what we might term her formal healing ministry, which was undertaken for the most part in the context of the missions described above or in prayer groups associated with churches of different denominations, Sanford healed in many informal situations as well. During World War II, for example, she became a Red Cross volunteer and worked in the Tilton Army Hospital at Fort Dix in New Jersey. The miserable plight of many of the soldiers in the hospital moved her to pray for their healing, a practice that was discouraged at the hospital. Time after time Sanford would take the opportunity to help individual soldiers by discreetly praying with them for healing. In the end, she was asked to leave the hospital because of these healing practices, which apparently were against hospital regulations.

Several years after her husband moved to Massachusetts to take a church in the town of Westboro, he and Sanford established the School of Pastoral Care. The aim of the school was to teach priests and ministers how to cultivate spiritual gifts, particularly the gift of healing. This was an aspect of the Christian ministry, the Sanfords felt, that was not being taught or even considered in seminaries throughout North America. Over a period of five days, Sanford and her husband would meet with a group of ministers and share with them their knowledge of spiritual healing. Through the School of Pastoral Care the Sanfords came to interest hundreds of clergy in the healing ministry.

Sanford's theology of healing emphasized the ever-present nature of God's power, which she often referred to as God's healing light. This power or light is available to anyone, as it underlies and pervades the entire creation. Access to this power, according to Sanford, is primarily through prayer accompanied by an absolute faith in God's healing power. Sanford also spoke of a spiritual person or self that abides with and in the physical body. For her, healing involved, first and foremost, healing this spiritual body, which was done through prayer and ritual.

Sanford's method of healing was rather simple and straightforward. She would first get a clear picture of what was wrong with the sick person. Then she would visualize this part of the person as healthy and whole. As she pictured the person restored, she would pray to God for healing and lay her hands on the part of the person that was afflicted. In many cases, Sanford and her "patients" reported feeling heat and a tingling sensation. Sanford's description of a healing gives a clear picture of the simplicity and informality of her healing method.

> I went to see a little girl who had been in a cast for five months following infantile paralysis. One day I placed my hands above the rigid knee in that instinctive laying-on of hands that every mother knows. (What mother has not soothed a crying baby with the laying-on of hands? And what lover of animals has never gentled a restive horse with the same soothing touch?) And I asked that the light of God might shine through me into the small, stiff knee and make it well.
>
> "Oh, take your hands away!" cried the little girl. "It's hot."
>
> "That's God's power working in your knee, Sally," I replied. "It's like electricity working in your lamp. I guess it has to be hot so as to make the knee come back to life. So you must stand it now for a few minutes, while I tell you about Peter Rabbit."[18]

Like Godfrey Mowatt, Agnes Sanford discovered and developed her healing powers while dealing with her own illness. Also like Mowatt, she did not heal by means of elaborate rituals or complicated techniques. It was primarily her ability to contact a healing power, which she referred to as God, through prayer and faith, that empowered her.

HEALING RITUALS

While the importance of individual, charismatic healers in the tradition of Jesus himself is clear throughout the history of Christianity, the church also developed healing rituals and sacraments that were administered, for the most part, by church officials. An indication that such rituals were a part of early church history is indicated in a passage from the letter of James in the New Testament:

> Is any among you sick? Let him call for the elders of the church, and let them pray over him, anointing him with oil in the name of the Lord; and the prayer of faith will save the sick man, and the Lord will raise him up; and if he has committed sins, he will be forgiven. Therefore confess your sins to one another, and pray for one another, that you may be healed. (James 5:14–16)

Here the act of healing has become sacramental and institutional. Healing power does not rest upon the charismatic nature of the healer but belongs to the church as an institution. It may be channeled or dispensed through the duly consecrated or appointed representatives of the church, in this case "the elders of the church." In later Christian tradition, bishops and priests became the people who were entitled to bestow healing sacramentally and ritually.

The institutionalization of healing is clear in the linking of healing to the sacraments. Baptism, confession, and communion came to be viewed as rituals that dispelled sickness and had protective qualities and powers. Baptism was believed to repel evil spirits that dwelled within a person or that might attack a person and cause sickness. Confession was believed to purify people and make them impervious to sickness. Communion was held to have cleansing power.[19] In addition, the rituals of exorcism, laying hands on the sick, anointing them with holy oil, and making the sign of the cross were all employed in combating sickness and restoring health. The rituals of laying hands on the sick and anointing them with oil (sometimes also involving making the sign of the cross) eventually came to be regarded as a sacrament as well, the sacrament of unction (later called extreme unction) or visiting the sick. The original intention of this set of rituals, the seventh sacrament, was to restore health and rid the communicant of sickness, not to prepare the patient for death, which eventually became its purpose.[20]

The theory of healing in these rituals is similar to the sacramental theology in Christianity. The church contains a superabundance of grace (earned by Jesus) that may be dispensed to members of the church by its consecrated leaders (bishops, priests, or ministers who are Jesus' representatives). This grace has healing effects that may cure sickness, in addition to refreshing the soul or renewing the spirit. For centuries, countless Christians sought relief from illness through the rituals of the institutional church.

The passage from the letter of James quoted above is significant also because it expresses an important theological view of illness and healing, a view that is almost entirely absent in the healing of Jesus himself as described in the Gospels but one that comes to dominate much of later Christianity. In this passage, the anointing of the sick with oil is said to forgive any sins the person may have committed. Conversely, the passage also says that by confessing sins to each other and praying for each other, sickness will be cured (James 5:16). The linking of sin, or morality generally, with illness is clear here, and confession of sin as a healing act is also emphasized. This is an understanding of illness and healing that we have seen in many traditional cultures. Indeed, it is a view found in almost every culture we have looked at.

While the passage from James does not indicate exactly how morality, or sin, is implicated in causing illness, or how confession helps in healing, it is clear in many other Christian sources that illness comes from God. Illness may be sent as punishment, as a form of discipline, to teach a lesson, or to test a person. Whatever the purpose, however, sickness has come to be understood as a divine visitation. This view is explicit in Gregory the Great's *Book of Pastoral Rule*, a work that was destined to become extremely popular among clergy for centuries (he was pope from 590 to 604).

In Gregory's view, God molds, tempers, fashions, and disciplines those he cares for by afflicting them with illness. Much in the same way that a sculptor fashions a beautiful statue by striking the rock with a hammer, God fashions human beings. For Gregory, illness should be looked on as a blessing, an opportunity to discipline and improve oneself. "The sick are to be admonished that they feel themselves to be sons of God in that the scourge of discipline chastises them."[21] God also can heal, of course, but healing is now clearly related to moral improvement, penance, and willingness to correct one's behavior.

Linking sickness with sin and divine punishment or visitation became such an accepted idea at certain periods in Christianity that physicians were instructed not to treat patients unless they had first confessed their sins to a priest. At the Fourth Lateran Council (1215) the church declared that because sickness was often caused by sin, a physician's first duty when called to take care of the sick was to summon a priest. The Council's decree said that once spiritual health was restored, bodily health would return. In the sixteenth century, the church required physicians to swear that they would stop treating a patient if, after three days, the patient had not made confession backed by a statement to prove it.[22] In the eighteenth century, Catholic physicians who treated patients who had not confessed were forbidden to continue to practice medicine.[23]

The attitude that sickness is a scourge sent by God either to teach a lesson or to punish or correct sinful ways is still found in contemporary Christianity. The Anglican *Book of Common Prayer*'s Office for the Visitation of the Sick expressed such ideas quite clearly as recently as 1972:

> Dearly beloved, know this, that Almighty God is the Lord of life and death, and of all things to them pertaining, as youth, strength, health, age, weakness, and sickness. Wherefore, whatsoever your sickness is, know you certainly that it is God's visitation. And for what cause soever this sickness is sent unto you; whether it be to try your patience for the example of others, and that your faith may be found in the day of the Lord laudable, glorious, and honourable, to the increase of glory and endless felicity; or else it be sent unto you to correct and amend in you whatsoever doth offend the eyes of your heavenly Father, know you certainly, that if you truly repent you of your sins, and bear your sickness patiently, trusting in God's mercy, for his dear Son Jesus Christ's sake, and render unto him humble thanks for his fatherly visitation, submitting yourself wholly unto his will, it shall turn to your profit, and help you forward in the right way that leadeth unto everlasting life.[24]

Perhaps the clearest example of the move away from a view of sickness as something caused by hostile spirits or Satan, or as something God opposes and wants to overcome, to a view of sickness as an instrument of God's punishment and education is found in the gradual change in the church's understanding of the sacrament of extreme unction. In the early history of the church, the rituals constituting this sacrament were meant to relieve the communicant of sickness. The sacrament was seen as a form of God's grace toward the sick. It was aimed at alleviating suffering and restoring health. The priest and communicant both expected the sacrament to bring about healing. By the twelfth century, however, the sacrament was seen primarily, if not exclusively, as preparation for death. The sacrament came to be known as extreme unction and is only used when a person is at the point of death. The sacrament is aimed, not at healing, but at preparing a person for death. In this sacrament, confession of sins, anointing with oil, and laying on of hands are all employed to prepare the soul for dying, not to heal physical sickness. In the words of Thomas Aquinas (1225–74): "Extreme Unction is a spiritual remedy, since it avails for the remission of sins. . . . the effect intended in the administration of this sacrament is the healing of the disease of sin."[25]

ENDNOTES

[1]In some ways these two theories are reflected in modern secular medicine's ideas about disease causation. One modern theory, which we might call the objective theory of disease, emphasises the invasion of the body by a foreign object—a germ or virus. Healing is the process of ridding the body of this alien presence. This is similar to the idea that disease is caused by a malevolent demon. The sick person is primarily a victim and not responsible for the illness. Another modern idea about disease causation says that illness arises due to the person's pathological behavior or habits, stresses, imbalances, or choice of a dangerous environment. The illness fits the sick person; the patient has "earned" the disease. Healing is the process of restoring harmony, changing or reforming one's life, possibly changing one's personality or approach to life. As in the Christian theory of illness as a divine visitation, illness "fits" the sick person; that is, it is related to his or her overall life history and pattern, and healing involves learning a lesson from the illness and reforming one's habits and attitudes.

[2]Cited in Morton T. Kelsey, *Healing and Christianity in Ancient Thought and Modern Times* (New York: Harper & Row, 1973), p. 164.

[3]Ibid., p. 193.

[4]Cited in ibid., pp. 190–91.

[5]Cited in ibid, p. 190.

[6]Cited in ibid., p. 229.

[7]Anonymous Life of St. Cuthbert, iv. 5, in B. Colgrave, *Two Lives of St. Cuthbert* (Cambridge: Cambridge University Press, 1940), pp. 117–19; cited in Wilfrid Bonser, *The Medical Background of Anglo-Saxon England: A Study in History, Psychology, and Folklore* (Oxford: Oxford University Press, 1963), p. 5.

[8]Kelsey, p. 231.

[9]Ibid., pp. 231–32.

[10]Ibid., pp. 235–37.

[11]Ibid., pp. 232–35.

[12]Indeed, the phenomenon of the "faith healer" has dominated certain periods and certain Christian movements in twentieth-century Christianity in North America. In the case of many of the more flamboyant "faith healers," healing has become the central focus of their ministries. See Chapter 12, "Contemporary Christian Faith Healers."

[13]The following section on Mowatt is based on Tom Harpur, *The Uncommon Touch: An Investigation of Spiritual Healing* (Toronto: McClelland & Stewart,1994), pp. 75–97.

[14]Ibid., p. 84.

[15]Ibid., p. 85.

[16]Agnes Sanford, *Sealed Orders* (Plainfield, N.J.: Logos International, 1972), p. 97.

[17]Ibid., p. 99.

[18]Agnes Sanford, T*he Healing Light* (St. Paul, Minn.: Macalestser Park Publishing Co., 1947), p. 31.

[19]Kelsey, p. 207.

[20]Ibid., p. 207.

[21]Cited in ibid., pp. 196–97.

[22]Ibid., p. 212.

[23]Ibid.

[24]Cited in ibid., p. 16.

[25]Cited in ibid., p. 209.

Chapter 11

Saints
and Healing Shrines

Like many cultures and traditions, Christianity is known for its healing shrines. Throughout its history, shrines associated with healing have been an important part of popular Christian piety. In most cases, Christian healing shrines are churches. In addition, most healing shrines (or churches) are associated with a saint who has a reputation for healing. Some of the most famous healing shrines in Christendom are associated with the Virgin Mary, queen of saints. Healing power at these sacred places is more or less constant, but at certain times, usually coinciding with the patron saint's feast day or with some day important in the Marian calendar, healing powers are considered intensified and particular shrines may be extremely crowded.

Churches became healing centers at a very early period in Christianity. In some cases churches were built on the sites of pagan healing shrines (or the shrines were simply converted into churches). The healing rituals of these pagan shrines often persisted, and the role of the former pagan priests was assumed by the new Christian priests. The priests, whether pagan or Christian, typically played three healing roles: (1) they looked after the sick, many of whom were insane, becoming their caretakers; (2) they acted as intermediaries conveying prayers to the healing deity of the shrine; and (3) they acted as exorcists, particularly in the case of mental disease.[1]

In some cases, Christian healing shrines are associated with particular kinds of illness.[2] The healing shrine at Gheel in Belgium, for example, is special for those suffering from mental illness. The shrine is sacred to Dympna, the patron saint of the mentally ill. Her biography is directly related to her role as patron saint of the mad and to Gheel as a sacred healing place for the mentally ill. Dympna refused to marry the man chosen by her father, preferring to lead a chaste, religious life. Her father, who was mad, became enraged at her resistance to his will and chopped off her head. Around 1200, a church was built on the place of her martyrdom, where her remains also were buried. For many years people came there for cures and underwent elaborate rituals, which included crawling under Dympna's tomb, which had been relocated inside the church. Many people also did this as a precaution against being attacked by mad people. Soon the mentally ill were flocking to Gheel for curing and a problem arose: what to do with all the mentally ill who were roaming the streets of the small town? In time, the people of Gheel began to open their homes to the mentally ill and incorporated them into the regular routines of their lives and the village. In this way, many of the mentally ill, especially the mentally retarded, who came to Gheel found healing in the sense of being incorporated into normal society. Gheel came to be known as the City of the Simple. It remains today one of the most effective places for treating the mentally ill and is now administered by the Belgian Ministry of Public Health.[3]

The rituals done at healing shrines differ quite dramatically. At some shrines, pilgrims sleep in the church or shrine in the hope of being visited or blessed by the presiding saint in a dream. This is very similar to the practice of incubation, which was common in the Mediterrean world at the time of Jesus, particularly in the cult of the Greek god of healing, Asclepius. When the pilgrim at the shrine or church is asleep, the saint is implored to either heal the person outright or reveal to the pilgrim how a cure might be found.[4]

Some of the most popular early Christian healing shrines were dedicated to saints who were physicians. If shrines had been healing temples to pagan healing deities such as Asclepius, Isis, or Serapis, they often were simply taken over by expanding Christianity and converted into churches. The presiding deity who had been approached for healing was identified with, replaced by, or converted into a Christian saint. In this way the healing cult was able to survive a change in religions. At the healing shrine, "new" Christian doctor-saints continued to practice medicine, as it were, by healing, diagnosing, and prescribing therapies to patients who came as pilgrims to seek their aid.[5]

Two of the most famous Christian healing saints were Saint Cosmas and Saint Damian. Cosmas and Damian were twins who were converted to Christianity in the third century. They were physicians and were said to have been able to heal simply by word or touch due to their great virtue. They were martyred in 287, and soon afterward miracles of healing began to be reported at their graves. A popular cult soon grew up around these two saints, and shrines sacred to them were erected in many places, although the center of the cult was in Constantinople. As in the case of the cult of Asclepius, Cosmas and Damian appeared to people in dreams, often in the context of incubation at one of their shrines, and either healed them right away or gave them directions for achieving a cure.

In harmony with Christian theology, Cosmas and Damian themselves did not have the power to cure, as the earlier pagan gods had had. Rather, they played the role of intermediaries, petitioning God on behalf of supplicants for healing. This is clear in the healing of Saint Theodore, who fell ill and petitioned Cosmas and Damian for help. They appeared to him in a vision and promised to intercede on his behalf with God. When the two saints returned from heaven, they brought an angel with them, who announced to Theodore that God was pleased with him and had decided that he might live a while longer. Cosmas and Damian then told Theodore to get up and return to his bishop's flock, which he did, completely healed.[6]

An undated chronicle of the healing miracles of Cosmas and Damian at the church at Byzantium (probably written between the fourth and sixth centuries) makes clear that their cult was extremely popular and that they treated a wide range of ills. Many pilgrims practiced incubation in this church and had visions of the two saints in which they performed surgery, gave medical advice (often in the form of dietary restrictions), or dictated prescriptions. The saints are also depicted as exorcising demons that caused madness and as curing infertility. They often cured people simply by touching them in their dreams. Just how popular this healing center was is indicated by the fact that pilgrims sometimes had to wait weeks or months to be treated. In one case a man is said to have stayed at the shrine for a year seeking a cure.[7]

This healing shrine, and others like it, resembled hospitals. They were institutions whose function was caring for and healing the sick. The medical staff were primarily priests, but many of them probably had rudimentary, if not sophisticated, medical knowledge and skill. These early Christian healing centers were forerunners of later Christian hospitals, which were staffed by members of religious orders.

In addition to incubation and prayers, bathing in special water (pools, rivers, or lakes) is important at many Christian healing centers. At some shrines, pilgrims undertake the stations of the cross or circumambulate the church or shrine as healing rituals. At many shrines, special healing services are conducted for the sick, sometimes during communion.

The healing dynamic of a sacred journey is also important in the effectiveness of Christian healing shrines, as it is in other traditions.[8] The prospect of undertaking a pilgrimage for healing galvanizes the sick person to seek healing; it mobilizes the person's energy, will, and resources toward getting better. Prior to and in the process of preparing for the pilgrimage, the pilgrim hears stories about the positive benefits of the healing shrine.

On the journey itself, the pilgrim is usually part of a group going to the same shrine, most of them with the same goal, namely, to get better. They may sing devotional hymns and tell stories concerning the healing effects of the shrine. In short, the expectations of the pilgrim are undoubtedly heightened during the actual journey. A spirit of *communitas* may well dominate the pilgrims, creating a special atmosphere in which the exceptional or unexpected may occur.

Pilgrims also may experience a liminal atmosphere, the feeling of being betwixt and between worlds, apart from and freed of the constricting structures of their normal world, of which their sickness is a part.[9] As liminal beings, pilgrims have the potential to find freedom from habits, expectations, and norms that constrict them. There is the potential to forge a new identity. This may include transcending one's attitude toward a debilitating, incapacitating, painful illness—in short, one may find healing.

LOURDES

The most famous of all Christian healing shrines is Lourdes in southern France. Millions of pilgrims and volunteers go there each year to seek healing or spiritual refreshment. The origin of Lourdes as a healing center is associated with Bernadette Soubrious (1843–79; later Saint Bernadette), who on February 11, 1858, had a vision of the Virgin Mary standing on a rock in a grotto above the river. Bernadette described the apparition as a beautiful young woman wearing a white dress with a blue sash. She appeared to Bernadette several times within the next weeks and eventually identified herself as the Virgin Mary. At one point she told Bernadette: "Go tell the priests to build a chapel on this spot. I want people to come here in procession. Pray—tell them to pray. Prayer and penitence. Go and drink in the spring and wash in it. I am the Immaculate Conception. I desire a chapel here."[10] At one point during this series of apparitions, the woman requested Bernadette to dig a hole in the sand; a spring came forth that still pours water that is believed to have healing powers.

At first Bernadette was regarded with some skepticism by her family and friends. But then people began to come to the grotto and to report they were healed. A blind man washed his eyes in the water and recovered his sight. A neighbor of Bernadette's brought her sick child, dipped her in the water, and the child recovered. People came in small bands and then in crowds. A small shrine was set up, and people began to make offerings to the Virgin Mary there. The local clergy at first remained aloof. Local authorities scorned Bernadette and closed the shrine to the public. However, in just four years, in January 1862, the church, after conducting an investigation, declared the apparitions valid and began a program to develop the shrine. Hotels sprang up, a church was built, and the water from the spring was channeled into pools in which pilgrims could bathe.

In 1871 the first French National Pilgrimage was organized and in 1872, the Rosary Pilgrimage. The National Pilgrimage is under the direction of the Assumptionist Fathers and the Rosary Pilgrimage under the Dominicans. A great many people who go to Lourdes make the journey as part of these large groups. These pilgrimages range from between twenty thousand and one hundred thousand people. Many smaller groups arrive from all over Europe and the world. In most cases these pilgrimage groups are organized by religious orders or local parishes and employ the help of pious volunteers. The case of Rose Martin of Nice, who visited Lourdes in 1947, is typical of hundreds of thousands of pilgrims. Having undergone an operation for uterine cancer, she continued to lose weight rapidly as cancer spread to other parts of her body. She was terribly sick and was cared for by the Sisters of the Misericordia, who used to visit her eight times a day to wash and dress her and comb her hair. They never accepted any money for this. They urged her to go to Lourdes and made all the arrangements. While at Lourdes, Rose gradually began to get better and eventually completely regained her health.[11]

The large pilgrimages are impressive affairs. A special White Train that carries the very sick is part of the French National Pilgrimage. Here is a description of its departure from Paris:

The White Train carries the "*grandes malades*," the utterly helpless and hopeless cases whom science has declared itself powerless to relieve. On the day of departure the Auster-litz Station in Paris looks like a vast hospital. Rows of stretchers are lined up—on them men, women, children all so white, so wan, so visibly sick unto death as to make one's heart ache. . . . The Cardinal Archbishop of Paris never fails to visit the *grandes malades* at the station, passing from one to the other. . . . Most of their charges are actually dying. Several have received the Last Rites, just before leaving home. But whatever their condition, every one of the *grandes malades* is a willing traveler and often a cheerful one. It is the onlookers who shed tears as they watch one stretcher after another carried into the train."[12]

Lourdes-bound trains often depart from the home station to the strains of the "Mag-nificat," the "Ave Maria," the "Song of Bernadette," or other devotional songs. Some-times these hymns resound throughout the length of the train for the entire journey to Lourdes. At one point on the Rosary Pilgrimage, twelve hundred sick pilgrims hold-ing candles are arranged at night in the form of a cross on the esplanade and recite the stations of the cross in unison.[13] In 1953, 515 trains brought two million pilgrims to Lourdes during the six-month season.

Many other pilgrims, of course, go to Lourdes in less dramatic contexts, on their own or with a few friends or family members. Many are not in search of healing. There are volunteers who return to Lourdes year after year to help the sick. They say they gain spiritual refreshment from serving the sick and seeing their faith. One vol-unteer said: "These few days at Lourdes each August fix me up for the whole year. I *live* for twelve months on what I get here in just this one week!"[14] Many of the vol-

Members of the English National Pilgrimage to Lourdes, 1969. Courtesy of Wilfred Seychell.

Wilfred Seychell of Canada, a *brancardier* **at Lourdes.** Courtesy of Wilfred Seychell.

unteers are members of organizations founded specifically to aid the sick at Lourdes. Shortly after large pilgrimages began going to Lourdes, three noblemen in the area founded the Hospittalers to help pilgrims. The Hospittalers are governed by the local bishop and enjoined to cultivate the virtues of charity, piety, and discipline. Each member is given a book containing guidelines for proper conduct. Members, called *brancardiers,* are enjoined to treat the sick with tenderness and to pray without ceasing. These volunteers are on duty from dawn till midnight but may have to answer emergency calls in the middle of the night. The *brancardiers* are the ones who help the sick on and off the trains and buses, wheel them around to the pools for bathing and to the grotto for prayer, and generally tend and nurse them during their stay at Lourdes.

The work of the *brancardiers* extends beyond Lourdes. The Hospitallers have associations all over France, indeed all over the world, that help organize pilgrimages to Lourdes and see to it that sick pilgrims are able to make the often long and arduous trip. Wilfred Seychell, a man in his seventies in a nearby town here in southern Ontario, has been a *brancardier* for many years. As often as he can afford to, he travels to Britain to help sick pilgrims make the train trip to Lourdes. He helps them get dressed, changes their linen, and tends to their needs on the trip and during their stay at Lourdes. The Hospitallers also raise money to help poor people make the pilgrimage.

There is also a large staff of voluntary medical personnel at Lourdes, charged with providing medical treatment to the thousands of sick who are there at any given time. Many of the volunteers are untrained and simply go to Lourdes to help out in any way they can. There are scores of teachers, lawyers, clerks, and school children who come year after year to help in their own way. Many of the volunteers are former Cures, individuals who claim to have found healing at Lourdes. None of these people are paid for the help they give.

Each day at Lourdes there are events in which most pilgrims take part: morning Mass in the basilica, baths in the pools, prayers at the grotto, the Procession of the Blessed Sacrament in the afternoon, and the torchlight procession at night on the esplanade. The most dramatic and important events of the day for the patients are bathing in the pools and the Procession of the Holy Sacrament. Some dramatic cures have taken place during a bath in one of the pools or during the procession. The activity is described this way by one writer:

> The morning trek to the Baths begins. The very sick are taken on stretchers, others are wheeled sitting up; the little carriages, each with its burden of agony, hopes and fears, rolled along by devoted stretcher-bearers or nurses. These are often praying aloud as they push their patients; the patients too are praying. . . . In front of the pools, relatives and friends with their rosaries, praying audibly. Songs and prayers are heard also at the Chapel of Bernadette around the corner.[15]

Each patient-pilgrim is stripped and completely immersed in the cold waters of the spring. Some of the most spectacular cures have taken place at just this point. In some ways, of course, the immersion in the pools is reminiscent of the sacrament of baptism. Traditionally, baptism is associated with the washing away of original sin and in the early church was associated with driving out demons. The curative symbolism of baptism is not difficult to appreciate, and immersion in the pools at Lourdes probably has baptismal associations for many participants.

Several spectacular cures have taken place during the daily Procession of the Blessed Sacrament. Hundreds of clergy proceed from the basilica down the long esplanade on which the sick are arrayed in rows. The sacrament is displayed as the clergy move along, and each patient is given communion. Again, we are reminded of the healing qualities implicit in the sacrament of the Eucharist. Ingesting the sacred elements, the communicant prays: "Lord I am not worthy to receive you, but only say the word and I shall be healed." The baths symbolize the washing away of impurities, incompleteness, sickness; the Eucharist symbolizes receiving the holy presence of the divine.

People who have experienced miraculous cures state that they felt great and sudden pain, followed by a feeling of total well-being and a voracious appetite. Some speak of having felt a superior force intervening in their bodies. One woman said: "I can neither forget nor explain—but it certainly proceeded from a force outside of and superior to my own nature." This woman had been paralyzed for seventeen years and suddenly was restored to health at Lourdes during the Procession of the Sacrament. She said the force that invaded her was so violent that she was flung right off

Blessing of the sick at Lourdes. Courtesy of Wilfred Seychell.

her litter.[16] Other famous Cures speak of being transported, of having altered consciousness, of not being aware of what was going on around them. One patient who
was cured said he was "no longer touching the ground." It has also been noted that
cures seem to take place "when the recipient is absorbed in the thought of God or of
some absent loved one. In such cases the person praying forgets all about himself—
his personal problems, tensions, fears, anxieties—and becomes single-pointed, overwhelmed by a great, impersonal, selfless feeling for his neighbor, and by faith and
reliance on a Higher Being."[17] Faith also seems to have played an important part in
the experience of some famous Cures. Many Cures mention their own faith or that
of a family member, friend, or religious people who were helping them.

      The vast majority of people who go to Lourdes do not experience any dramat-
ic physical cure, and many critics of Lourdes (and other religious healing cults) have
suggested that more harm than good is done at such places. Imagine, the critics say,
the great disappointment of the majority of people who go to healing shrines and experience no physical improvement. On the other hand, defenders of Lourdes say there
is another side to the experience that should not be forgotten, and that is the healing
of the spirit or soul that so many pilgrims to Lourdes mention. A pilgrim who had
been to Lourdes many times said: "Of the uncured none despair. All go away filled
with hope and a new feeling of strength. The trip to Lourdes is never made in
vain."[18]

      Just how healing can take place at Lourdes (and any other healing shrine)
without any physical curing is illustrated in the story of a clerk named Lemarchand
from Brest, who went to Lourdes hoping for a cure of his legs, crippled since birth.

He arrived on pilgrimage with his sister and went to the grotto. He increasingly became absorbed in the other sick people.

> I still prayed for my cure, but on the second day, I began to feel ashamed of myself. On my right, a blind man sat rigid in his chair; on my left lay a consumptive. I looked around at all the sufferers and then up to the green mountains and higher to the sky. I could see; and I could move about; I had the free use of my ears and tongue and arms. I had not known disease—and I was praying for my cure! I started praying for the blind man and the consumptive. Since that moment I have felt that I should think of others and not of myself.[19]

The following year he and his sister returned, and she began work as a volunteer nurse. He felt useless and offered himself for clerical work. He knew English, and his services were accepted. "I felt like a new man. I, even I, was doing something to help the sick. Perhaps it sounds foolish to speak of the happiness I have found at Lourdes, I who went there to be cured and still a cripple. But I have found contentment, and my soul has been cured. And, for more persons than anyone knows, Lourdes has done the same thing."[20] The process of healing in many cases involves patients coming to terms with their physical impairment. In many cases the healer's primary

The grotto at Lourdes.
Courtesy of Wilfred Seychell.

task is helping sick people to adjust their expectations, to adopt a realistic view of their capabilities and the future. This is exactly the kind of healing experienced by Lemarchand at Lourdes.

Finally, it should be mentioned that the physically healthy also benefit from a pilgrimage to Lourdes (and probably to most healing shrines). A Protestant writer was present during the Annual Rosary Pilgrimage's formation of a cross at night on the esplanade, when twelve hundred sick people hold candles and recite the stations of the cross, identifying, one supposes, with the sufferings of Jesus. A large crowd of pilgrims surrounded this living symbol of suffering, a cross composed of the sick. The author then noticed that one of the sick was looking directly at her and in fact was praying for her, indeed, that many of the sick were praying for the well. When the writer commented on this to one of the *brancardiers*, he said: "But yes, madame. The gift of the sick to the well here at Lourdes is perhaps greater than the gift of the well to the sick. We *brancardiers* are constantly aware of it!."[21]

Perhaps the gift of the sick that the *brancardier* refers to is mentioned by Lemarchand when he says that at Lourdes he began to think of others and not himself. At Lourdes, pilgrims seeking healing are instructed to pray for others. This meditational process draws their attention to pilgrims who are more desperate than they themselves and helps them frame their illness in a new context. The sick praying for the well, furthermore, also impresses upon many at Lourdes the fact that illness is not only physical, that mental torment and anguish can be as incapacitaing and painful as physical sickness. It impresses upon the physically well that they also may be in need of healing, that they may lack the mental repose, dignity, and acceptance of life's constraints and limitations that many of the desperately sick possess.

ENDNOTES

[1]Mary Hamilton, *Incubation or the Cure of Disease in Pagan Temples and Christian Churches* (London: Simpkin, Marshall, Hamilton, Kent, 1906), pp. 116–18.

[2]This is also the case in India. People suffering from mental disorders seek relief at the Balaji temple in Rajasthan.

[3]William A. R. Thomson, *Faiths That Heal* (London: Adam and Charles Black, 1980), p. 238.

[4]Hamilton, pp. 109–18.

[5]Ibid., p. 119.

[6]Ibid., pp. 119–21.

[7]Ibid., p. 126.

[8]See the Zinacanteco and Hindu materials discussed earlier.

[9]See Victor Turner, *Process, Performance, and Pilgrimage: A Study in Comparative Symbology* (New Delhi: Concept Publishing, 1979).

[10]Ruth Cranston, *The Miracle of Lourdes* (New York: McGraw-Hill, 1955), p. 8.

[11]Ibid., p. 252. Unlike most people who go to Lourdes, Rose Martin was miraculously cured there.

[12]Ibid., p. 183.

[13]Ibid., p. 191.
[14]Ibid., p. 79.
[15]Ibid., pp. 30–31.
[16]Ibid., p. 267.
[17]Ibid., p. 271–72.
[18]Ibid., p. 140.
[19]Ibid., p. 142.
[20]Ibid.
[21]Ibid., p. 191.

Chapter 12
Contemporary Christian Faith Healers

One of the most flamboyant and dramatic expressions of healing in Christianity in recent times is found in a group of individuals referred to as faith healers. While healing by charismatic individuals is nothing new in Christianity (going back to Jesus himself and evident to some extent in almost all periods of Christian history), the popularity and notoriety of faith healers during the last forty years or so in North America has associated dramatic, charismatic healing with Christianity. It is faith healers that many people think of first when they associate religion and healing today.

The background for most of the contemporary faith healers in North America is the Pentecostal and charismatic revival movement that has taken place primarily in Protestant Christianity beginning in the late nineteenth century. An important part of this movement has been its emphasis on healing, often referred to as spiritual healing, miraculous healing, or faith healing. Unlike healing in traditional Roman Catholic contexts, Protestant faith healing puts relatively little emphasis on sacred shrines or sacramental healing. Rather, it usually takes place in the context of preaching, which is one of the central features of Protestant Christianty.

There are two emphases in Pentecostalism that are central to most faith healers. First, and as the name suggests, Pentecostalism stresses a type of spirituality that was expressed at the feast of Pentecost in the Book of Acts when the Holy Spirit descended upon the early Christians and empowered them with a variety of miraculous gifts: prophecy, speaking in tongues, and healing. Pentecostalism affirms that the Holy Spirit is active in modern times, just as it was among early Christians, and that the faithful still enjoy these miraculous gifts. Second, Pentecostalism understands divine healing in the context of conversion, or spiritual renewal—what is termed

Baptism of the Holy Ghost. Healing comes about in the context of spiritual transformation and renewal; indeed, it is a sign of such transformation. Spiritual healing
is symptomatic of the "signs and wonders" of a religious community in which God
is active. Pentecostals strive to reclaim and cultivate the vitality of the early church,
in which spiritual healing was common.

In this century, the relationship often has been strained between the best-known
faith healers and both established Pentecostalism and other Protestant denominations stressing divine healing. Established Pentecostalism has actively supported
and cooperated with some faith healers at certain points in their ministry (Oral
Roberts was a member of a Pentecostal church early in his career), but it has also criticized or opposed others for both their theology and their practices. So, while most
faith healers may be understood to fit within the Pentecostal movement's emphasis on
divine healing in the context of spiritual renewal, many have founded their own sects
or organizations and chosen to remain independent of any established religion. Many
of the most famous faith healers have been independent, itinerant preachers on the margins of established religion. Indeed, some of these faith healers see in their wandering lifestyle an imitation of Jesus' own ministry. The immense tents they used to haul
with them from town to town for their meetings were dramatic symbols of this aspect
of their ministry.

Two important early figures in the contemporary faith-healing movement in North
America were Alexander Dowie and Aimee Semple McPherson. Dowie, who was born
in Scotland in 1847, came to Chicago in 1893 and began preaching about divine healing. He attracted much attention, and was even arrested, because of his scathing denun-
ciations of sin and corruption in the local economic and political structures. He
founded his own church and was soon attracting large crowds. In 1896 he pur-
chased six thousand acres of land north of Chicago on which to build the new
Jerusalem, a city of the righteous. In just two years he convinced ten thousand people to move to his new heaven on earth. Dowie established a publication entitled *Leaves
of Healing* that soon had a large international circulation and featured his emphasis
on divine healing. Dowie claimed to receive many divine revelations and compared
himself to the prophet Elijah and to the early Christian apostles. Dowie was one of
the first preachers to draw widespread attention to divine healing in twentieth-century
America. For Dowie, divine healing was part of the creation of a new society, a holy
city. It was a sign of religious renewal.[1]

Aimee Semple McPherson was an itinerant preacher who emphasized revival-
ism and healing. She had remarkable success and was known all over North America at the height of her career. She was a great beauty and had a galvanizing effect
on her audiences. In 1923 she established herself in Los Angeles, where she built a
large church and began publishing a monthly magazine that described her ministry.
She founded her own sect, the Foursquare Gospel Church, which emphasized a
return to Christian fundamentals, including the cultivation or renewal of charismatic
gifts such as healing.[2]

THE POST–WORLD WAR II HEALING REVIVAL: GENERAL CHARACTERISTICS

Shortly after World War II there was a dramatic outburst of charismatic healing, which continues till this day, although in rather subdued form. It featured many popular and powerful preachers, including A. A. Allen, Jack Coe, Velmer Gardner, T. L. Osborn, A. C. Valdez, Mildrid Wicks, Morris Cerullo, Tommy Hicks, O. L. Jaggers, H. Richard Hall, David Nunn, Franklin Hall, Robert Schambach, David Terrell, William Freeman, Jimmy Swaggert, Kathryn Kuhlman, and the most famous of all, Oral Roberts.

The beginning of this movement is usually traced to William Branham, who received a call to preach and heal in May 1946. In 1947 he began to hold large rallies all over the United States, and reports of miracles spread. In city after city, day after day, Branham preached about spiritual renewal, discerned or intuited illnesses of those attending his rallies, and pronounced them healed. He often spoke about communicating with angels and sometimes healed the sick by exorcising spirits. Most of the prominent faith healers who came after Branham admitted to being inspired by him, and it is also clear that many sought to imitate him.

Although there are many faith healers who have been active in North America since World War II, and although they have differing, often distinctive, styles, there are several characteristics that apply to most, if not all, of them.

1. With some exceptions, the physical environment of revivalist healing meetings emphasizes the itinerant, transient nature of the faith healer. While it is true that some revivalists have established churches or headquarters where they conduct many of their services, most healers, even those with a home base, travel widely and conduct their rallies "on the road." Perhaps the most striking symbol of the itinerancy of the faith healers was the huge tents in which they used to conduct their meetings. Many faith healers shunned churches or public buildings (most buildings were far too small for them) in preference for these temporary, portable shelters, which could accommodate tens of thousands of people and were hauled all over North America. These tents were often set up in farmers' fields, outside town. Especially in the case of tent rallies, we can see that the faith healers preferred a healing context that was on the edge of the everyday world, that was impermanent, temporary, liminal. Such a setting required those attending to step outside their normal world into a special place where habitual routines and normal rules and regulations could be left behind. The tent and the liminal atmosphere helped provide a setting in which normal boundaries and routines could be stretched or shattered. In such a setting, anticipation of drastic transformations might result in healing.

2. Many faith healers emphasize the theme of entering a special time during which the Holy Spirit is active. In harmony with Pentecostal theology, most faith healers cultivate the theme of reentering, recapturing, or re-creating the atmosphere of the early Christian church in which signs and wonders were commonplace. In a book-

let distributed by the Oral Roberts organization on its healing crusades, those who plan to attend meetings are specifically instructed to read the Gospels and to put themselves in the place of the individuals whom Jesus healed.[3] Like the emphasis on creating a liminal space for healing, this emphasis on experiencing the faith of the early church stresses the importance of creating a liminal time in which healing can take place. The faith healer takes pains to remove people from their normal settings by emphasizing the re-creation of a special atmosphere in a special place. The preaching of many faith healers also emphasizes the "end times," the theme that the world is about to enter a time when God or Jesus will dramatically intefere in human history. Signs and wonders herald this cosmic event. Dramatic healings are understood as a part of this universal, transformative event. The model for re-creating this atmosphere of intense faith and expectation is the description of the early church in the Book of Acts, in which the Holy Spirit is described as blessing people with miraculous gifts, in particular, the gift of healing.

3. Most prominent faith healers are masters at arousing intense faith and expectation in those attending their services. Indeed, it is this aspect of their ministries that has led to their being called faith healers, a term that many object to. They carefully and usually successfully arouse hope in those who seek healing from them. In some cases these healing crusades distribute detailed instructions in advance to people who intend to attend their services. A typical set of instructions written by R. F. DeWeese, an associate minister of the Oral Roberts movement, prepares people for spiritual healing as follows:

> If I were coming to the crusade for healing, I would begin now to prepare myself. If I did not know Jesus Christ as my Saviour, I would ask Him to forgive my sins, and to come into my life . . . I would concentrate on God's love for me and that He wants to heal me. I would pray and read several chapters in the Gospels and Acts each day. As I read the accounts of healing by our Lord, I would put myself in the place of those Jesus healed and try to believe as they did. I would study the Scripture concerning healing and also read Brother Roberts' book, If You Need Healing, Do These Things . . . I would plan to attend every service of the crusade. . . . As I filled out my prayer card . . . I would be willing to be healed any time or place that pleased God, whether on the ramp, down in the prayer line, or just sitting in the audience. Faith alone is not enough. We must know how to release our faith in order to receive healing. We can do this through a point of contact. This is something you do, and when you do it, you release your faith toward God for healing. When Brother Roberts lays hands on you, this may be your point of contact. . . . To sum up, if I were you: I would come expecting a miracle, I would believe that it is God's will for me to be healed. I would build up my faith by attending both afternoon and evening services and listening to the Word of God preached. I would use a point of contact to release my faith. And, I would let my faith go to God and accept my healing from Him.[4]

Prior to the meeting, the seeker after miraculous healing is instructed to vividly imagine the event actually taking place, to imagine the precise moment and act of the preacher that will bring this about, and to anticipate it fervently. The person is also instructed to re-create the atmosphere of Jesus' own ministry, to imagine him- or herself present with Jesus as he heals. In other words, the faith healer often gives prior instructions to those coming to a healing meeting that arouse expectations of getting better. The instructions aim at filling the person with faith in the ability of the healer to bring about a cure.

At the meeting itself, the leader takes pains to further arouse people's expectations. It is typical for people to give testimonials concerning their miraculous cures at the hands of the preacher. Dramatic tales are told of healings. Often the leaders themselves have tales to tell of their own miraculous healing. Oral Roberts, for example, was dramatically healed at a revivalist meeting when he was a teenager and has often related this story to his audiences. The healing evangelist Harold Woodson often began his meetings by telling dramatic stories of healings at his earlier meetings. Then he would ask his audience: "How many of you believe that some miracle working power is in this tent tonight? Lift up your hands to heaven . . . I believe the miracle working power of God is here tonight. To set men and women free, to deliver, to heal, to open the eyes of the blind." Another evangelist, Don Steward, was in the habit of saying at the beginning of his services: "Now the Lord has already spoken to me tonight about what he is going to do. In a few minutes we are going to feel the glory of God begin to rise in this service. Jesus Christ is going to come with healing in his wings . . . The power of God is going to touch you."[5] Kathryn Kuhlman also often opened her services with statements assuring her audiences that miracles would happen. At a rally in Los Angeles, for example, she said at the beginning of the service: "My friends, I am sensitive enough to the Holy Spirit to know that wonderful things are going to happen today. Miracles—very special ones—are going to happen in this place this afternoon."[6]

It probably is not surprising that so many people report healing in this heightened, often frenzied, atmosphere. The huge crowds, the singing, the testimonials, the healings of others present, and the passionate preaching and praying of the evangelist create a context conducive to dramatic psychological and physical transformation—in short, miraculous healing.

4. Most faith healers frame miraculous or spiritual healing in the context of spiritual renewal or conversion. Theologically, most faith healers agree with the Pentecostal idea that the atonement (how Jesus saved humanity) includes the salvation of the body as well as the soul, that deliverance includes physical healing.[7] They believe that Jesus' own healings described in the Bible are illustrations of this and that such healing still takes place today through the activity of the Holy Spirit. Theologically, most faith healers believe that it is God's intention for people to be healthy. Health, however, is understood to be a reflection of one's relationship to God. If one is reconciled to God, dedicated to God, accepting of God's grace, one opens oneself to God's healing power. If one is alienated from God, closed to God's grace, one can block God's healing power. The emphasis in much evangelical healing is on spiritual renewal, getting right with God, on what is often called being born again. Part of this emphasis is on confessing and repenting of one's sins. William Branham often claimed that at precisely the moment people confessed to him they were healed.[8] Heal-

ing, that is, is seen as a sign or result of spiritual renewal, conversion, or salvation. Often people at healing meetings are urged to come forward to declare their dedication to the Lord. These altar calls, as they are termed, set the context for healing. In the act of making a commitment to God, one experiences spiritual and physical renewal.

5. Many faith healers understand illness to be caused by spirits and heal by means of exorcism. Throughout the faith-healing movement, a common theory of disease causation is that Satan afflicts people with illness by sending spirits that actually enter their bodies to make them sick. Like Jesus himself and the apostles, revivalist healers combat sickness by casting out evil spirits. Here is an account of William Branham healing a girl who was deaf and mute: "As I watched Brother Branham minister to the sick, I was especially captivated by the deliverance of a little deaf-mute girl over whom he prayed thus: 'Thou deaf and dumb spirit, I adjure thee in Jesus' name, leave the child,' and when he snapped his fingers, the girl heard and spoke perfectly."[9]

Oral Roberts early in his healing career attributed many diseases to demon possession and often healed by exorcism. It was A. A. Allen, however, more than any other faith healer, who attributed most diseases to demons and was a specialist in exorcism as a means of healing. Allen claimed that demons had "filled the insane asylums, penitentiaries, prisons, and courts to over capacity."[10] In his book *Curse of Madness*, he argued that almost all of Jesus' healings involved exorcism of demons. Allen included in the book several drawings of demons done by a woman possessed by many demons until he cast them out.[11] Allen's publication, *Miracle Magazine,* contained many accounts of him exorcising demons. In the case of Hugh Chrisman, a forty-three-year-old hermaphrodite, who claimed that he had been to many medical specialists in an attempt to rid himself of his bisexual condition, Allen healed him by exorcising his female half, which departed Chrisman in the form of a female spirit. After this exorcism, Christman claimed, his female characteristics completely disappeared, and his masculine features and characteristics were strengthened.[12]

6. Closely related to exorcism is the ability of some faith healers to discern a person's physical and spiritual condition, which may be directly related to his or her health or illness. William Branham had the ability of "discernment"—he could vividly picture details about a person's life and physical condition without having met the person previously. At his rallies, which attracted thousands of people at a time, he would "discern" an illness in the large audience, and usually a person would come forward. Branham would then pray over this person, often spending a long time "discerning" details of her life, particularly traumatic events connected with illness. It was as if he could see directly into the spiritual, psychological condition of people and heal them through physical touch and his empathy.[13] Other healers who followed Branham enjoyed the same ability, which within faith-healing circles is understood to be a special gift of the Holy Spirit, the gift of knowledge. Richard Hall often claimed to be able to know in precise detail the nature of peoples' lives and sickness and said that this ability was a revelation of God to him.[14] At her healing rallies, Kathryn Kuhlman routinely announced that she had "discerned" a miraculous healing in the

audience and invited the person to come forward to confirm her intuition. More often than not, a person from the audience would report that he or she had undergone the cure that Kuhlman described to the audience.[15]

7. Most prominent faith healers are powerful preachers. In this respect they often see themselves as following the model of the apostles who first spread the gospel of Christianity. Many faith healers have a strong prophetic strain. They are prophetic in two ways. First, they see themselves as being the spokespersons of God, the classic definition of a prophet in the biblical tradition. They often claim to be inspired by and to speak for God. Second, they are prophetic in condemning the sinful ways of the world and of individuals. They invoke divine law and promise divine punishment for sin. In this prophetic mode, many faith healers become intensely passionate and succeed in prompting great numbers of people to make "altar calls" in which they repent of their sins and dedicate their lives to God.

Many faith healers are extremely effective public speakers, with dramatic styles and charismatic personalities. Some have flamboyant mannerisms and techniques to stir up the excitement and expectations of their audiences. Often, they directly involve their large audiences in some fashion. Franklin Hall, for example, insisted that his audiences sit with "head up and eyes open," because after many years of research he had determined that they would have a "400 percent greater faith in coming to the Lord with head up and eyes open." He wanted no slouchers in his audience and expected them at least to appear attentive. He would invite his audiences to raise their right hands and say "Hello, Jesus," and then to raise their left hands and greet Jesus again. Hall also claimed that one could detect the presence of Jesus by his pleasant fragrance and often invited his audience, after greeting Jesus, to smell his fragrance. "Now take a deep sniff," he would tell his audience. "Doesn't that smell good? . . . Oh, you can take this fragrance with you and it will go over the lot. It gets in your house, makes it bug proof. It makes you a Holy Ghost exterminator."[16]

8. Almost without exception, the prominent faith healers have claimed that their healing powers are not their own but come from God. They see themselves as chosen by God to undertake healing ministries, to bring God's gifts to those who suffer. They see themselves as God's instruments through whom he brings healing and other miraculous gifts. Kathryn Kuhlman used to instruct her audiences not to try to touch her. "I have no healing power, no special magic," she would say. "Reach out to touch Him [referring to God]," she would urge them. "He is the source of all healing power."[17] She told one interviewer: "I have nothing to do with these healings. The miracles are produced by the power of God."[18] According to almost every faith healer, it is divine healing power that mades them effective, and this power has been bestowed upon them by God at some critical moment, usually when they were called to their ministries, or else it is bestowed upon them just prior to or during their healing services. In many cases faith healers understand their role as advocates of their audiences, for whom they pray to God for healing. Their claim is not that they themselves have the power to heal but that they have God's sympathetic attention.

9. In some cases, faith healers speak of their relationship to divine powers and exhibit techniques (especially exorcism) that are reminiscent of shamanic motifs and

healers. Shamanic motifs are especially clear in the case of William Branham. Like many shamans, he had a dramatic encounter with a spiritual being who bestowed upon him his healing power and mystical insight. He described this encounter himself many times to his audiences:

> Then along in the night, at about the eleventh hour I had quit praying and was sitting up when I noticed a light flickering in the room . . . As the light was spreading, of course I became excited and started from the chair, but as I looked up, there hung the great star. However, it did not have five points like a star, but looked more like a ball of fire or light shining down upon the floor. Just then I heard someone walking across the floor, which startled me again . . . He appeared to be a man who, in human weight, would weigh about two hundred pounds, clothed in a white robe. He had a smooth face, no beard, dark hair down to his shoulders, rather dark-complexioned, with a very pleasant countenance, and coming closer, his eyes caught with mine. Seeing how fearful I was, he began to speak. "Fear not. I am sent from the presence of Almighty God to tell you that your peculiar life and your misunderstood ways have been to indicate that God has sent you to take a gift of divine healing to the people of the world. If you will be sincere, and can get the people to believe you, nothing shall stand before your prayer, not even cancer.[19]

Branham also maintained a close relationship with a being whom he described as an angel whose presence he believed to be necessary for him to heal. Like a shaman, Branham's special powers were related to a relationship he cultivated with a spiritual being, a kind of helping spirit or spirit ally. This being, or angel as Branham referred to it, empowered Branham to see directly into the spirit world. Describing this aspect of his ministry, F. F. Bosworth, an admirer of Branham, wrote:

> He does not begin to pray for the healing of the afflicted in body in the healing line each night until God anoints him for the operation of the gift, and until he is conscious of the presence of the Angel with him on the platform. Without this consciousness, he seems to be perfectly helpless. But when conscious of the Angel's presence, he seems to break through the veil of flesh into the world of spirit, to be struck through and through with a sense of the unseen.[20]

The angel enabled Branham to "see" people's sickness and their moral or spiritual condition. Like a shaman, Branham was a soul doctor, one who had special insight into people's inmost lives. Like a shaman, Branham, with the help of his angel, could enter into, or see into, the spiritual world, where sickness arises and is dealt with. Branham's "gift of knowledge," which enabled him to intuit the details of a person's life and discern illness, suggests a special ability to relate to or enter into the spirit world, which is one of the classic characteristics of a shamanic healer. Other faith healers as well, such as H. Richard Hall, Oral Roberts, and Kathryn Kuhlman, professed a special ability to discern illness, which they claimed was a divine gift. David Terrell, H. Richard Hall, Oral Roberts, and several other healing revivalists often said that God talked directly to them. David Terrell said: "God spoke to me just as plain as anyone could speak. I actually heard His voice with my own ears and there's not a devil in hell or on earth that can make me doubt my calling."[21]

Kathryn Kuhlman also had the uncanny ability to discern people's sickness and to vividly picture healings in her huge audiences. In this state she said that she felt especially close to the Holy Spirit. She described this state as a kind of altered consciousness in which she could not remember what she thought, said, or did. "There is a point where I become so sensitive to the Holy Spirit that I can go ten minutes and I can't tell you what I've called out or what I've said."[22] She even spoke sometimes of having the experience of being "out of body," detached from her circumstances, as if looking on from outside herself and being astonished at what she is saying and doing.[23] It is as if she were taken over by the Holy Spirit. This mood or state is reminiscent of shamanic trance, in which the shaman has special, intense rapport with the spirit world and is able to discern the spiritual condition of people.

Exorcism of disease-causing spirits is also remininiscent of shamanic healing. William Branham, Oral Roberts, and especially A. A. Allen often healed by means of exorcism. As in many cultures where shamanic healing dominates, some faith healers assume that illness is related to spirits. For these faith healers, illness is primarily a spiritual matter. Not only may illness be caused by malevolent spirits (usually related in some way to Satan), but one's actions may be implicated in demon-caused illness. That is, some faith healers believe that immorality, sinful actions, make one more vulnerable to demonic attack. Healing becomes a matter, then, not only of exorcism but of repentence and a commitment to a righteous, God-fearing life. This linking of illness with conduct is often a characteristic of shamanic healing.

10. Many prominent faith healers were from low social classes and economically depressed backgrounds. William Branham was born in a dirt-floor cabin in the mountains of eastern Kentucky and grew up in extreme poverty. His father was a drunkard.[24] Oral Roberts was the fifth child of poor parents.[25] A. A. Allen was born in Sulphur Rock, Arkansas, to a very poor family. His father was a drunkard, and his mother lived with a series of men during his youth.[26] T. L. Osborn was one of thirteen children raised in poverty on a farm during the Depression in Oklahoma.[27] Jack Coe was abandoned by his parents and raised in an orphanage.[28] William Freeman was born in a log cabin in Missouri to a very poor family.[29]

Not surprisingly, faith healers also appealed to the poor and outcasts of North America. Derek Prince said: "The Pentecostal movement was the child of poverty and rejection."[30] Just as their healing rallies were often held on the physical margins of society, in tents outside town in farmers' fields, so the healing revivalists appealed to those living on the margins of society. A striking characteristic of many of the early healing crusades, which frequently were held in the American South, was the interracial nature of the audiences. It is not clear how this remarkable development came about. The faith healers themselves can hardly be considered social activists and rarely preached about social justice or the plight of blacks. They did not preach interracial harmony. When it was apparent, however, that their crusades were attracting both blacks and whites, they welcomed the situation and took it as a sign that the spirit of the early church was present. Like the early church, in which there was "neither Jew nor Greek, male nor female," the healing crusades seemed to be able to break down ordinarily stubborn social barriers.

The evangelist healer Don Steward was probably the most insistent on identifying himself and his followers as social outcasts. He told his audiences that if they were healthy, rich, treated well by their relatives, and belonged to nice, fancy churches it was unlikely he had anything to give them. But if they were poor, rejected, and from the wrong side of the tracks, then he had a message for them, which was, "Jesus is here to touch you." Steward was proud to call his followers "outcasts" and said: "There are very few places they can go and worship the way we do . . . We consider it a privlege and a blessing to be an outcast. . . . It puts you on the in-crowd with God."[31]

11. Finally, some prominent faith healers are suspicious, even resentful, of doctors and modern medicine. Some faith healers speak of "Dr. Jesus" as the only effective physician and implore their audiences to put their faith in him rather than in secular, medical doctors. Indeed, to put faith in medical doctors implies a lack of faith in Jesus, according to some faith healers. Jack Coe, for example, was strongly opposed to the medical profession and said that those who sought its help were looking in the wrong place for healing.[32] The more common position, however, is that of Oral Roberts, who finds no conflict between medical and spiritual healing and often boasts about having physicians among his followers.[33]

ORAL ROBERTS AS A HEALER

Surely the most famous (some might say infamous) revivalist faith healer in modern times in North America is Oral Roberts. Roberts began his healing ministry in 1947 and continues to appear before millions throughout North America on television, where healing remains one of his concerns.[34] Roberts was born in 1918. His father was a Pentecostal minister, and he was raised in an atmosphere in which spiritual healing was not exceptional. His family and religious background in many ways primed him for his later healing ministry. His theology and his interest in and understanding of spiritual healing are firmly grounded in Pentecostal tradition. Typical of Pentecostal theologians, Roberts thinks of spiritual healing as a gift of the Holy Spirit and evidence that God is active in the present day just as he was in the early church. Also typical of Pentecostal thinking is Roberts's view of illness as caused by Satan and as something that God is absolutely opposed to.

Roberts's interest in spiritual healing to a great extent is related to his own experience of being miraculously healed at a revival meeting. At age seventeen Roberts became extremely ill with tuberculosis. He had been in robust health prior to this and very active in school sports. Both Roberts and his family were devastated by his illness. For months he lay in his bed, too weak to do anything but drink and eat. He coughed violently many times each day, spraying blood about the room. His family despaired and thought he would surely die. Throughout his illness, his friends and family, especially his father, would gather to pray for him. He often earnestly joined in himself. During one of these prayer sessions in his bedroom, Roberts experienced an exhilarating conversion experience. As his father prayed aloud for his son, Roberts beseeched Jesus to save him. Then, according to Roberts, a bright light enveloped his father, and his father's face was transformed into a different face, which Roberts identified as Jesus' face. Roberts felt that he had been visited by Jesus himself and declared himself born again. His family all wept tears of joy.[35] He did not recover his physical health until later, however.

Some months after his conversion, Roberts's older brother, Elmer, and his wife attended a revivalist healing meeting in a huge tent in the nearby town of Ada, Oklahoma. The healer-revivalist heading this meeting was George W. Moncey. Moncey was a fiery preacher who roamed the countryside promising divine healing. Elmer and his wife were so impressed by what they saw that they rushed back to the town of Stratford, where Roberts lay sick in bed in his parents' home, and insisted that Oral be taken to Moncey's tent to attend a healing service. Elmer and Oral's father dressed Oral and carried him to the car and laid him on a matress in the back seat. He was too weak to walk by himself and weighed only 120 pounds, although he was over six feet tall. On the way to the meeting, Elmer and his wife, Ora, talked excitedly about the meeting they had attended and the people they had seen healed. Elmer was certain that Oral would be healed. Listening to the excited conversation in the front seat, Oral remembers that he also became convinced that he would be healed by God.

It was a steamy July night, and the tent was crowded when the Roberts group arrived. Elmer had brought a rocking chair for Oral, and he placed it in one of the aisles. Moncey preached for over an hour, and Oral was impressed by his dramatic, flamboyant style and remembers that he thought he was in the presence of a man who really knew God. There was a long healing line of over two hundred people, and only after Moncey had prayed over each one of them, which resulted in several healings, did he approach Oral, seated in his chair. Moncey stood in front of the boy and at first prayed that God might heal him. Oral was helped to his feet by his parents while Moncey prayed for him. Oral then sat down again in the chair, and Moncey appeared to be about to leave. But then Moncey turned back to the boy, and there followed this scene remembered by Roberts:

> Brother Moncey said words that I think I can quote . . . pretty accurately . . . because they were so different and they were so penetrating. He did not pray, "O Lord, heal this boy." . . . He spoke to another power and he said, "You foul tormenting disease, I command you in the name of Jesus Christ of Nazareth, come out of this boy. Loose him and let him go free!"[36]

Roberts then felt a force moving through his body, which he described as "electricity going through me," or "like a kind of warm liquid feeling that came up and came all the way up my lungs." His lungs cleared, and he was able to breathe deeply. Many in the crowd knew Oral, and soon they were shouting "Glory" and "Hallelujah" as it became clear that something dramatic had happened to Oral. Oral got out of his chair and jumped up on the stage and shouted loudly: "I'm healed! I'm healed!" He then spoke about the glories of God, testifying about what God had accomplished in healing him. Up to this point in his life, he had been impaired by a severe stutter, but as a result of this dramatic healing he spoke freely and clearly. Oral and his family returned home rejoicing.[37]

Like several healers we have considered, Roberts was intimately acquainted with severe illness and successfully survived it; he gained knowledge of illness directly, by suffering it himself. In this sense, he is yet another example of the "wounded healer," a person who himself has suffered from sickness and has gained deep insight and compassion as a result of the experience. The dramatic healing of Oral Roberts was also important in his life because it set a model for thousands of healings he himself would precipitate in his crusades. It gave him confidence that dramatic spiritual healings could actually take place in the right circumstances for people who were open to the possibility, as he had been. The timing of his healing also helped form his conviction that divine healing is directly related to conversion and salvation. Indeed, most of Roberts's crusades explicitly aimed at bringing people to a dramatic spiritual renewal or commitment to Jesus. To some extent, healing was a secondary emphasis during these crusades. What mattered was the condition of people's souls. Physical healing was understood by Roberts as a byproduct of renewed faith or conversion. In his own case, his conversion had prepared him for physical healing. By committing himself to Jesus, he had opened himself up to divine healing power.

Roberts's call to a healing ministry was also dramatic and involved direct contact with God, whom Roberts said spoke clearly to him on several occasions. In one case, Roberts was attending a sociology class in which the professor ridiculed some biblical stories. Roberts was shocked, but instead of protesting he let his mind wander until, as he says, "It seemed I was alone in the presence of God." He then heard a voice, which he identified as God's, that said: "Son, don't be like other men. Don't be like other preachers . . . Be like my Son, Jesus Christ, and bring healing to the people as he did."[38]

This dramatic experience precipitated a period of intense prayer and searching by Roberts. For several weeks he sought solitude. At one point he went to study at the church where he was pastor and lay face down on the floor with his hands clasped together in prayer. He called on God to speak to him again and command him what to do. In this state of concentration, he felt alone with God. "I was just with the Lord. Was no longer aware of anything physical. It was like He took eternity and held it and stopped it. Like everything was suspended. I felt like I wasn't touching anything."[39] Then, according to Roberts, God spoke to him again in an audible voice, "like a military commander, words of crisp command, clear and strong. 'Stand upon your feet,' the voice said. 'Go and get in your car.'" Oral dutifully got in his car. "Then God said, 'Drive one block and turn right.'" As Oral drove home following God's commands, he received a second call. The voice said: "From this hour your ministry of healing will begin. You will have my power to pray for the sick and to cast out devils."[40]

This remarkable story is strongly reminiscent of shamanic healers, who heal by establishing rapport with a guardian or helping spirit. Like a shamanic healer, Roberts establishes direct contact with the spirit world and is adopted by a spirit (God) by means of whose powers he heals. Also like shamanic healers, Roberts heals by means of combating demons, by exorcising them through superior spiritual power or with the help of a superior spirit being. In the early years of his ministry, exorcisms were a routine part of Roberts's healing services. He adopted a vigorous, aggressive attitude toward sickness, which he often said came from Satan and not God, and would shout at demons to leave a person and sometimes would strike people quite hard in his attempts to heal them. He often said in a loud voice before individuals in the healing line came forward to be touched by him: "Devil, take your hands off God's property."[41]

In one particularly dramatic encounter, Roberts was assaulted by a woman. She punched Roberts, shouted at him, and tore buttons off his coat in her fury. Roberts finally managed to place his hand firmly on her forehead, and from that instant, he said, the woman became still, feeling the power of God surge through him. Roberts received the gift of knowledge at this moment and was able to discern that the woman was possessed by forty or fifty spirits, which he commanded to leave her. "When those demons came out they shook her body as though she had a chill. And suddenly, as they left her, she screamed a blood-curdling yell, and then she was as quiet and calm as you are. And she looked about and cried, 'I am free.'"[42] Like a shaman, Roberts is able to see directly into the spirit world and exercise power over it. Also like a shaman, Roberts often heals by means of combating spirits who bring disease. He is reminiscent of Jesus as a healer in these respects too.

Roberts insists that he has no healing powers of his own, that it is God through whom or by means of whom he heals. This is how he once described himself as a healer: "You must understand that I am two persons. One is just when I am myself, and the other is when the Spirit of God takes possession of me, and I feel the presence of God, usually after my sermons. Then I can do things of which I am not normally capable. I am still in control of my faculties, you understand. I can still think and act. But there is a spirit in me that is different."[43] A particularly dramatic scene in Jacksonville, Florida, illustrates how Roberts would be overcome or "possessed" by healing powers. A small boy who had been born without a hip socket had been brought forward for healing.

> The miracle started and all of a sudden I cried out that my right hand was like it was on fire. My hand was burning like you were sticking it with a thousand pins . . . Suddenly I jumped to my feet. I didn't say anything and the crowd jumped and here they came and completely engulfed the platform and me. People were pushed up in wheelchairs. They came out of the wheelchairs and just kept right on walking. . . . Collins [he is addressing Collins Steele, one of his staff], the next day you fellows picked up armloads of crutches and eyeglasses and hearing aids . . . It started and stopped in five minutes.[44]

The carefully planned and orchestrated setting that Roberts created for healing was a revival meeting. These meetings were usually held in tents, and an intense, frenzied atmosphere often developed. Roberts himself once said: "Angels walk the grounds, the Lord walks the aisles, people feel the Holy Ghost and fire under the tent. Many people have said, 'Brother Roberts, when I walk on the grounds I feel the presence of God.'"[45] Two central features of such meetings were crucial in all of

Oral Roberts. Courtesy of the Oral Roberts Library and University.

Roberts's healing crusades. The most prominent feature of any revivalist meeting is the sermon, and Roberts's meetings were no different. Roberts was a dramatic and effective preacher. And what he preached (and still preaches) was a personal commitment to God, a transformation of one's personal life, an invitation to be "born again." Roberts often stressed that the primary goal of his crusades was to bring people to Jesus as their savior. This was also, however, very clearly linked in his mind to healing. Just as he had been "born again," or saved, prior to his own dramatic healing as a youth, so he felt that people should prepare themselves for healing by making a commitment to God. This was important, he thought, in "releasing their faith in him" as God's healing agent.

The second feature of most revival meetings that Roberts incorporated into his healing crusades was the altar call, the point at which individuals in the audience are invited to come forward and make a public commitment to God. In Roberts's healing services, however, the altar call also involved, and eventually primarily became, the healing line, consisting of those people who had come forward to be healed. Because so many healings took place in the line, this became the dramatic high point of Roberts's services. Partly because of the huge numbers of people who entered the healing line in the hope of receiving Roberts's touch, the line soon became quite ritualized. Originally Roberts would spend several minutes with each person, inquiring about their illness and their lives, before touching them with his hands. This intimate, personal approach, however, was soon given up because of the overwhelming number of people who came forward. One night in Columbia, South Carolina, for example, an estimated ninety-three hundred people came through the healing line. Often Roberts conducted services several times each week and spent hours with those who gathered in the healing line to receive his blessing. He remembers one evening when "we formed a healing line, over three thousand came through it. We were caked with dust and mud. Our whole bodies, our eyes, our hands, and I had prayed until my arm literally ached."[46] This was an exhausting experience for Roberts, and sometimes he had to be supported by his assistants in order to complete praying and laying hands on all those in the healing line.

Eventually Roberts developed a style that required only a few moments with each person in the healing line. He would firmly place his hands on an individual and make a short prayer and then move to the next person. In some cases, it appeared that Roberts actually struck people with his hands. Roberts once commented on his forceful approach in the healing line:

> I pray with what some call authority, because the spirit is upon me and because I hate sickness, I hate disease, I hate evil, and when I am close to someone who is sick I suffer and I want to help him, I feel that if I do not pray for them I will burst. I put my hands on people in the healing line with force because I want to drive that evil out of them. I have tried to do it gently and it doesn't work.[47]

Roberts and many other modern faith healers have been criticized as greedy charlatans or, less severely, as flamboyant showmen. There have been outrageous abuses and trickery by some faith healers,[48] and Roberts himself in the later stages of his ministry has become almost totally preoccupied with raising money, which has led him to preach a capitalistic message of "seed faith," according to which money donated to his cause will be multiplied by the Lord many times over.

Nevertheless, it is clear that much of what happens in a typical faith-healing service is not much different from what we have seen in traditional healing scenarios. There is a built-up expectation in those who attend these services, often cultivated by those sponsoring the service. The faith healer may have an exaggerated reputation in which the person seeking healing has invested immense faith and hope. Faith healers take pains to create an appropriate atmosphere for healing, cultivating an enviroment in which enthusiasm and even frenzy are encouraged. The temporary setting, testimonials, hymn singing, and preaching all contribute to an atmosphere in which the people expect God to act and bestow blessings and miracles.

Faith healers also explicitly frame illness in a meaningful context. Illness is sent by Satan or evil spirits, or it is inflicted by God as punishment for sin. A restoration of health is often directly related to a commitment to Jesus, to conversion, to being born again. One cannot be healthy unless one is open to God's healing power. And finally, faith healers almost all incorporate into their healings a dramatic ritual that usually includes physical contact with the sick.

HEALING THEMES IN KATHRYN KUHLMAN

For many years Kathryn Kuhlman was one of the best-known faith healers in North America, rivaling even Oral Roberts in popularity. She was born and raised in Missouri and came from a Methodist background. At the age of fourteen she had a dramatic conversion experience during a service in a small Methodist church. She trembled and sobbed as she sat in her pew and felt that the power of God had come over her. She says that on the way home from church "everything looked brighter, more beautiful. My feet didn't touch the sidewalk. Then suddenly I knew what it was: Jesus had come into my heart. . . . This was the beginning of everything."[49]

At the age of just fifteen she preached her first sermon, and at sixteen she undertook an itinerant ministry, traveling from town to town, sometimes even having to hitchhike. She said of this period in her life: "I would find any empty building, advertize the services, set up benches, and the people would come—strictly out of curiosity to see a red-headed, teen-age girl preacher."[50] In 1946 she had another dramatic encounter with what she referred to as the Holy Spirit and says that she had the experience of dying and being reborn and of becoming completely filled with divine power. She said of this experience: "That afternoon, Kathryn Kuhlman died. And when I died, God came in, the Holy Spirit came in. There, for the first time, I realized what it meant to have power."[51]

After spending nearly twenty years as a traveling evangelist, she settled down in a small church in Franklin, Pennsylvania, in the 1950s. In 1954, members of her congregation began to report healings at her services. In 1955 she moved to Pittsburgh and rented the Carnegie Library auditorium for her services. She continued to conduct her "miracle services" there for twenty years, as well as traveling throughout North America to undertake healing crusades. Her ministry also eventually involved extensive television and radio networks.

Like most other healing evangelists, Kuhlman framed her healing services in the context of a Christian theology that emphasized faith, forgiveness, and conversion. While she sometimes expressed astonishment at the people whom God chose to heal during her services (for example, those claiming no faith and those saying they only attended her services out of curiosity), her services were replete with evangelical, Protestant themes in which a clear attempt was made to call people forth to a commitment to God. She understood healing to be an expression of focusing on God, praising and praying to God, becoming completely dependent upon God, vowing to serve God, and giving up self-centeredness to assume Christian charity. It was as if this opening up to God allowed divine power to infuse the individual.

Like many other faith healers, Kuhlman was in the habit of laying hands on people who came forward for healing during her services. Almost always, people whom she touched staggered or completely collapsed. They fell backward into the arms of a waiting assistant, the official "catcher," whose job it was to see that no one was injured. This phenomenon, which is also evident with many other faith healers and in small healing groups (discussed below), is referred to as "going down under The Power."[52] One witness to her services described the phenomenon as follows:

> Some fall with their backs rigid, as in cataleptic swoon or hypnotic trance. Others double over, as though they had been punched in the solar plexus. Still others crumple like empty sacks.
>
> The sensations experienced by the subjects are variously described as "like being hit by lightning," "a thousand needles going through you all at once," "a cool breeze blows over you and then you're out," "an immense peacefulness." Most of those who experience the phenomenon seem to agree that it leaves a feeling of well-being and euphoria that sometimes lasts for several days.[53]

It is quite likely that this phenomenon was learned by those attending Kuhlman's services and that most people going forward expected to feel something when she touched them. What is important to note, though, is that this phenomenon reinforced the idea that Kuhlman had healing power, or (as she would insist) that she was an instrument for the healing power of God. The sight of people collapsing under her touch dramatically illustrated to all attending her services that she put people in direct contact with some force that had healing effects.

This is a central theme in many of the materials we have looked at in traditional healing scenarios. Healers are effective because they are able to put patients in contact with some kind of healing force or power. Healers are conduits of such power or are able through ritual or gestures to attract such powers for the benefit of their patients.

Another striking feature of Kuhlman's role as a healer was her ability to discern illness and healings in those attending her services. In this respect, she is reminiscent of William Branham (discussed above). During her services, she suddenly would begin to announce or proclaim that certain conditions had just been healed. Sometimes she gave specifics of the person's condition, how it arose, when it arose, and what its symptoms had been. Sometimes she specified exactly in which part of the auditorium the healing had taken place. The following "discernments" are typical:

> "Somebody's ear has opened. It happened not more than two minutes ago. On the ground floor, over to my right. A middle-aged woman. You didn't even expect to be healed but you are." . . . "Diabetes is being healed. To my right in the first balcony somebody is being healed of diabetes at this very moment. Don't be frightened, that heat in your body is the power of God." . . . "And a growth has disappeared. It's a man up there in the top balcony. Examine your leg and you'll find that the growth that was behind your knee is gone. God has healed you while you sat there." . . . "A blind eye is clearing. Somebody has a cataract and the cataract is slipping. It's the right eye. That's up in the first balcony to my left. The cataract is melting even as I speak."[54]

It is as if she knew exactly who the person was who had been healed. Indeed, she said that she had vivid pictures of these healings, which were repeatedly verified when people came forth to "claim their healings." When asked how she could possibly know these things, she replied: "The Holy Spirit tells me."

This ability of Kuhlman sent a clear message to those attending her services: that she had special insight, intuition, or telepathy that enabled her to see directly into people in the most intimate ways, permitting her to perceive changes in their bodily

Kathryn Kuhlman. Courtesy of the Kathryn Kuhlman Foundation.

and mental conditions. Again, as we have seen in many of the cultures discussed in earlier chapters, it is precisely the healers' ability to see into the spirit world, or into realms of reality not ordinarily visible to other people, that makes them effective. Like many traditional healers, especially of the shamanic type, Kuhlman seemed able to see directly and deeply into people's physical and spiritual condition.

Furthermore, Kuhlman's intuitive (or divine) ability to discern functioned only under certain conditions. In fact, this ability arose almost exclusively during her healing services, when it seems that she entered an altered state of consciousness. She herself said that during these periods she had out-of-body experiences, sometimes could not remember what she said or did, and was not aware of her surroundings. She also said that during these periods she behaved spontaneously and did things that surprised her.[55] According to her own understanding of these periods, she was overcome by the Holy Spirit, which guided her. In terms of shamanic healers whom we have looked at in earlier chapters, Kuhlman's behavior during her periods of discernment resembled a shamanic trance in which the healer's spirit is freed from the ordinary limitations of the body and can travel and see into the spirit world and understand spiritual matters more intensely. The shamanic theme of being able to see into the spirit world is clearly suggested in descriptions of Kuhlman during her services.

ENDNOTES

[1]See David Edwin Harrell, Jr., *All Things Are Possible: The Healing and Charismatic Revivals in Modern America* (Bloomington: Indiana University Press, 1975), pp.13–15.

[2]Ibid., p. 16.

[3]Ibid., p. 92.

[4]Cited in ibid., p. 92.

[5]Ibid., pp. 91–92.

[6]Allen Spraggett, *Kathryn Kuhlman: The Woman Who Believes in Miracles* (New York: World, 1970), p. 8.

[7]Harrell, *All Things Are Possible*, p. 85

[8]Ibid., p. 38.

[9]Ibid., p. 64.

[10]A. A. Allen, *Invasion from Hell* (Miracle Valley, Ariz.: A. A. Allen, 1953), p. 6; cited in ibid., p. 88.

[11]A. A. Allen, *The Cure of Madness* (Miracle Valley, Ariz.: A. A. Allen, 1963), pp. 53–73; cited in Harrell, *All Things Are Possible*, p. 88.

[12]Cited in Harrell, *All Things Are Possible*, pp. 198–99.

[13]See ibid., pp. 36–39.

[14]Ibid., pp. 210–11.

[15]Several examples of this are shown in the Canadian Film Board film *Healing* about a Kathryn Kuhlman rally in Ottawa.

[16]Harrell, *All Things Are Possible*, p. 213.

[17]Canadian National Film Board film *Healing*.

[18]Spraggett, p. 154.

[19]Gordon Lindsay, *William Branham: A Man Sent from God*, 4th ed. (Jeffersonville, Ind.: William Branham, 1950), p. 77; cited in Harrell, *All Things Are Possible*, pp. 27–28.

[20]F. F. Bosworth, "Looking at the Unseen," *The Voice of Healing* (January 1950), p. 4; cited in Harrell, *All Things Are Possible*, p. 37.

[21]"The Ministry of a Prophet," *The End Time Messenger* (July 1966), pp. 2–5; cited in Harrell, *All Things Are Possible*, p. 237.

[22]Spraggett, p. 124.

[23]Ibid., pp. 124–25.

[24]Harrell, *All Things Are Possible*, p. 28.

[25]Ibid., p. 42.

[26]Ibid., pp. 66–67.

[27]Ibid., p. 63.

[28]Ibid., p. 58.

[29]Ibid., p. 75.

[30]Cited in ibid., p. 237.

[31]Ibid., p. 205.

[32]Ibid., p. 101.

[33]Ibid.

[34]The best book on Oral Roberts is by David Edwin Harrell, Jr., *Oral Roberts: An American Life* (Bloomington: Indiana University Press, 1985). The following summary of Roberts's ministry is based on this book.

[35]Ibid., pp. 33–34.

[36]Ibid., p. 7,

[37]Ibid.

[38]Oral Roberts, *My Story* (Tulsa, Okla.: Summit Book Co., 1961), p. 80; cited in Harrell, *Oral Roberts*, p. 66.

[39]Cited in Harrell, *Oral Roberts*, p. 67.

[40]Oral Roberts, *My Life*, p. 95; cited in Harrell, *Oral Roberts*, p. 67.

[41]Harrell, *Oral Roberts*, p. 101.

[42]Cited in ibid., p. 105.

[43]Will Oursler, *The Healing Power of Faith* (New York: Hawthorn Books, 1957), p. 186.

[44]Oral Roberts, *The Holy Spirit in the Now*, 3 vols. (Tulsa, Okla.: Oral Roberts University, 1974), vol. 2, p. 28; cited in Harrell, *Oral Roberts*, p. 106.

[45]Oral Roberts, *Oral Roberts' Best Sermons and Stories* (Tulsa, Okla.: Oral Roberts University, 1956), p. 37; cited in Harrell, *Oral Roberts*, p. 90.

[46]Oral Roberts, Chapel Transcript (Nov. 15, 1967), p. 24; cited in Harrell, *Oral Roberts*, p. 106.

[47]Oursler, p. 187

[48]For a telling critique of the faith healers, see J. Randi, *The Faith Healers* (Buffalo, N.Y.: Prometheus Books, 1987).

[49]Spraggett, p. 133.

[50]Cited in Harrell, *All Things Are Possible*, p. 190.

[51]Spraggett, pp. 135–36.

[52]Ibid., p. 11.

[53]Ibid.

[54]Ibid., pp. 10–11.

[55]Ibid., pp. 124–25.

Chapter 13

Healing in Contemporary North American Christianity

Many people associate religious, spiritual, or faith healing in contemporary North American Christianity primarily with the flamboyant healers we discussed in the previous chapter. However, although statistics are difficult to come by, such healing is far more common in small Christian groups associated with a local church. Prayer groups that focus on healing, healing services, rituals that are part of regular services, and individuals who heal in private or in small groups are more the rule than the exception when it comes to religious healing in contemporary Christianity. Flamboyant faith healers such as Oral Roberts and Kathryn Kuhlman have gained the publicity, but most religious healing is done in small, local groups in unspectacular, undramatic fashion.

Much of the local, small-group, routine religious healing in contemporary Christianity is related to the Pentecostal and charismatic revival movements. Like many of the faith healers we discussed above, local, small-group religious healing assumes many of the themes that are central to the Pentecostal and charismatic movements. Of particular importance to healing are the assumptions that God bestows gifts of the spirit (charismatic gifts) on those who worship him (as he did at Pentecost among the early Christians) and that it is primarily the power of God that heals or enables an ill person to understand and learn from illness. In this sense, religious healing is related to the biblical accounts of the early church; healing services often seek to imitate what is understood to be early biblical Christianity (as was also the case with the faith healers discussed above). In short, much of the local, unspectacular spiritual healing in contemporary North American Christianity is somewhat sectarian in nature, being part of the Pentecostal and charismatic revival movements.

At the same time, however, religious healing remains an important part of the mainline Christian tradition in North America. The Order of Saint Luke in the

Anglican (or Episcopal) Church, which centers on the visitation and healing of the sick, and the existence of healing rituals in the Anglican *Book of Common Prayer* and the Methodist *Book of Worship* indicate an interest in healing outside the Pentecostal and charismatic movements in contemporary Christianity. Agnes Sanford, one of the most important religious healers of the modern period, was an Anglican layperson and was only tangentially related to the Pentecostal movement, even though she was known and admired by them. She was what might be called a mainline Christian healer, who affirmed a theology in which the healing power of God is latent in every individual, waiting to be awakened or cultivated. It is not so much a special gift of the spirit as it is an intrinsic part of God's creation.

ILLNESS AND HEALING UNDERSTOOD
IN A THEOLOGICAL CONTEXT

A striking feature of religious healing in contemporary Christianity is the centrality of providing a theological framework within which illness and healing can be understood. As we have seen in many cases discussed earlier in the book, one of the primary roles played by healers and healing rituals is to frame illness in a meaningful context. Indeed, healing itself can often be understood as consisting primarily or only in this. To come to an understanding of what one's illness means, how it fits a larger biographical or social pattern, is tantamount to finding healing. Healing is the process of combating the heightened fear and anxiety associated with illness and affirming that the human suffering associated with disease is not proof that life is meaningless and chaotic. This is a central, if not the central, feature of religious healing in contemporary Christianity.

In the broadest sense, religious healing relates sickness to a divine scheme or purpose. It makes sense of what might otherwise appear to be a frightening, meaningless, dangerous experience by providing an overarching theology in which illness has significance. While there are sophisticated theological systems with long histories associated with almost every group in which religious healing takes place, there are a few rather straightforward theological assertions that are central to understanding religious healing in most groups and for most individuals.

First, illness (and by implication healing) is related to one's overall life experience. It usually is not understood to be random (as it often is in modern, "secular" medicine). Traditional Christianity tends to relate illness to a human being's sinful nature or to specific sinful actions or thoughts. In its simplest form, the idea is that sin causes sickness, either directly, in a kind of cause-and-effect way, or as a punishment from God. As one leader of the charismatic healing movement put it: "The basic source of a sickness is the primordial evil which weighs upon man and can only be lifted by a power beyond our human intelligence and activity."[1] This passage refers to "original sin," Christianity's idea that the basic nature of human beings is sinful. It is the human tendency to rebel against, ignore, or resist God's will that makes human beings susceptible to illness. It is also common to relate sickness to individual sinful actions or to a pattern of such actions. In the following quotation, the individual attributes illness to the habit of not turning over one's life to God.

> I really believe it [sickness] is the result of sin. I really do. I really do. I mean we pollute our bodies with additives or whatever, you know. You can't see the direct link. But for example like when I had my first job, I had severe stomach problems after I was first married and you know, really bad. I was in and out of the hospital and stuff . . . and that was just worry and anxiety and that sort of thing . . . all from not turning it over to Jesus and trusting the Lord.[2]

Another person put it this way:

> Sin is probably the root cause; it's probably the only cause. Sin—either your own sin or the sins of others around you or just the sin factor in the world. Not being in tune with the Lord. Not being disciplined enough to hear Him speak and direct your life . . . Disregarding the laws of God, being not in tune with Him, committing sin. Subtle sins, like hatred of another person that you're not fully aware of. That's sin. Harboring a grudge, letting your temper fly in such a way that you then have guilt. . . . It's because of sin that we derive all the illnesses and evils of the world.[3]

In the case of sin as the cause of illness, the individual is encouraged to "own" his or her illness, to take responsibility for it. The individual is told that he or she has control over illness because it is the individual's actions that bring on the sickness. Healing is the process of admitting one's sinful nature or actions and trying to do better. Often healing is understood to necessitate a renewed commitment to God.

The second dominant theory of illness is that it is caused by Satan or evil spirits. The central theological idea here is that there exists a power in the world that opposes God and is constantly working to thwart his will. This power, in the person of Satan or evil spirits, is always seeking to undermine human commitment to God and often attacks human beings in the form of sickness. This theory tends to disassociate God from sickness and also tends to relieve the individual of blame for his or her illness. When sickness is understood to be the result of hostile spirits, the ill person is understood to be a victim. Here is how one person understands the idea:

> I believe that it's coming from Satan. And he uses it in all sorts of ways to . . . zap you with something. You know, all of a sudden you feel fine, then tomorrow morning you wake up with something horrible, and you've probably been exposed to it. I mean illness is in the realm of Satan. And however you get it—whether it's through sin or exposure or neglect or whatever—that all is Satan's territory.[4]

Another person said this about Satan and illness:

> I think Satan does his best. I think it's time we recognized that the power of evil lives in the world and that we as individuals have to cope with the evil that's in the world today. And again that's another thing, another advantage of having a prayer community. It's because we gather together for strength and you sort of get to be invincible in a group. If you try to hit it out on your own, I mean obviously, you just can't with those devils. You just don't stand a ghost of a chance. You know, I know a lot of people don't

believe the devil exists, but I really don't think things would be as bad as they were, the evil in us, the evil in man. The evil that's in man is the evil that's an extension of possession of the devil. The devil is using that person just like God can use us . . . I do believe that a lot of evil, a lot of sadness and sickness in this world is brought on by Satan. I think it's in his scheme of things to turn us against God.[5]

While both passages clearly relate Satan or devils to illness, it is interesting to note that both individuals relate Satan to basic human depravity or sin, and by extension to the theory of illness as caused by sin. It is also interesting that in the second passage individuals are portrayed as far from helpless in combating Satan's power. If one joins a prayer group and combines efforts with other devotees, Satan can be held at bay. The implication, again, is that ultimately one is responsible for one's illness, which is directly related to whether one is a member of an effective prayer or healing group.

GROUP STRUCTURES AND PRACTICES

In sharp contrast to the huge healing rallies that dominated the crusades of such famous faith healers as Oral Roberts and Kathryn Kuhlman are the small healing and prayer groups and routine, unspectacular healing services and rituals that dominate most religious healing associated with local churches. Healing is often private, the services are low key, and the leaders are often laypeople who claim no special healing power.

A particularly striking difference from the famous faith healers is the low profile of the leaders in the local healing groups. Healers such as Oral Roberts and Kathryn Kuhlman were understood to have unique, strong healing powers. Despite what they themselves might have said about the source of their healing powers, they were perceived by people as having a powerful healing touch or presence. Their charisma strongly affected the healing process. In the small, local groups, although clergy may play leadership roles, there is an insistence on the democratization of routine healing. Healing is something that anyone can do for another person and that one can do for oneself. It is a natural ability given by God to all human beings. It only has to be recognized and cultivated in order to become effective.

Healing itself, similarly, is understood to be a normal part of spiritual development. The emphasis in the small groups is usually placed, not on dramatic physical healing, but on small changes in attitude, habit, and daily routine. While the small local groups do not deny the possibility of dramatic physical cures as a result of their efforts, they concentrate on healing as a maturing of one's spiritual life. Healing is not so much (if at all) a change in one's physical condition as it is a fuller understanding of how illness fits into one's spiritual sojourn.

Groups that cultivate religious healing meet regularly (often weekly) and consist of a few members who pray for those who have made requests for help. Meetings may be independent of any regular church service or ritual, or they may be directly tied to such services. It is quite common, for example, for the healing group to meet to help those having requests right after a regular Sunday service or for the clergyperson to have a short healing service in the sanctuary right after the normal Sunday service.

Prayer is by far the most common and central healing activity of these groups, no matter what the denomination. Group members may pray for a person who is present and ill, or they may pray on behalf of someone who is not present but for whom someone has come with a request. Sometimes members of the healing group, especially if they are Pentecostals, "speak in tongues," which is understood to be a special type of prayer. Prayer may be silent or spoken.

Many other healing practices are also used by these groups. In Roman Catholic groups, the sacraments often play a central role in healing services. Of particular importance is the sacrament called anointing of the sick. This ritual used to be called extreme unction and was used primarily to prepare people for death. In recent years, however, the sacrament has been reinterpreted to play the role it originally played in early Christianity, namely, healing the sick. The emphasis in the revised sacrament is away from hearing the confession of those who are on the verge of death and toward ministering to anyone who is sick and wishes a ritual of healing. The trend is also away from performing the sacrament in private (which was appropriate for hearing confession) to performing it with members of the family or other sick people present. This new communal emphasis stresses the importance of affirming family and community solidarity in the healing process. In this sacrament, a priest anoints sick people with holy oil and invokes prayers asking for healing. One such prayer reads:

> May your blessing come upon all who are anointed with this oil, that they may be freed from pain, illness, and disease and made well again in body, mind, and soul.

> Father, may this oil, which you have blessed for our use, produce its healing effect, in the name of our Lord Jesus Christ.[6]

The sacraments of Penance and the Eucharist also have healing themes and sometimes are oriented specifically to healing. In the sacrament of Penance, the priest may discuss people's past lives with them in an attempt to heal oppressive and painful memories. This is sometimes referred to as the healing of memories. The emphasis of Penance in such cases is on reconciling the penitents' relationships with others, on healing or restoring relationships. There is the recognition here that personal relationships are implicated in much sickness. The Eucharist, the central ritual drama of Roman Catholicism, has a healing theme and may be performed during services held specifically for healing. The most explicit reference to healing in the Eucharist is the prayer said just before receiving the sacred elements:

> Deliver us, Lord, from every evil,
> and grant us peace in our day.
> In your mercy keep us free from sin
> and protect us from all anxiety . . .

Lord Jesus Christ,
with faith in your love and mercy
I eat your body and drink your blood.
Let it not bring me condemnation,
but health in mind and body.
Lord, I am not worthy to receive you,
but only say the word and I shall be healed.[7]

Perhaps the most common healing ritual act besides prayer that is used in almost all healing groups no matter which denomination is the laying on of hands. The laying on of hands is an ancient practice in Christianity and symbolizes the conferring of God's grace or blessing. Laying on of hands is prescribed for healing services in the Methodist *Book of Worship*:

> Laying on of hands, anointing with oil, and the less formal gesture of holding someone's hand all show the power of touch, which plays a central role in the healings recorded in the New Testament. Jesus often touched others—blessing children, washing feet, healing injuries and disease, and raising people from death. Biblical precedent combines with our natural desire to reach out to persons in need in prompting us to touch gently and lovingly those who ask for healing prayers. Such an act is a tangible expression of the presence of the healing Christ, working in and through those who minister in his name.[8]

Laying on of hands, or touching, as a healing act is common in many cultures. In the most general sense, the laying on of hands in both Christian and non-Christian contexts symbolizes the transference of energy or power from one person to another. In a healing context, the person touching (the healer) transfers energy or power to the supplicant or sick person. In contemporary Christian religious healing, the laying on of hands is central. Many famous faith healers employ the technique in their healing lines. Perhaps the person with the most famous healing touch is Oral Roberts. In small, informal, local groups also, the laying on of hands is common. In almost every situation in which it is used, the laying on of hands is accompanied by a prayer in which healing is requested. The following prayer, with instructions, from the Methodist *Book of Worship* is typical:

> *If there is laying on of hands, a leader, who may be joined by others,
>   lays hands*
> *upon each person's head, in silence or using these or similar words:*
> *Name*, I (*we*) lay my (*our*) hands on you
> (*These hands are laid upon you*)
> in the name of the Father, and of the Son, and of the Holy Spirit
>   (*in the name of the holy and triune God*)
>   (*in the name of Jesus, the Christ, your Savior and Healer*)
> [*for specified purpose*].
> May the power of God's indwelling presence heal you of all illnesses—
>   of body, mind, spirit, and relationships—
> that you may serve God with a loving heart. Amen.[9]

As the act of laying on of hands is usually understood to symbolize the transmission of God's power, it is not surprising that many people attest to a physical sensation when the ritual is performed. One leader of a healing group said: "It's like a real mild current of electricity in your hand and you feel it kind of tingly and the heat."[10] Another person described the sensation as follows: "It's almost like cobalt; it's like the power of the Lord working through the person who's laying on hands and then it's through the hands directed into the person who's being prayed for and it's just like the Spirit, the power of the Lord going through that person right into the other person."[11]

A striking characteristic of the laying on of hands in large, public healing crusades is the collapse of individuals after being touched. This is commonly referred to as being "slain in the spirit" and is said to be caused by the infusion of the Holy Ghost into the recipient's body. It is as if the recipients have been knocked out by the energy being transmitted from the healer. This phenomenon is also evident in local healing groups. One Pentecostal minister described this common experience as follows: "Many times when I pray for people, they feel the power of God coming into them, and—nine out of ten—it just knocked them right on the floor. I didn't do it. I just laid my hand barely on them. It was God's healing power going through me into them, effecting a healing and cure and undoing the works that Satan had done in their body."[12]

It is not surprising, given the fairly common idea that illness is caused by Satan or evil spirits, that exorcism figures in the practices of many healing groups. Exorcism can take the form of a ritual performed by a duly ordained Catholic priest according to established liturgical guidelines, which is fairly uncommon, to a more informal ritual in which a healer (either lay or clerical) combines laying on of hands, anointing with oil, or making the sign of the cross (or all three) with a prayer or invocation of the name of Jesus abjuring Satan or a demon to leave an afflicted person. Exorcism is sometimes referred to as the deliverance ministry and is regarded as a special form of healing requiring a special gift.[13]

INNER HEALING AND DISCERNMENT

It is clear that the term *healing* covers a wide range of experiences, conditions, and events in the context of Christian healing groups. Minor physical maladies such as headaches, colds, and cuts, as well as serious conditions such as hepatitis, arthritis, and cancer, are certainly mentioned as being healed. But healing also applies to many conditions or situations that are physical only in a tangential sense; it can apply to almost every facet of a person's life.

In the most general sense, healing refers to a continuous spiritual growth or development, the goal of which is to achieve an intense rapport with God. In this sense, *health* might be defined as "oneness with God."[14] As one person put it: "I think that a really healthy person has got to have a good relationship with the Lord. Or else I don't think that they're really healthy, totally."[15] Another expressed it this way: "I think to be truly healthy . . . well, I believe that if a person is healthy, they're one with the Lord. They're relaxed, relaxed in Him and resting in Him."[16] People who have anchored their lives in faith and trust in God are considered healthy in the sense of being meaningfully oriented in life. Even if such a person is physically ill, even terminally ill, he or she is basically healthy. In this sense, health is not necessarily related to physical health and in some cases may not be related to physical health at all.

As one would expect, *illness* is also defined very broadly and may not bear any relationship to physical disease. Illnesses are often personal shortcomings, particularly relating to one's faith in God. Lack of faith and trust in God, for example, is often said to be a problem in need of healing. Self-centeredness, indifference to others, hatred of others, jealousy, and other problems relating to personal relationships are also often mentioned as areas that are in need of healing or that have received healing.

Related to the healing of human relationships is what many groups refer to as the healing of memories. This usually involves people telling (or confessing) traumatic past events to a counselor or priest or discussing relationships or situations that are particularly troublesome, painful, or debilitating. To some extent, this resembles psychotherapy, in which past life events are remembered, evaluated, and fully acknowledged. In the healing of memories, the emphasis is often on reconciliation and forgiveness of those who have abused or harmed one. Of particular interest are visualization and imaging techniques such as calling forth and walking back. *Calling forth* involves recalling in vivid fashion a painful memory, reexperiencing the event, praying for its healing, and "giving it over to the Lord." *Walking back* is the process of gradually leading a person back through his or her life, pausing at every sad or uncomfortable memory, and praying over it.[17] Another technique involves imagining Jesus at one's side in difficult situations and calling on his power to heal the memory.[18] Jesus is often pictured or imagined as approaching supplicants, reaching out and touching them, embracing them, and speaking a word of forgiveness or comfort. He is sometimes pictured as reconciling two people by putting his arms around both of them and bringing them together in a three-way embrace.[19] The kinds of memories healed include early childhood experiences of parental neglect or abuse, harmful sibling relationships, and failed romantic relationships.

Healing also sometimes involves what is called discernment. Discernment is the process or experience of coming to a true or complete understanding of one's illness. Discernment is often accomplished or experienced by the healer, to whom the inner condition of the "patient" is revealed by God or the Holy Spirit. The patient, in turn, experiences realization about her spiritual condition. Discernment enables the healer and the supplicant to focus their healing efforts (prayer, touch, or imaging) to bring about positive change more effectively. Discernment may reveal a particular personality trait, attitude, or relationship that is inhibiting a person's spiritual growth. Discernment is reminiscent of the shaman's ability to see into a person's soul and assess his spiritual condition as part of the healing process. It also relates to healing as self-knowledge in some contemporary schools of psychotherapy.

DEVELOPING AND UTILIZING DIVINE HEALING POWER

The democratization of religious healing in local churches tends to minimize the special healing powers of particular individuals. In these groups, it is often assumed that anyone can cultivate and use healing power, which is latent within each person. To put the matter in a more theological way, it is assumed that any individual can cultivate attitudes or habits that permit God to heal through her. Healing energy is understood to be a given, inherent in the creation, something with which God has infused the world that is at the disposal of human beings if they can understand how to use it.

Agnes Sanford, one of the most famous Christian healers in North America, understood God's energy to pervade every particle of creation and to reside within each human being: "Knowing then that we are part of God, that His life within us is an active energy and that He works through the laws of our bodies, let us study to adjust and conform ourselves to those laws. When we do this with understanding and common-sense, we can speed up the natural healing forces of the body."[20]

Prayer, according to Sanford, is the way in which we put ourselves in touch with this energy by becoming aware of it. Prayer is the acknowledgment that we are part of a living power that goes beyond our individuality and personal limitations. It affirms that we are connected to an underlying energy that empowers and enlivens us and that is the basis of our ongoing health and vitality. Having put ourselves in touch with this divine energy by becoming conscious of it, the next step, according to Sanford, is to affirm that power infusing our bodies. When one senses that one is energized, as it were, one can then direct this energy to healing oneself or others. When healing others, certain rituals or gestures, especially the laying on of hands, are important, as they symbolize the transference of the healing energy.[21]

According to most people involved in local healing groups and rituals, the most congenial setting in which to activate healing energy and direct it effectively is a loving community. This community may be the family or local church but is usually spoken of as the local prayer or healing group itself. Composed of like-minded people bent on healing each other or people outside the group, it is understood to provide the best context for arousing healing energy and facilitating its free flow. Although healing may take place between an individual healer and supplicant while they are alone, the group context is nearly always said to be more effective and powerful.[22]

The healing power of a supportive, loving group is something we have already seen in other contexts. In many cultures, healing practices and rituals are public events necessitating the participation of family members and friends, who often have important roles to play in the patient's healing. Healing becomes a community or group project. It is not understood to be something the patient should or can do by herself. In scenarios where group participation is important, it is affirmed that the illness implicates the group as a whole, which must take responsibility for bringing about a restoration of health. In local Christian healing and prayer groups, a strong support community is made available in which illness can be treated cooperatively. To a great extent, it is the community setting that makes the groups as effective as they are. They surely provide something that is almost entirely lacking in allopathic biomedicine, which is so strongly focused on the isolated doctor-patient relationship, which tends to neglect entirely the patient's role as a member of various communities. By framing illness in a meaningful context, and by providing the patient with a support community, these groups often meet needs that are ignored or neglected in secular medicine.

A dominant theme in local Christian healing groups is the relationship of healing to divine power or energy and, conversely, of illness to its lack. The theme is not distinctively or peculiarly Christian, of course. We have seen in many healing scenarios the importance of reestablishing harmony with cosmic forces, of reconnecting individuals with divine energy, and so on. In the Christian context, the idea is that God's power, which is normally available to all individuals, maintains individuals in health. This divine dispensational power is thought of either as inherent in creation or as a free-flowing gift of God to all members of the believing community (the church).[23]

This power is often mediated through individuals (saints, clergy, or other individuals who are special conduits of divine power) and groups (particularly local healing groups). Opposing this divine energy that maintains and stimulates health and protects against illness are forces such as Satan, evil spirits and individuals, and the human tendency to sin. In the context of the healing group, the central aim is often understood to be to enhance the flow of divine energy and to combat the evil forces that inhibit its flow. To be right with God, to be open to God's will and purpose, to be established in a faithful relationship with God, is usually understood as critical in keeping open the channels through which God's healing energy can flow. To yield to weakness, to live in ways that are offensive to God, to be less than steadfast in serving and relying on God, creates a barrier against God's healing power or makes one vulnerable to negative forces that prevent God from touching one with healing energy.

ENDNOTES

[1]Francis MacNutt, *The Power to Heal* (Notre Dame, Ind.: Ave Maria Press, 1977), p. 129.

[2]Cited in Meredith B. McGuire, *Pentecostal Catholics: Power, Charisma, and Order in a Religious Movement* (Philadelphia: Temple University Press, 1982), p. 150.

[3]Cited in Meredith B. McGuire, *Ritual Healing in Suburban America* (New Brunswick, N.J.: Rutgers University Press, 1988), p. 47.

[4]Cited in McGuire, *Ritual Healing*, p. 49.

[5]Cited in McGuire, *Pentecostal Catholics*, p. 150.

[6]Cited in Francis MacNutt, *Healing* (Toronto: Bantam Books, 1977), p. 252.

[7]Cited in ibid., p. 266.

[8]*United Methodist Book of Worship* (Nashville, Tenn.: United Methodist Publishing House, 1992), p. 614.

[9]Ibid., p. 621.

[10]McGuire, *Ritual Healing*, p. 64.

[11]McGuire, *Pentecostal Catholics*, pp. 136–37.

[12]McGuire, *Ritual Healing*, pp. 64–65.

[13]See Agnes Sanford, *The Healing Gifts of the Spirit* (Philadelphia: J. B. Lippincott, 1966), pp. 193–209; McGuire, *Ritual Healing*, pp. 65–66; and McGuire, *Pentecostal Catholics*, pp. 133–35.

[14]McGuire, *Pentecostal Catholics*, p. 153.

[15]Ibid.

[16]Ibid., p. 155.

[17]Michael Scanlan, *Inner Healing: Ministering to the Human Spirit through the Power of Prayer* (New York: Paulist Press, 1974), pp. 47–48.

[18]McGuire, *Pentecostal Catholics*, p. 138.

[19]Scanlan, p. 69.

[20]Agnes Sanford, *The Healing Light* (St. Paul, Minn.: Macalestser Park Publishing, 1947), p. 34.

[21]Ibid., pp. 21–22.

[22]See Sanford, *The Healing Light*, pp. 148–59, and Scanlan, pp. 63–70.

[23]McGuire, *Pentecostal Catholics*, pp. 174–83.

PART THREE
Modern Medical Culture

INTRODUCTION

There can be no doubt that modern medicine has fewer religious features than the healing traditions, cultures, and scenarios we have looked at so far. Indeed, one of the chief features of modern medicine, as we shall see, is its claim to be rational and scientific, by which is meant that it does not presume mystical or religious causes or therapies. Modern medicine largely defines itself as nonreligious, even antireligious, when it comes to its philosophy and techniques of healing. Nevertheless, many of the features we have seen in premodern or nonmodern healing contexts persist in modern medicine and indicate that, in some ways at least, there is a dimension to modern medicine that is not modern at all.

The aim of the following chapters is to demonstrate these continuities and also to suggest that modern medicine has its own ideology, "myths," and rituals. My aim is not to undermine its credibility by showing that there are traditional, nonscientific elements in it. My primary purpose is to suggest that modern medicine relies on techniques, symbolism, and rituals for part of its efficacy in much the same way as traditional, religious medical systems do and that in this sense we might think of it as having implicit religious (or at least symbolic) dimensions.

We will look first at some of the dynamics operating in modern psychotherapy to suggest that healing in this context involves many characteristics of premodern healing. In psychotherapy (at least where drugs and surgery are not involved), the healer basically persuades the patient to get better; the healer talks the patient into getting well. In this process, many techniques are used that we have seen in traditional healing systems and societies. It is primarily the dynamic between the healer and the patient that is important here, and little that is specifically modern, or even scientific, is central to the process.

Second, we will look at the placebo effect and studies that show how powerful the human imagination is in the disease and healing processes. I argue that the dynamics operating in the placebo effect are operating in all aspects of modern modern medicine; furthermore, techniques and procedures that enhance the placebo effect are readily apparent in the delivery of modern medicine. The placebo effect is a particularly clear example that rituals and symbols are powerful in effective healing.

Third, we will examine some of the distinctive features of modern medicine in an attempt to suggest that it is just as ideological (or mythological) as other medical systems and that an important part of modern medicine is cultural, as distinct from scientific. Modern medicine has made clear choices in what to emphasize and what to deemphasize in its approach to illness, and these choices or tendencies lend it a distinctive character that has little to do with its scientific nature.

Fourth, an attempt will be made to illustrate that modern medicine, which often claims to have delinked medicine and morality, to have disassociated sickness from sin, has defined and arbitrates an implicit morality. We will try to show how morality in contemporary North America has been medicalized or strongly related to issues of health and illness. Although they prefer to be thought of as practical scientists, we will suggest that physicians actually play priestly roles by defining and enforcing the underlying morality of modern North American culture.

Finally, we will look at a new and fairly large genre of modern literature in which people from a wide variety of backgrounds tell about their own illnesses. In these writings, which have been termed *pathographies,* we find the authors struggling to frame their illnesses in a meaningful context. In some cases, they are helped in this process by medical professionals. In other cases, they get no help from the medical establishment and consequently are critical of modern health professionals. The concluding chapter suggests that perennial human questions concerning the nature of human existence and human destiny arise in the context of serious illness, and they persist, no matter how hard we try to disassociate them from healing in the modern context. In essence, these are religious questions, and any healing culture or system that tries to ignore them, or fails to deal with them, leaves an important part of the healing process incomplete.

Chapter 14

Aspects of the Healer/Therapist's Role in Modern Psychotherapy

No matter how much we might wish to assert modern medicine's absolute difference from all other medical systems, the healer-patient relationship still remains at the heart of much, if not most, modern medical healing. No matter how much emphasis we might wish to place on modern medicines and therapies as constituting the superior efficacy of modern medical practice, it is still the interaction between medical personnel and patients that is critical to much, if not most, of the success of modern medical treatment. And what is important to note is that much, if not most, of the healer-patient dynamic in modern medicine is neither particularly modern nor scientific. Many aspects of this relationship are quite clear in other medical systems that we have looked at. To a great extent, the healer in modern medicine (whether a physician, nurse, or some other medical professional) employs techniques and approaches found in premodern or nonmodern medical systems.

The extent to which this is the case is readily apparent in psychotherapy that does not use drugs, psychosurgery, or electric-shock therapy. In such psychotherapy, the healer, in one way or another, persuades the patient to get better. It is the healer-patient dynamic alone that brings about healing. In trying to discern those aspects of modern medicine that are similar to the nonmodern systems we have looked at so far, it is helpful to look first at psychotherapy, because it enables us to focus on those aspects of modern medicine that are separate from modern drugs and physical therapies such as surgery, which are often credited with giving modern medicine its superior efficacy. It allows us to focus on the healer-patient dynamic alone.

Many psychotherapists attribute the success of their treatment to modern theories of human behavior, recent discoveries concerning the human unconscious, and recently developed therapies. Nevertheless, much of what constitutes psychotherapy involves techniques and approaches that we have seen in premodern medical sys-

tems. Indeed, much of what is considered modern is not modern at all. The case for
the centrality of nonmodern techniques and the relative insignificance of modern
psychoanalytic theory as central to the healer-patient dynamic in modern medicine has
been presented in the classic work on modern psychotherapy by Jerome Frank, *Persuasion and Healing*. According to Frank, it is not the therapist's knowledge of
psychoanalytic theory or of psychotherapeutic techniques that has the most influence
on the patient; it is the attitudes, opinions, and expectations of the therapist that are
most important in the healing process. According to Frank, the psychotherapist's healing "magic" is not very different from the traditional healer's magic. In both cases,
he argues, healing is brought about by means of the healer persuading the patient that
he can get better.

In healing situations where persuasion is important, which Frank argues includes
all forms of psychotherapy, a crucial factor is the involvement of the patient. The more
involved the patient gets in his own therapy, the more likely that dramatic and last-
ing change will come about. Frank cites several experiments that demonstrate this
point.[1] In many therapeutic situations the patient is urged to play different roles, to
identify with a certain person or attitude, to remember and reflect upon specific
details of his life, to talk about painful details of his life, and so on. In this way the
patient becomes actively involved with certain points of view that might help alter
behavior, attitudes, self-images, and so on that the therapist perceives to be unhealthy.
The emphasis in many forms of psychotherapy is on the patient talking about himself, which forces the patient to become strongly involved in solving his own problems. The point here is that the therapist does not offer the patient a magic formula,
a "silver bullet," or some miracle drug for restoring health. The therapist puts the patient
to work in healing himself.

Another factor in the psychotherapeutic healing process is the transference of
the therapist's feelings, ideas, and expectations to the patient. Even in so-called
nondirective therapy, in which the patient is supposed to explore her own life without direction from the therapist, the therapist nevertheless, willy-nilly, conveys her
approval or disapproval, expectations, and ideas to the patient in a variety of ways.
What is clear is the great extent to which the patient is attentive to the healer and the
healer's expectations and approval. No matter how neutral or uninvolved the therapist may try to be, her attitudes are picked up by the patient and have a very strong
influence on the therapeutic process. The therapist subtly guides the patient to behave
in ways that conform to her expectations, even when the therapist is consciously
trying to exert no influence whatsoever. In a case cited by Frank, it is clear that, even
in nondirective therapy, the therapist's responses to patients were easily classified as
approving or disapproving and that the number of statements patients made after
the eight sessions with the therapist that were disapproved by the therapist dropped
sharply, from forty-five percent to five percent. Conversely, statements they made that
were approved by the therapist during the same period rose from one percent to
forty-five percent.[2] If the therapist unintentionally transfers her attitudes and expectations to the patient in nondirective therapy, how much more powerful and effective
such transference must be in directive therapies.

Another factor in the psychoanalytic or psychotherapeutic relationship that Frank sees as important is the therapist's concern for the patient's welfare. Again, this has little to do with psychiatric or psychoanalytic theory or technique. It has to do with establishing a relationship in which the healer can express sympathetic feelings for the patient. This is largely accomplished by a process of selectivity, whereby the therapist selects and encourages as patients only those toward whom he is sympathetic. Most therapists have success with certain types of patients and certain types of illnesses. Some therapists actively seek out alcoholics, for example, while others carefully avoid them. Psychotherapists tend to gravitate to people whom they regard as ideal patients. These are individuals who share many of the same values as the therapist and who suffer from conditions the therapist is confident of curing. Healers probably have exercised this kind of selectivity (consciously or unconsciously) at all times and places to some extent. It is probably also the case, although Frank does not discuss this, that patients tend to shy away from healers whom they find unsympathetic to their conditions and situations.

A related factor in much psychotherapy, Frank says, is combating demoralization. Most patients who seek psychotherapy, Frank says, are discouraged. They are depressed and feel helpless to improve their own plight. It is often the principal job of the therapist to instill in the patient a sense of personal worth and hope about the future. Healing becomes the process of raising the patient's morale and restoring self-esteem. Frank lists several components of treatment that are successful in combating demoralization, all of which are also found in nonmodern healing situations. First, he says, it is important to establish an "emotionally charged, confiding relationship."[3] Second, it is important to establish a healing setting, a context in which the patient feels confident that healing can take place. In psychotherapy this is usually the therapist's office or a hospital. Third, it is important for the therapist to frame the patient's problems in a "rational, conceptual scheme, or myth."[4] That is, the therapist must "make sense" of the patient's situation. And finally, the therapist must provide a procedure (or ritual) that involves the patient in his own healing. Each of the components of successful psychotherapy, of course, is common in many of the healing scenarios we have looked at in premodern cultures.

Two of these components of successfully combating demoralization should be elaborated. Providing a healing context in psychotherapy often means surrounding the patient with impressive, prestigious symbols. A modern medical center itself is one such symbol. Controlled access to the therapist is another important part of establishing a powerful healing context. A patient may have to wait some months before seeing the therapist, and there are usually induction rituals that must be performed prior to this. The patient must undergo preliminary interviews, which often define and create specific expectations, which the therapist is confident of fulfilling. Waiting rooms and receptionists serve as a kind of outer circle surrounding and protecting the inner sanctum, the therapist's office, where therapy will actually take place. In the office itself, shelves containing heavy medical tomes line the walls, framed gilt-edged certificates from prestigious institutions adorn the walls, and the therapist himself is dressed in dignified fashion. There is a hushed solemnity to the therapist's

McMaster University Medical Center. Courtesy of Archives, Chedoke-McMaster Hospitals, Faculty of Health Sciences.

office. In short, the patient is placed within a carefully designed healing setting, often after a long wait during which expectations are aroused about the healing power of the therapist.

Setting the patient's illness in a meaningful context involves relating the patient's condition to a theory of psychoanalysis or psychology, that is, to a general theory of human behavior. These theories are often mythical in nature in the sense that they purport to reveal the answers to the mysteries of human behavior or existence but remain unproven or are incapable of being proven. They are similar to worldviews or ideologies. They provide a framework for understanding the complexities and subtleties of human existence, and it is within such a framework that a therapist will place a patient's problems. This framing of the patient's illness accomplishes two things. First, it provides his illness with a name or label, thus removing much of the mystery of the illness and removing the patient's sense of isolation. By labeling the illness, the therpist reassures the patient that he is not alone or unique. Second, by putting a label on the illness, the therapist locates the illness in the realm of what is potentially treatable. The illness is domesticated, as it were.

Closely related to Frank's view that psychotherapy primarily involves combating demoralization is the approach of Victor Frankl. Frankl, who spent some months in a Nazi concentration camp during World War II, noticed that people who were able to maintain a strong sense of hope and had a clear and positive understanding of what their lives meant had a much better chance of survival than those who had lost hope or who were overwhelmed by a sense of meaninglessness. He also noted that these two things were often related. That is, hopeful individuals had a strong sense of purpose, and those who were not hopeful often had no sense of purpose. Frankl's therapeutic approach is to combat depression, demoralization, and low self-esteem by helping patients reinterpret their lives and their life situations in a positive fashion. His aim is to help them affirm that their lives are meaningful and have some significance. This may involve helping individuals reconstruct a positive, affirmative account of their lives that is less burdened with guilt and recrimination. Although this approach is often premised on the idea that reviewing one's life is a means of gaining true insight into one's character, when the aim is to stress the positive, life review involves very selective memory and exaggeration. The aim is not so much to recapture the patient's past in accurate detail as it is to help the patient rethink her own self-image in a more positive vein.[5] Another important part of Frankl's approach, which he calls *logotherapy* (therapy aimed at constructing meaning), is to help patients find in illness, misfortune, even impending death, an underlying or ultimate purpose in their existence. To live without purpose and without hope, Frankl says, is to be truly ill. Restoration of health in this case means discovering meaning in one's life. To some extent, the role of the therapist in combating demoralization is to instruct the patient in what to believe about herself and what to ignore, minimize, or forget. The therapist helps the patient construct a new self-image. There is nothing particularly new or modern about this process. Healers in most premodern cultures are adept at relating patients' behavior to their illness and prescribing behavior modification as a means of combating or avoiding illness.

A final important aspect of psychotherapy concerns the self-confidence of the therapist and the patient's corresponding respect for the therapist. Frank emphasizes the importance of psychoanalytic or psychiatric theory in providing the therapist with confidence. It is not primarily the theory itself that is efficacious, Frank suggests, it is the fact that the healer has access to arcane, esoteric, special wisdom that she believes is powerfully effective. This gives her great self-confidence. This, in turn, gives the patient confidence in the therapist. It makes the patient eager to please and comply with the healer in his own cure. The careful, often meticulous, attention healers take in many cultures to project an impressive, powerful image is something we have noted earlier. The same factor is recognized as important in psychotherapy.

It is difficult to find much in all of this that is specifically modern or scientific. Those factors that Frank stresses as central in psychotherapy are all found in premodern medical cultures. According to Frank, the chemistry of the healer-patient relationship that is at the heart of the healing process in psychotherapy consists of factors that are well-known as efficacious in many non-Western, premodern contexts.

It is also important to note that these factors operate, to some extent, in other aspects of modern medicine. Even though drugs, surgery, diet, or other physical therapies may be involved, the nonphysical aspects of the healer-patient dynamic are also working in the healing process. It is probably just as important for a patient to have confidence in her surgeon prior to surgery or in her internist while undergoing drug therapy as it is for the patient to have confidence in a therapist while undergoing psychotherapy. Combating demoralization may be just as important in the former cases as in the latter. In both cases, the factors that Frank says are at the heart of the healer-patient dynamic are positively implicated in the healing process. Another way of putting this would be to say that much of what makes modern medicine work is not modern at all.

ENDNOTES

[1]Jerome D. Frank, *Persuasion and Healing: A Comparative Study of Psychotherapy* (New York: Schocken Books, 1974), pp. 110–13.

[2]Ibid., p. 129.

[3]Ibid., p. 40.

[4]Ibid., p. 42.

[5]See Victor E. Frankl, *The Doctor and the Soul: From Psychotherapy to Logotherapy* (New York: Random House, 1986; originally published 1955).

Chapter 15

The Placebo Effect: Ritual and Symbol in Modern Medicine

A placebo is an inert substance (often a sugar pill) having no pharmacological property; it is given by a doctor to a patient to help and often please the patient (hence the term *placebo*, "I shall please," from Latin). Sometimes the placebo is not a substance at all. It may be surgery, or a regime of behavior, including diet and physical exercise, or elaborate (and expensive) diagnostic procedures that the patient insists upon having (patients often consider them therapy). In short, a placebo is anything prescribed by a doctor or healer that the doctor or healer believes has no medical effect on the condition from which the patient suffers (or complains). The *placebo effect* is the resulting improvement in the patient.

The powerful effectiveness of placebos has led some to define the placebo effect as a person's ability to translate expectations about the future into reality, especially concerning the body and physical health generally. The placebo effect is important for our purposes at this point, because it clearly illustrates the great extent to which modern medical procedures (like procedures in all other medical cultures) have ritualistic and symbolic aspects that contribute to their efficacy. Although some critics of premodern medicine have said that any positive effects to be found in these systems is "simply due to the placebo effect,"[1] it should not be forgotten that the placebo effect also operates in modern medicine and may very well account for the positive benefits of many therapies.

We should also realize that the placebo effect, which we shall see is directly related to the faith and hope patients give to their doctors, also operates when placebos are not being used. That is, patients' hope and faith in doctors and in medicines and procedures prescribed by them are always at work in healing situations and often have positive effects. While doctors and patients alike might be inclined to attribute all healing effects to the medicines and procedures employed, it is obvious that the patient's trust and faith in the doctor is also a factor (often a crucial factor) in getting better.

EXAMPLES OF THE PLACEBO EFFECT

The importance, breadth, and strength of the placebo effect have been summarized as follows: "Many papers have demonstrated the importance and magnitude of the placebo effect in every therapeutic area. Placebos can be more powerful than, and reverse the action of, potent active drugs. The incidence of placebo reactions approaches 100 percent in some studies. Placebos can have profound effects on organic illnesses, including incurable malignancies. Placebos can often mimic the effects of active drugs."[2] Conditions for which placebos have been shown to give some relief include "cough, mood changes, angina pectoris, headache, seasickness, anxiety, hypertension, depression, and the common cold."[3] Placebos have been shown to "lower blood sugar in diabetics"[4] and to help shrink tumors in some patients.[5] They can also mimic the effects of active drugs. Placebos can create peak effects hours after the "drug" is taken, can create a cumulative effect over a period of time, and can create carryover effects when the "drug" is stopped.[6] That is, patients taking a placebo often experience the effects that the physician tells them they will experience and that are appropriate to a certain active drug.

Perhaps the best-known example of the placebo effect is in the treatment of warts. When a doctor paints warts with colored dye and tells the patient that the wart will disappear as the dye fades, the therapy is as effective as any other procedure, including surgical removal. As one author has said: "Apparently the emotional reaction to a placebo can change the physiology of the skin so that the virus which causes warts can no longer thrive."[7]

In one study, eighty-eight people suffering from arthritis were treated with placebos instead of aspirin or cortisone. As many patients reported improvement as would normally report positive effects from the usual drugs. Some of the patients who reported no improvement from the placebo tablets were given placebo injections. Of these, sixty-four percent reported improvement. They said that as a result of the injections they experienced pain relief, slept better, ate better, and had reduced swelling in their joints.[8] Although both the tablets and injections were placebos having no medical ingredients whatsoever, in modern medical culture injections are perceived to be a much more powerful medical treatment than a pill. Patients' expectations for the injections were undoubtedly higher than for the tablets. They were anticipating a more powerful effect, and hence many experienced improvement with the injection when they had not with the tablets. We can see quite clearly here the symbolic significance of medical procedures. Injections symbolize a more intense, concentrated, direct medical intervention than taking a pill.

Placebo studies have shown that people view tablets as more powerful than pills, capsules as more powerful than tablets, and injections as more powerful than capsules. Such studies have also shown that medicines with a bitter or unpleasant smell or taste

Pharmacy. Courtesy of Chedoke-McMaster Hospitals. Photograph by Peter Foulds.

are considered more powerful than tasteless and odorless medicines. If a medication is touted as "new and improved" or is in a special package, patients also perceive it to be more effective. The cost of a medication is also relevant: the more expensive a medication is, the more effective it is deemed to be. The appearance, type, and cost of medications all seem to carry symbolic meanings for patients.[9]

Not surprisingly, then, placebo surgical procedures can have extremely strong positive effects. The general perception is that surgery is the most dramatic, radical, and intense modern medical therapy. Some years ago (before there were requirements for full disclosure in the United States), a study was undertaken on patients suffering from heart pain. At that time, a surgical procedure was used that involved tying a mammary artery. This was supposed to increase blood flow to the heart, thus alleviating pain. The procedure was eventually discovered to be of no use in actually increasing blood flow to the heart. Nonetheless, about forty percent of the patients undergoing this procedure reported improvement. They could endure more exercise without discomfort, and even their electrocardiograms indicated improvements. In one case, a surgeon actually did mock operations on half of the patients he was treating.

The patients were given an anesthetic, and an incision was made in their chest, but the artery was not cut or tied. The mock surgical procedure was just as effective in bringing about symptomatic relief as the actual procedure.[10]

Another experiment compared the effectiveness of a placebo to morphine. The subjects suffered from postoperative pain. Half the group were treated with morphine and the other half with a placebo. Fifty-two percent of those given morphine reported relief, while forty percent of those receiving the placebo reported relief. That is, the placebo was seventy-seven percent as effective as morphine. The study also discovered that the placebo was more effective than morphine in cases of severe pain.[11] In another study, patients addicted to morphine were given placebo injections that they believed to be morphine, and they did not suffer withdrawal symptoms. Only when the injections were stopped did the patients suffer withdrawal symptoms.[12]

VARIABLES AND THE PLACEBO EFFECT:
SETTING AND EXPECTATIONS

Several studies have shown that the placebo effect is related to the setting in which therapy takes place. The more convincing the healing context, the more likely the placebo effect will operate. A particularly important variable in this respect is the interest of the medical staff. Studies have shown that patients improve dramatically in hospitals and institutions when the staff take a keener interest in them. For example, when a "new" drug or therapy is introduced and tested (in fact it is a placebo in these studies), the staff perks up and shows more interest in the patients. The patients, in turn, respond favorably and improve, which further stimulates the staff, and so on, creating an ongoing healing setting in which patients get better. In one study a marked improvement occurred in psychiatric patients before any drugs or placebos were even administered. It seemed clear in this study that the patients were responding to the increased attention of the staff. Staff apathy, it seems, can greatly impede healing, while staff interest (quite apart from the medications and therapies employed) can greatly enhance the healing process.[13]

Just how effective the attitude of the medical staff can be on patients is illustrated in an experiment undertaken on rats. In the study, the experimenters were told that they would be working with rats that had been specially bred for intelligence or dullness, although in fact all the rats were from the same genetic strain. The experimenters performed learning experiments on the rats. The data the experiments obtained confirmed their expectations. That is, rats that they thought were smart did better in the experiments, while the "dumb" rats did poorly. One author commented on this experiment: "If scientists can somehow communicate their own expectations and attitudes to rats, it seems reasonable to assume that physicians can unknowingly communicate expectations and attitudes to patients, altering the patients' therapeutic outcomes as a result."[14]

In psychotherapy, considerable importance is placed on introducing the patient to the healer and the healing setting in preparation for treatment. Jerome Frank compares these induction procedures to rites at religious healing shrines:

> Most mental health clinics put the patient through some sort of intake procedure. Traditionally this consists of one or more interviews with a social worker, the purpose of which is to determine the patient's suitability for psychotherapy and to prepare the patient for it. Implicitly, the intake interview may also heighten the importance of the psychotherapist and psychotherapy in the patient's eyes by appearing to be a probationary period in which the patient's worthiness to receive this form of treatment is determined. In this sense it may not be too far-fetched to liken the intake procedure to the preparatory rites undergone by suppliants at faith-healing shrines, with the intake interviewer in the role of acolyte and the therapist as high priest.[15]

Therapists also typically decorate their offices carefully. Their offices are often located in medical centers or hospitals and have such "props" as book-lined walls, a large picture of the founder of their particular healing school, a large couch, and framed certificates from reputable institutions. These details present the patient with an impressive setting and the therapist with a powerful mystique. In such circumstances, the placebo effect is likely to be greatly enhanced.[16]

It is clear that such dynamics also operate in other medical contexts unrelated to psychotherapy. Most medical professionals take care to surround themselves with appropriate props, and patients typically must undertake induction procedures before seeing the physician, such as making an appointment to see the doctor, who may be a specialist, months in advance. During this long wait, positive expectations may be aroused to the point where the patient regards the doctor as a magical healer, which enhances the placebo effect. After having undergone elaborate induction rituals, after having waited for a long period to actually meet the healer, the patient is very likely to expect miracles from the doctor. The placebo effect suggests to us that a good part of many medical "miracles" concerns positive patient expectations—in some cases carefully aroused by the healer.

The ways in which patients seem able to adjust getting better to external constraints also illustrates how the placebo effect operates in terms of the realization of expectations. For example, patients' ability to pay and the amount of time a doctor can spend with patients often set limits within which patients are expected to get better. In one study, it was shown that the median time it took patients to get better in a mental hospital declined as the number of days covered by insurance companies dropped from sixty-five to thirty days.[17]

One study turned up interesting results concerning patients' expectations and their attitudes toward their doctors in relation to the placebo effect. In the study, a group of fifteen adult outpatients diagnosed as psychoneurotic were given a placebo and told exactly what it was. The instructions given to the patients were: "Many people with your kind of condition have also been helped by what are sometimes called sugar pills, and we feel that a so-called sugar pill may help you too. Do you know what a sugar pill is? A sugar pill is a pill with no medicine in it at all. I think this pill will help you as it has helped so many others. Are you willing to take this pill?"[18] Patients were instructed to take the pills three times a day for a week and return for assessment. Fourteen of the patients reported significant improvement. (The fifteenth did not return because her husband ridiculed the treatment.) Interviews with the patients revealed that some of them did not believe the pills were placebos, while others did. This made no difference in whether they reported improvement, however. In both cases, the patients said they believed their doctor would not tell them to do something that would not help them get better. One patient said that she thought her doctor was concerned about her avoiding addiction to drugs and therefore prescribed a sugar pill. No matter what the rationalization, all the patients said they trusted their doctor to prescribe what was best for them and hence expected to get better.

THE ROLE OF THE HEALER IN THE PLACEBO EFFECT

Perhaps the most crucial variable in creating a context in which the placebo effect can operate is the healer. We have mentioned at several points in this book the importance to the healing process of healers conveying to patients their confidence that a cure is possible, even likely, and their expectations concerning when and how the patients will get well. Even when a healer seeks not to convey *any* feelings, ideas, or instructions to a patient, as in nondirective psychotherapy, it is clear that the therapist transmits expectations and biases that are picked up by the patient and acted upon. It is hardly an exaggeration to say that in many cases the healer teaches the patient how to get better. The patient's role is to learn how to get better from the healer. Sometimes this process is quite obvious and self-conscious on the part of the healer. Here is a description of how some mental-health experts deal with their patients at the beginning of therapy:

> The therapist tells the patient at length about the power of the treatment method, pointing out that it has been successful with comparable patients and all but promising similar results for him too. The patient . . . is given a straightforward rationale for the way in which the specific treatment procedures will "remove" his symptoms. . . . The explicit positive and authoritarian manner in which the therapist approaches the patients seems destined, if not designed, to establish the therapist as a powerful figure and turn the patient's hopes for success into concrete expectations.[19]

In the healing process, particularly in psychotherapy, an important role of healers is to inform the patient about the nature of treatment, to educate the patient concerning the goals of therapy, and to provide the patient with realistic expectations. It is important in this process to conduct "anticipatory socialization interviews" or "role induction interviews" to prepare the patient for therapy. These interviews shape the patient's expectations in terms of what the therapist anticipates will happen.

In relation to the placebo effect, this education (or indoctrination) is helpful, perhaps even vital, in guiding the specific nature of the placebo effect. The role of the healer here is primarily that of teacher or guide. Patients, desiring to get better, expecting to get better, come to the healer because they think they cannot get better by themselves. The healer describes and defines what restored health will be like and

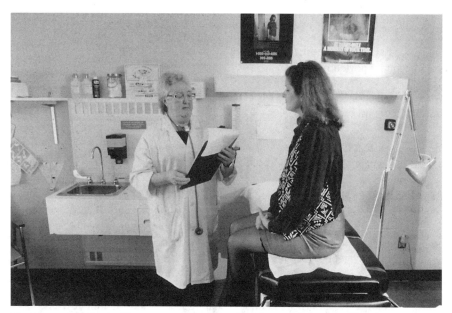

Doctor and patient. Courtesy of Chedoke-McMaster Hospitals. Photograph by Peter Foulds.

when patients might expect to achieve this improvement, thus providing them with realistic expectations and goals. In short, the healer defines the goal for patients and describes the kinds of behavior that will indicate that the goal has been achieved. The patient then imitates these characteristics. To a great extent, it has been suggested,[20] the particular form of therapy is not very important. Here is where the role of the placebo can be clearly understood. Therapy and medication, from the patient's point of view, represent the healer's authority, power, and concern for the patient.

Several studies have shown the crucial role of the healer in the placebo effect. In one study, patients who had had wisdom teeth removed were treated for pain. Half were given steroids (the normal medication), and the others were treated with ultrasound, which was applied by massaging the patients with an ultrasound traducer. The ultrasound treatment was as effective as the steroids. The levels of ultrasound were varied, and to the surprise of the researchers, no ultrasound at all, just massaging the patients with the traducer, proved more effective than any frequency of ultrasound. The researchers thought that it was simply the massaging effect of the traducer that alleviated the patients' pain and swelling. However, when the patients were instructed to massage themselves with the traducer, the swelling did not go down, and the pain did not lessen. It seemed that a doctor, or someone in a white coat (a researcher), was necessary for the technique to work.[21]

The attitude and status of the healer also affect the placebo effect. In one study, patients with bleeding ulcers were divided into two groups. One group was given a placebo by doctors who told the patients that they were being treated with a new drug that would certainly help their condition. The second group was given a placebo by nurses and told that not much was known about the effects of the drug. Seventy percent of the patients in the first group reported relief; only twenty-five percent of the second group reported relief.[22]

CONCLUSION

The placebo effect demonstrates the symbolic nature of much medical treatment and helps us understand the potency of many rituals and practices, in both modern and nonmodern medicine, that seem to have no proven medical effectiveness. The placebo effect demonstrates that healing often involves a lot more than just biological changes brought about by medical treatment. Put another way, the placebo effect suggests that most medical treatment, in either modern or nonmodern medicine, is symbolic in some sense and produces positive healing effects in patients quite apart from pharmacological, surgical, or other medical benefits attributed to the therapy.

We might think of the placebo effect as being symbolic in two differing, but complementary, ways. First, it is symbolic of patients' ability and intention to heal themselves. Second, it illustrates the symbolic nature of medical treatment itself. The placebo effect clearly illustrates the ability people have to make themselves better. It shows that much healing is something patients accomplish themselves. The placebo effect seems to demonstrate peoples' ability to translate their expectations and intentions into physical, biochemical changes.[23] People seem to be able to translate their wish to get better into actually getting better. When we realize that many dramatic physical changes are brought about by therapies that have no proven medical benefit, we must assume that people are able to heal themselves with the help of symbols and rituals.

The power of the symbols and rituals brings us to the second sense in which the placebo effect is symbolic. Placebo therapy, whatever it might use (pills, tablets, capsules, injections, surgery, diet, or some other treatment), is symbolic of the healers' power, authority, wisdom, and concern for the patient. The medication or therapy used by the patient symbolizes the healing potency of the doctor (or healer). It is never merely medicine or therapy; it is symbolic of the healer in a physical way. Whether or not the medication is active and effective, the placebo effect operates for the benefit of the patient, if the patient has faith in the doctor. Indeed, the placebo effect might be thought of as the tangible expression of the patient's faith and trust in the healer.

Ironically, the placebo effect seems to illustrate the point that faith in one's doctor has the power to awaken one's own "inner doctor," who actually does the healing. In this sense, the doctor's or healer's primary role is to stimulate patients to heal themselves. They need the healer to tell them what to do. What is remarkable is that often, no matter what the healer prescribes, it seems to have positive effects. The healer's role is often primarily catalytic. This dynamic is probably something that all sensitive, experienced healers in all cultures understand very well.

ENDNOTES

[1]A. K. Shapiro has stated, for example, that the "history of medical treatment until relatively recently is the history of the placebo effect"; "The Placebo Effect in the History of Medical Treatment: Implications for Psychiatry," *American Journal of Psychiatry* 116: 303; cited in Jerome D. Frank and Julia B. Frank, *Persuasion and Healing: A Comparative Study of Psychotherapy*, 3d ed. (Baltimore: Johns Hopkins University Press, 1991), p. 134.

[2]A. K. Shapiro, "The Placebo Response," in J. G. Howells (ed.), *Modern Perspectives in World Psychiatry* (Edinburgh: Oliver and Boyd, 1968), p. 599; cited in Howard Brody, *Placebos and the Philosophy of Medicine* (Chicago: University of Chicago Press, 1980), p. 10.

[3]H. R. Bourne, "The Placebo—A Poorly Understood and Neglected Therapeutic Agent," *Rational Drug Therapy* (November 1971), pp. 1–6; cited in Brody, p. 11.

[4]D. L. Singer and D. Hurwitz, "Long-Term Experience with Sulfonylureas and Placebos," *New England Journal of Medicine* 277 (1967): 450–56; cited in Brody, p. 11.

[5]B. Klopfere, "Psychological Variables in Human Cancer," *Journal of Projective Techniques* 21 (1957): 331–40; cited in Brody, p. 11.

[6]L. Lasagna, V. G. Laties, and J. L. Dohan, "Further Studies on the 'Pharmacology' of Placebo Administration," *Journal of Clinical Investigation*, 37 (1958): 533–37; cited in Brody, p. 12.

[7]Jerome D. Frank, *Persuasion and Healing: A Comparative Study of Psychotherapy* (New York: Schocken Books, 1974), p. 140.

[8]Norman Cousins, *Anatomy of an Illness as Perceived by the Patient: Reflections on Healing and Regeneration* (Toronto: Bantam Books, 1981), pp. 59–60.

[9]P. D. Wall, "On the Relation of Injury to Pain," *Pain* 6 (1979): 263; R. Melzack, "Folk Medicine and the Sensory Modulation of Pain," in P. D. Wall and R. Melzack (eds.), *Textbook on Pain*, 2d ed. (Edinburgh: Churchill Livingstone, 1989), p. 895.

[10]H. K. Beecher, "Surgery as Placebo," *Journal of the American Medical Association* 176 (1961): 1102–7; cited in Frank and Frank, pp. 135–36.

[11]Cousins, p. 59.

[12]Ibid., p. 60.

[13]Frank and Frank, pp. 142–43.

[14]Brody, p. 17, commenting on an experiment discussed in R. Rosenthal, "On the Social Psychology of the Psychological Experiment: The Experimenter's Hypothesis as Unintended Determinant of the Experimental Results," *American Scientist* 51 (1963): 268.

[15]Frank and Frank, p. 150.

[16]For a discussion of psychotherapy as involving primarily placebo therapy, see Jefferson M. Fish, *Placebo Therapy: A Practical Guide to Social Influence in Psychotherapy* (San Francisco: Jossey-Bass, 1973).

[17]Frank, p. 158

[18]Ibid., pp. 149–50.

[19]M. H. Klein et al., "Behavior Therapy: Observations and Reflections," *Journal of Consulting Clinical Psychology* 33 (1969): 262; cited in Frank, p. 162.

[20]Frank and Frank, passim.

[21]I. Hashish et al., "Reduction of Postoperative Pain and Swelling by Ultrasound: A Placebo Effect," *Pain* 83 (1988): 303–10.

[22]Cousins, p. 57.

[23]Ibid., p. 56.

Chapter 16

The Ideology of Modern Medical Culture

Modern medicine is usually described as rational and scientific. As rational, it insists upon viewing disease and healing as explicable and understandable on the basis of natural laws. Modern medicine denies the activity of spiritual or divine beings in the origin or curing of disease. Although disease may seem to afflict people unpredictably, although the course of a disease may seem peculiar in a particular situation, this is explained as due to lack of sufficient knowledge of natural law rather than to the presence of mysterious beings or forces that transcend natural law. In this sense, modern medicine inherits an approach to disease that goes back to Hippocrates and the ancient Greeks and that is also seen in certain aspects of classical Muslim, Indian, and Chinese medical systems.

As scientific, modern medicine insists on understanding the nature of disease on the basis of knowledge obtained from scientific observation, investigation, and experimentation, on knowledge that has been established empirically and can be demonstrated publicly. Medical treatment and practice, according to this definition of modern medicine, are not based on tradition, myth, or ritual. Modern medicine is not symbolic or ritualistic; it is scientific in the sense of proceeding on the basis of "hard" facts gleaned from scientific investigation. As rational and scientific, furthermore, modern medicine claims to be universally applicable. It is not culture specific and is efficacious in any social or cultural context.

To a great extent, modern medicine is undeniably rational and scientific. Other features of modern medicine, however, features that are obvious and admitted to be typical by those inside and outside the medical establishment, features that are often held to be rational and scientific, point to a more ideological or mythological dimension of modern medicine. In other words, some characteristics of modern medicine that are looked upon as evidence of its rational and scientific nature are not necessarily either rational or scientific. These characteristics help us begin to glimpse what the ideology or mythology of modern medicine might be and also help us begin to discern the outlines of what may be called modern medical culture. My aim here is not to demonstrate that modern medicine is irrational and unscientific because it contains irrational and unscientific practices or beliefs. My aim is to try to perceive the ideology that underlies modern medicine. This ideology is thought of and referred to both inside and outside the medical establishment as rational and scientific, but it is also more (or less) than this, having cultural (or ideological) aspects that are very important and fundamental to understanding the distinctive nature of modern medicine.

MODERN MEDICINE AS ALLOPATHIC

An important, if not central, feature of modern medicine is suggested in the term *allopathic*, which is the technical term often used to define the nature of modern medicine. Literally, *allopathy* refers to the treatment of disease by producing effects that are different from those produced by the disease. *Allopathic medicine* is the term often used to refer to "regular" medicine as opposed to *homeopathic medicine,* which treats disease by trying to induce an effect similar to the disease. These terms, *allopathy* and *homeopathy*, in their literal meanings are not so helpful in thinking about the nature of modern medicine. What is important and significant, however, is that

Surgery. Courtesy of Chedoke-McMaster Hospitals. Photograph by Peter Foulds.

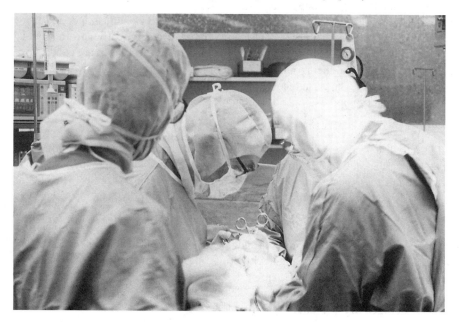

the term *allopathy* implies a struggle against disease, an approach that seeks by means of intervention to abruptly change the symptomatic progress of the disease.

Two of the most important forms of therapy in modern medicine are characteristic of allopathic medicine: drugs and surgery (radiation and laser therapy might be understood as extensions of these approaches). To a great extent, the internist and the surgeon are the dominant figures in modern medicine. The former is the expert in administering drugs (poisons, sometimes) that often drastically affect the inner workings, balance, and systems of the mind and body. The latter, the surgeon, is the expert in eliminating (or replacing) diseased parts of the body or rearranging the body so that it can overcome the incapacitating aspects of disease. In the most obvious type of imagery, modern medicine prefers an aggressive approach to disease. The most typical kinds of therapies—drugs and surgery—attack disease.

Disease itself is often thought about in such a way in modern medicine that an aggressive approach seems appropriate and obvious. In the history of medicine there have been, generally speaking, two ways of thinking about disease. One is what has been called the ontological idea, in which diseases are thought of as separate entities that exist in themselves. The other way is to think of disease as an abnormal physiological or ecological state within an individual. In the ontological view, disease is thought of as separate from the individual; in the ecological view, disease is thought of as an expression of the individual. It is the ontological view that has dominated allopathic medicine. In this view, disease is objectified in such a way that it bears little intrinsic relationship to the patient's personality or way of life. Medical professionals and laypeople both speak of a person "having a disease" and of doctors "treating a disease."[1] Perceived as a separate entity, disease is thought of as something that enters the body from outside and attacks it.

The ontological view of disease, of course, is as old as humankind, and there are many examples of it in the materials we have discussed earlier in this book. Object intrusion and affliction by spirits as theories of disease causation are good examples of the ontological theory and are found in many traditional cultures. It is not a modern idea at all. The germ theory of disease (which in some respects is quite modern) is also a very good example of the ontological view of disease, and is thus also quite traditional.

What is important for our purposes here, though, is the fact that the ontological idea of disease (whether expressed in terms of the germ theory or some other theory), so popular and prevalent among both physicians and laypeople in our culture, justifies, indeed mandates, heroic, aggressive measures against disease. The patient is often viewed as an innocent victim of a foreign invasion. A person's sickness is not self-engendered. It is an affliction, an insult, and an enemy to be sought out and destroyed. In this way of thinking, the physician plays the role of a fighter, a warrior, the secretary of defense, who musters and directs a team to defeat an enemy invasion. The disease is typically bombarded with drugs, blasted with radiation, scorched with lasers, cut off or cut out. The patient becomes the battlefield where the foreign invader and the medical warriors do battle. In this scenario, the patient often plays, or is encouraged to play, a fairly passive role.

MODERN MEDICINE AS MECHANISTIC

Another central characteristic of modern medicine is that it is highly mechanistic. Its mechanistic nature is usually traced back to René Descartes (1596–1650). He viewed the human organism as consisting of a physical body that was mechanical in nature and an animating spirit or soul that inhabited the body. By viewing the body as mechanical, Descartes encouraged the study of human beings along the same principles used in the study of the nonhuman, inanimate world. This helped simplify the study of human beings. A central principle of viewing them as mechanical was the division of the body into discrete parts. Each part was analyzed separately so that complicated problems became manageable. "To a very large extent the history of modern medical science consists in an attempt to pursue the reductionist analysis until it reaches into smaller and smaller fragments, or simpler and simpler functions. The study of life has thus become almost identified with the study of the molecules of which the body is made."[2]

Thinking about the human body on the analogy of a machine has resulted in the tendency to view it as a series of discrete parts and systems instead of as a complex whole. Thinking about the body as a machine has encouraged the attitude that health maintenance, healing, and therapy are engineering problems. Healing and therapy tend to be seen as the process of repair. Taken to its extreme form, the engineering view of health and healing leads to the notion that the proper approach to disease is the replacement of worn-out or diseased parts.

The predilection for viewing the human body as a machine also tends to emphasize healing and therapy as primarily a physical matter. In its tendency to focus mainly on the physical body, modern medicine is often referred to as biomedicine, suggesting its interest (and competence) in the biological aspects of the human organism. The mental aspects of illness—patients' doubts, fears, demoralization, and so on—are considered subsidiary problems that are either peripheral to the disease process or best left to the devices of patients' families, religious specialists, or social workers. It is the mechanical organism that is the primary focus of interest and treatment.

The mechanistic approach to medicine is also seen in the increasing importance of machines in diagnosis and therapy. A wide range of machines is now available to monitor (and display in various ways) most bodily functions and rhythms. Patients in hospitals are often connected to sophisticated and expensive machines that are part of this technological approach to diagnosis and therapy. For many patients the machines probably symbolize the power of modern medicine, and it is probably often the case that simply being attached to a machine has positive, healing effects.

The most spectacular example of the importance of machines in modern medicine is the increasing use of and research into artificial organs. While it is unlikely that any (or many) medical professionals see mechanical replacements of human organs as being superior to biological organs, this tendency to use machines to correct, replace, or supplement bodily functions and processes no doubt appeals to many people in our culture, for whom the machine represents a superior phenomenon to the body or to living organisms. The case of the "six-million-dollar man," the hero in a

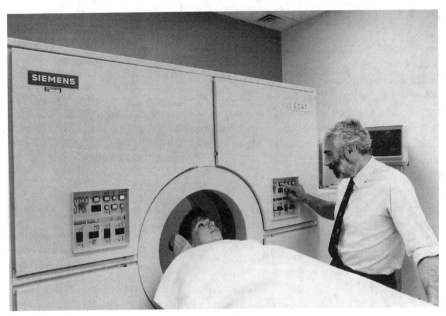

CAT scan. Courtesy of Chedoke-McMaster Hospitals. Photograph by Peter Foulds.

television series some years ago, is revealing. In this series, the hero, who had been terribly injured in an accident, was reconstructed using computer chips, wires, circuitry, and plastics. He was consistently superior to the standard, biological product. He was stronger, faster, could see better, hear better, and so on.

There is a strong tendency in our culture to admire machines and to use machine imagery and language when talking about ourselves. The application of the mechanistic model does not stop at the human body either. The mind also is understood on the analogy of a computer. That is, the mind is understood to function like a machine. Much of behavioral psychology is based on the assumption that the brain can be programed to respond in predictable ways, that the mind is essentially an extension of the physical brain, and that it operates in the same way. The popularity of mind- and mood-altering drugs that affect chemicals in the brain reinforces the image of the mind as lending itself to an engineering approach when treating mental illness. Mental problems become reduced to physical therapies. It is often assumed that, mentally as well as physically, human beings are mechanistic in nature.

MODERN MEDICINE AS INDIVIDUALISTIC

Modern medicine is also strongly individualistic. It is individualistic in the sense that it tends to locate or concentrate on disease in the individual person. Individuals and their diseases are usually thought of as only tentatively related to a wider physical or social environment. Medical science and practice tend to concentrate on disease when it makes its concrete appearance in an individual. Medical science does not tend to seek the wider environmental causes of diseases with an eye to prevention. This is clear in the allocation of health resources. Huge amounts of money and energy are invested in high-technology cardiac units, for example, while comparatively little effort is given to studying and treating environmental causes of heart disease and other modern blights. That is, the wider environment is simply taken as a given. It is not generally analyzed scientifically for sources of pathology in the population. In this respect, much of modern medicine concentrates on curative treatment of individuals instead of preventive medicine that would affect populations.

The emphasis on individual treatment as opposed to an environmental approach to disease can be illustrated with reference to what a study of bunions might be like in a modern medical context. Why some people are susceptible to bunions and some are not could be the subject of a very involved study. Genetic differences might be studied. The amount of walking and standing might be studied. Diet, weight, and build might also be studied as contributing factors in the formation of bunions. The different kinds of shoes people wear might also be studied. What might be missed entirely in such a study, however, is the fact that in populations where shoes are not worn at all, bunions do not exist. Indeed, shoes are the cause of bunions.

Similarly with many of the diseases that plague modern people, genetics, diet, personality, exercise, and a host of other variables are studied and probed in an attempt to discover the immediate causes of these diseases. Generally not investigated

Patient and medical technician. Courtesy of Chedoke-McMaster Hospitals. Photograph by Peter Foulds.

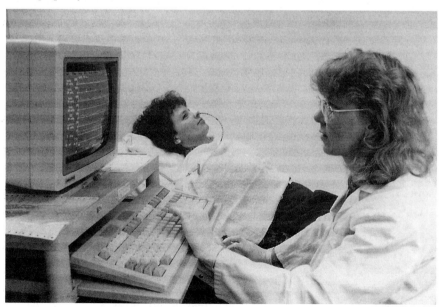

or called into question is modern industrial society. The individual, not the wider environment, is the focus of interest and treatment in modern medicine. Family, friends, enemies, bosses, colleagues, job dissatisfaction, boredom, loneliness, isolation from natural rhythms, pollution, crowding, and many other aspects of human life in contemporary society are disregarded in favor of isolating the individual biological organism as the locus of disease and therapy.

These features of modern medicine lead to a typical healing scenario: a patient in a high-tech hospital hooked up to a variety of machines, whose various fluids are taken for elaborate laboratory testing, who is surrounded by highly trained experts in specific diseases or bodily parts or systems, and who is administered strong drugs or scheduled for surgery. I am not suggesting that this healing scenario is not extremely effective. It is illustrative, however, of a particular medical ideology that is allopathic, mechanistic, and individualistic and not necessarily rational or scientific. The aggressive, mechanistic, and individualistic features of modern medicine are probably more cultural than rational or scientific.

It is also quite clear, as we have suggested above, that modern medicine, like any other medical culture, has symbolic and ritualistic features. I do not want to suggest that symbolic or ritualistic treatment is ineffective, but symbolic and ritualistic features of modern medicine are not rational and scientific in the ways it usually likes to claim. In this respect, I think we find essential continuities between modern medicine and nonmodern, non-Western, nonscientific medical systems, which we acknowledge to be highly symbolic and ritualistic. The symbolic value of doctors' white coats, of prescriptions written in an illegible scrawl filled with Latin terms, of routine physical checkups, are only some of the most obvious examples. It has also been suggested that our most sacrosanct ways of dealing with one of our most serious and common diseases are primarily symbolic and ritualistic and function mainly to reassure the patient, family members, doctors, and the population as a whole that something effective can be done. I refer to heart attacks and their treatment in high-tech cardiac units in hospitals.

In modern medicine the surehandedness of the technical response to heart attacks, the complexity of cardiac-care units, and the skill of the professionals who work in them are impressive and familiar to the public. The array of machinery, the heartbeat illustrated on an oscilloscope, the sound of the beating heart magnified, the lines feeding medications into the patient, the hushed intensity of the medical professionals are very impressive and convince us of the effectiveness of the medical approach being employed. Expensive cardiac units continue to be built and are a high priority in most areas. Indeed, the quality of local medical care is often related directly to the distance to such a unit. If such a unit is not nearby, medical care is deemed poor.

The effectiveness of cardiac units in terms of what they claim to achieve, however, has been called into question in a study comparing the effectiveness of such units with simple treatment at home.[3] How could this possibly be? The effectiveness of the cardiac unit is based on controlling erratic, arrhythmic heartbeats associated with heart attacks. By monitoring the heart electronically, it is assumed that doctors can

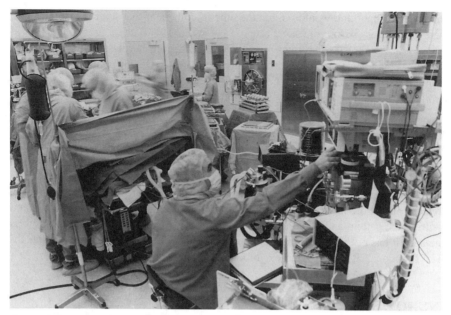

Operating room. Courtesy of Chedoke-McMaster Hospitals. Photograph by Peter Foulds.

get an early warning of potentially fatal patterns and intervene (with drugs, massage, or surgery) to prevent the collapse of the heart. Dangerous rhythms sometimes can be avoided or reversed by means of such interventions, thus saving the patient. What is not usually acknowledged, though, is that the heart is easily excited by emotion. Taking a patient to a cardiac-care unit, usually in dramatic circumstances, hooking him up to imposing machines and surrounding him with a cluster of intense and intent medical professionals, enclosing him in a strange environment away from familiar surroundings and family, might possibly be worse than the disease itself. The fear and apprehension aroused by the dramatic treatment might themselves induce arrhythmic, dangerous patterns in the heart. Perhaps this is why the study found simple home treatment as effective as treatment in a hospital.[4]

A more rational and scientific approach to prevention and treatment of heart disease and heart attacks might concentrate on lifestyle, habits that adversely affect the heart, education of the public, and more emphasis on low-tech home treatment. The cardiac unit in all its awesome technological complexity, however, seems here to stay. Perhaps this is because, in addition to any actual positive effects the unit may have in preventing heart attacks and helping heart-attack patients recover, the cardiac unit functions in an important symbolic and ritual fashion. In this respect, the cardiac unit has been compared to rituals in traditional medical cultures. "Both are active responses to forces threatening well-being. . . . The operators work in ways that are credible (and admired) in their wider cultures. Their activities provide means of coping with some threat which, if not coped with, would leave its victims exposed, and equally important, would remind the other members of that society that they, too, were defenceless before the same threat."[5]

Doubts are also sometimes raised about the various heroic and highly technological therapies used in the treatment of cancer and AIDS. It is important to keep in mind, however, the beneficial healing effects these treatments have on the patient, family members, friends, medical staff, and the wider culture in their role as coping mechanisms. It is reassuring and comforting—it is therapeutic—to know that something is being done in a dangerous, life-threatening situation. And in our culture, if that something is highly technological, highly professional, even grossly interventionist, all the better for the patient, who often holds to this medical ideology. Viewed in this way, some modern medical technology can be understood as performing nontechnical medical functions such as exerting control over a dangerous situation, engaging the patient and the healer in rituals that are believed to alter a situation in flux, and assuring the patient and all concerned that help is available. Medical technology, as one author has put it, "to an increasing extent . . . is serving as a mask for nontechnical functions. It carries a large symbolic load."[6]

ENDNOTES

[1]René Dubos, "Medicine Evolving," in David S. Sobel (ed.), *Ways of Health: Holistic Approaches to Ancient and Contemporary Medicine* (New York: Harcourt Brace Jovanovich, 1979), p. 22.

[2]Ibid., p. 33.

[3]See H. G. Mather et al., "Acute Myocardial Infarction: Home and Hospital Treatment," *British Medical Journal* 3 (1971): 334–38.

[4]See John Powles, "On the Limitations of Modern Medicine," in Sobel (ed.), pp. 73–75.

[5]Ibid., p. 74.

[6]Ibid., p. 76.

Chapter 17

The Medicalization of Morality: Modern Medicine as Secular Religion

In dealing with modern medicine in this book, my aim has been to try to show connections between nonscientific, traditional, religious medical systems and modern, scientific medicine. I have tried to show that the claim to uniqueness of modern medicine—that it is based on scientific truth and therefore is not culture specific—breaks down at many points. In this vein, I would like to look at another area of modern medicine that suggests connections with nonscientific medical systems. We have seen in most nonscientific medical systems a strong tendency to relate morality to sickness and health. In recent times, a process has been taking place that we might call the medicalization of culture, according to which many areas, behaviors, and problems formerly deemed legal, religious, social, or political have been brought within the orbit of medicine. In many cases this illustrates a clear relationship between modern medicine and morality. Modern medicine, like nonscientific, religious medical systems, is very much involved in defining, defending, and arbitrating moral order.

THE MEDICALIZATION (OR "HEALTHIFICATION") OF CULTURE

Contemporary North American culture shows a preference for medical imagery and language to describe areas of human life that not many years ago were described in moral, criminal, legal, religious, economic, or political terms and images. A wide range of phenomena that in the past were not thought of in medical terms are now routinely referred to in terms of health, sickness, and healing. For example, we often speak of sick economies, healthy relationships, cancerous political movements, pathological social acts, the cancer of terrorism, and the plague of drug abuse. This is the semantic expression of the medicalization (or "healthification") of culture, in which we see an increasing preference for using medical (or health) terms and ideas to think about and describe reality.

The term *health* itself, or similar terms and ideas, is also increasingly being used to describe the ultimate aim of human existence, that is, the ultimate human Good. The aim of individual life is to achieve and maintain health, broadly defined, and the aim of a society or culture, similarly, is often said to be to create a healthy atmosphere for citizens. An example of the tendency to think of health as the chief aim of human life and the most lofty of social, economic, and political goals is the World Health Organization's definition of health: "Health is a state of complete physical, mental, and social well-being and not merely the absence of disease and infirmity." Health broadly defined like this easily becomes identified as an overarching moral good: what is healthy is good. Conversely, what is bad or undesirable is unhealthy, sick, ill, or diseased.

The medicalization of culture is also seen in the strong tendency to describe and treat the mysteries and primary functions of human life in medical terms. Birth, sex, eating, lactation, menstruation, menopause, aging, dying, and death are typically thought about in medical terms, approached as medical problems, and referred to as illnesses or as having unhealthy "syndromes." Increasingly, the age-old human mysteries of birth, maturation, sex, and dying, which in all cultures are hedged about with religious rituals supervised by religious specialists, are becoming medical issues hedged about with medical rituals supervised by medical specialists. We are quite accustomed to hearing about "eating disorders"; many medical professionals regard obesity as an illness. Similarly, we hear of sleeping disorders that are subject to medical treatment. Nearly every physiological process, and many physical characteristics, are now spoken of in medical terms as if they might be pathological and liable to medical therapy. A wide range of personality "disorders" are also spoken of as pathological and treatable by "mood" drugs that promise to render personalities more socially acceptable. Similarly with behavioral patterns: we hear of sexual addiction, drug addiction, addiction to violence, and so on, and are told that such behaviors, which are deemed pathological, are subject to effective medical treatment. In general, living is seen as the process of resorting to a variety of medical therapies that will retain, restore, or strengthen one's health. Medical treatment has become, in the eyes of many both inside and outside the medical establishment, a panacea promising a kind of secular salvation called "health."

The doctor–patient relationship, in addition, is confessional in nature, resembling the relationship between a layperson and a priest. It is to their doctors that many people tell their deepest secrets. People often tell their doctors what they would never tell their spouses, children, parents, or closest friends. In this sense, for many people the role of the confessor and spiritual advisor has been medicalized.

Such things as diet and exercise also have been medicalized in the sense that they are understood to contribute to good health. Increasingly, we are encouraged to eat a healthful diet and to exercise regularly so that we can maintain or achieve good health. Proper eating and exercise are encouraged not so much as ends in themselves as means to the end of achieving or maintaining health. A "good" meal for many people no longer means a delicious meal presented in a pleasant atmosphere accompanied by congenial conversation but, rather, a meal that avoids or includes types of food that are thought to cause or forestall feared diseases. Similarly with sports, many people discuss their participation in sports or physical exercise in terms of leading a "healthy lifestyle," rather than in terms of intrinsic enjoyment, of mental, physical, and spiritual exhilaration and satisfaction. Indeed, many confess to having taken up sports or exercise for health reasons, often at the advice of their doctors.

Jobs, work, and career are also spoken of by many people in terms of health. People speak critically of their jobs or their careers in terms of the bad effects they have on their health. Work or professions that are reputed to be full of stress are typically referred to as dangerous to one's health, while jobs that are described as favorable, good, or rewarding are also described as good for one's health. "I'm sick of my job" is a common expression, and people often speak of a "healthy" career change.

Relationships—romantic, family, and otherwise—are often described as tending to make one healthy or sick, and they are often defended, criticized, or evaluated in terms of health and sickness. Such sentiments as these are common: "It was a healthy move for me when I moved away from home and got away from my father." "It made me sick the way he tried to manipulate me in that relationship." "I had a healthy relationship with my uncle." To hear many people speak, relationships are not pursued or appreciated or suffered because of the intrinsic worth of human communication, affection, love, or moral responsibility. They are pursued, appreciated, or suffered relative to their effects on health, however that may be defined or thought of.

The semantic expression of the medicalization of culture is more than merely metaphoric. There is a moral overtone to the use of medical terms in the examples I have given. To a great extent, what is perceived to be good or desirable in a moral and social sense is described as "healthy," while what is perceived to be bad or undesirable in a moral and social sense is termed "sick" or "unhealthy." At a linguistic level, that is, the language of sin and virtue, of good and bad, seems to be giving way to the language of "health" and "sickness." This does not necessarily mean, however, that ideas of sin and virtue have changed.

THE MEDICALIZATION OF DEVIANCE

That the medicalization of culture is deeper than just semantic and that the process has strong moral implications is made clear by looking at certain areas in which medicalization has been instrumental in defining and treating what is considered deviant by our culture. In a variety of areas and in a variety of ways, new illnesses have been "discovered" and are being treated by medical professionals, "illnesses" that in previous generations were thought of in terms of social, behavioral, moral, or criminal terms. These new "illnesses" almost always involve areas of what might be called social deviance, involving actions or habits that are in conflict with social norms and values. Medicalizing these problems, however, has not entirely removed the moral stigma, and it is not difficult to detect an implicit morality operating in each case. These illnesses are not just "incapacitating" or "dysfunctional"; they are "bad," "wrong," or "deviant" and often are spoken of in terms suggesting that they present grave threats to the social and moral fabric or our culture.

The process of medicalizing deviance is not new, as is clear from two cases in the nineteenth century. Dr. Samuel Cartwright, an established physician in the southern United States, described a disease he named "drapetomania" in a prestigious medical journal. The disease only afflicted slaves, and its primary symptom was the uncontrollable urge to run away from their masters.[1] In Victorian England, medical texts described masturbation as a serious illness or addiction that could be treated successfully with surgery.[2] More recently, in the former Soviet Union, political dissidents were "diagnosed" as mentally ill, as suffering from "paranoia with counter-revolutionary delusions" and "manic reformism."[3]

It is perhaps easier to discern and understand the moral implications and innuendoes of the medicalization of deviance by looking at examples from the past or from other cultures. What is clear in the examples just given is that there really was no medical problem or issue at all, that the issue was entirely political, social, or moral. Designating and treating those conditions as illnesses, medicalizing them, was a social and political act.

It is harder for us to see that a very similar process continues today in our own culture. The designation of a condition as an illness or a disease is often essentially a social act, whereby society labels that condition undesirable in some way. In our culture, such labeling is usually applied to biophysical phenomenon, but not always. Many physical conditions, such as baldness, are not deemed illnesses, while others whose biophysiological component has been hotly debated, such as hyperkinesis, alcoholism, and homosexuality, have been deemed illnesses, at least until recently.

Deeming a condition or behavior an illness and treating it with medical therapies is often thought to be a morally neutral process. On the whole, most of us tend to think of this process as involving strictly scientific judgments disassociated from ideas of sin and virtue, right and wrong. However, in many cases it is clear that such labeling does imply moral judgments and that, in the process of labeling, medical professionals are playing the role of moral arbiters, that is, playing the role of judging what is acceptable and unacceptable, what is good and what is bad, what is allowed and what should be prohibited or punished. A few examples from the literature on the medicalization of deviance should help clarify how this process works and the ways in which morality is involved.

HYPERKINESIS

In 1957, Maurice Laufer was conducting experiments with stimulants on children who were described as having behavior problems. Laufer coined the term *hyperkinetic impulse disorder* to describe the apparent inability of some male children and adolescents to sit still and pay attention in certain social (especially educational) situations. Laufer claimed that this disorder was the result of "minimal brain injury," although he was never able to show any organic basis for the "disease."[4] A drug that had recently been synthesized, methylphenidate (Ritalin), was prescribed for the treatment of this disorder and deemed effective. The success of the drug in calming wild behavior in children was advertised aggressively by pharmaceutical companies. The ads, which appeared in most medical journals, explained how easily hyperkinesis could be diagnosed and how effective the new drug was in treating it. Whether hyperkinesis is a "real disease" is an interesting question but one that would take us too far afield at this point. What is important to note is that a type of behavior that before 1957 probably would have been dealt with by family or school officials suddenly was labeled an illness that was medically treatable. In labeling a certain kind of fairly common male child and adolescent behavior a disease and treating it medically, the medical establishment was exercising social control, and medical professionals were acting as moral arbiters.

Many people would object to drugging young boys in order to impose social control on them. Few object, however, to treating an illness. It seems rational, scientific, and unrelated to the imposition of moral controls. In the case of Ritalin and hyperkinesis, however, the two processes—social control and medical treatment—are closely related, and the former is being accomplished by resort to the modern medical establishment and its prestige.

ALCOHOLISM

The medicalization of dealing with the consumption of alcohol in amounts that lead to inebriation or antisocial behavior is another example of the way in which morality and medicine have become intertwined in modern medicine. In this case, unlike the case of hyperkinesis, there were strong pressures outside medicine to label excessive drinking an illness. Prior to the medicalization of excessive alcohol consumption, such behavior was deemed a weakness of character, antisocial, socially harmful, and sometimes criminal. It was dealt with primarily in terms of moral contempt, social marginalization, or, in extreme cases, incarceration, which forced the offender to abstain. In the late nineteenth and early twentieth centuries, a movement to view excessive drinking as an illness, termed *alcoholism*, gained considerable momentum. Excessive drinking during this period came to be regarded as a major social problem. Through the efforts of the Temperance Movement, the production and sale of alcohol were declared illegal in the United States. The antidrinking movement began to advocate that excessive drinking be regarded as a disease. They hoped to gain scientific legitimation for something they saw as a serious social problem. To redefine the problem in medical terms, to speak of it as a public-health problem, gave the movement to ban alcohol an air of scientific legitimacy.

For many who sought to medicalize alcoholism, including alcoholics themselves, an important goal was to come to an understanding of the problem that excluded moral condemnation. It was thought that treating alcoholism as an illness would decriminalize and humanize the problem. This campaign was successful in the sense that the majority of physicians (and the public) agree that alcoholism is a disease. Nevertheless, there is much evidence that many doctors continue to view it as a moral problem as well. They describe alcoholics as weak in character, lazy, morally bankrupt, even criminal, and refuse to treat them or do so only reluctantly.[5] Medicalizing an old problem that is redolent with moral issues does not automatically remove it from the sphere of morality. Even those who agree that it is more enlightened, more humane, and more scientific to think of alcoholism as an illness tend to make moral judgments about those who are labeled alcoholics.

HOMOSEXUALITY

Attempts to medicalize homosexuality offer another example of how medicine and morality often become intertwined. For thousands of years, homosexuality has been considered morally objectionable. It is condemned in the Bible, and Christianity and Judaism over the centuries have generally followed the biblical view. Homosexuality has been a criminal offense until very recently in the West. In the past century there was a move toward viewing it as pathological, as a sickness that could be treated. Only now is homosexuality being demedicalized, primarily as a result of the Gay Liberation Movement, which strongly objects to labeling homosexuals as sick.

The term *homosexuality* was coined in 1869 by a Hungarian physician, K. M. Benkert, who was opposed to the legal repression of same-sex sexual behavior. He spoke of same-sex sexual behavior as an illness that involved a degeneration of the nervous system. Under the inspiration of Sigmund Freud, the psychiatric establishment carefully and elaborately defined homosexuality as an illness. Although the movement to medicalize homosexuality was usually presented as humane by the psychiatric and medical establishments, their publications often described homosexuals in judgmental terms that implied a moral perception of the issue.

Dr. Edmund Bergler, a psychoanalytical psychiatrist who was a particularly persuasive advocate of homosexuality as a disease in the 1950s and 1960s, while insisting that homosexuals were not criminals, described them in terms redolent with moral judgment. They were, for example, according to him, "psychic masochists" who strove for "defeat, humiliation, and rejection" because of their early failure to master the oral stage of psychodynamic development; they were "regressed personalities." They were terrified of women and fled from them to other men. They were characterized by "an unfounded megalomaniacal conviction" that they were superior persons, they were "depressed neurotics,' and they were essentially unreliable.[6] Charles Socarides, another important advocate of homosexuality as a disease, described same-sex sexual behavior among men as "aggressive, self-destructive, and typified by paranoid feelings, a 'masquerade of life' in which the actors are 'tormented' individuals."[7]

The American Psychiatric Association at first agreed to label homosexuality an illness[8] and then later, under pressure from the Gay Liberation Movement, decided to demedicalize the behavior. This indecision points out the extent to which labeling homosexuality as sick was (and still is) a political and moral process. A brief statement by a gay activist, which was shouted at a group of psychiatrists at an American Psychiatric Association meeting in San Francisco in 1970, suggests how the medicalizing of homosexuality was regarded by the "patients" themselves: "You are the pigs who make it possible for the cops to beat homosexuals: they call us queer, you— so politely—call us sick. But it's the same thing. You make possible the beatings and rapes in prisons, you are implicated in the torturous cures perpetrated on desperate homosexuals."[9] In the face of mounting rage on the part of the homosexual community, the medical establishment changed its official view and by 1973 was describing homosexuality as a behavior of choice that did "not necessarily constitute a psychiatric disorder."[10]

In some cases, people whom the medical establishment views as patients view themselves as victims of it. In some cases, what the medical establishment views as treatment or therapy, patients view as punishment.[11] The rather startling difference of opinion between patients and those treating them should give us pause when thinking about the extent to which modern medicine is morally neutral and above political, social, and economic influences in defining and treating illness.

CONCLUSION

The process of labeling many conditions as illnesses is often a moral process, or a process that has moral implications. A condition may be defined as an illness primarily because it deviates from a socially accepted norm. As deviant, the condition is considered undesirable, a condition from which the "patient" should seek relief. Childhood wildness, same-sex sexual behavior, excessive alcohol consumption, taking drugs, violence against children, and many behavior patterns that are deemed "sick" are cases in point. It is not so much a matter of the medical establishment inventing a morality to go along with its increasing involvement in what were formerly nonmedical areas as it is a case of the medical establishment inheriting a morality and enforcing that morality "in the name of humane, scientific, rational medicine." The pretense that the medicalization of cases such as those discussed above is morally neutral, that the process is strictly a scientific one, is not the case. Modern rational, scientific medicine, like every other medical culture discussed in this book, is involved in defining and arbitrating morality. Indeed, modern medicine seems to be becoming more, not less, involved in defining and arbitrating morality as it expands its domain into areas formerly not deemed medical at all.

ENDNOTES

[1]S. W. Cartwright, "Report on the Diseases and Physical Peculiarities of the Negro Race," *N.O. Med. Surg. J.* 7 (1851): 691–715; cited in Peter Conrad and Joseph W. Schneider, *Deviance and Medicalization: From Badness to Sickness* (St. Louis: Mosby, 1980), p. 35.

[2]A. Comfort, *The Anxiety Makers* (London: Thomas Nelson & Sons, 1967), and H. T. Englehardt, Jr., "The Disease of Masturbation: Values and the Concept of Disease," *Bull. Hist. Med.* 48 (Summer 1974): 234–48; cited in Conrad and Schneider, p. 35.

[3]Peter Conrad, "Soviet Dissidents, Ideological Deviance, and Mental Hospitalization" (presented at Midwest Sociological Society Meetings, Minneapolis, 1977); cited in Conrad and Schneider, p. 35.

[4]For a discussion of hyperkinesis, see Conrad and Schneider, pp. 155–60.

[5]H. A. Mulford, "Alcoholics, Alcoholism, and Iowa Physicians," *Journal of the Iowa Medical Association* 54 (1964): 623–28; cited in Conrad and Schneider, p. 98.

[6]E. Bergler, *Homosexuality: Disease or Way of Life?* (New York: Hill & Wang, 1956); cited in Conrad and Schneider, p. 189.

[7]C. W. Socarides, *The Overt Homosexual* (New York: Grune & Stratton, 1968); cited in Conrad and Schneider, p. 191.

[8]See its definitions of homosexuality as a variation of "Sociopathic Personality Disturbance" in its *Diagnostic and Statistical Manual of Mental Disorders* (1952 and 1968 editions).

[9]Cited in D. Teal, *The Gay Militants* (New York: Stein & Day, 1971); cited in Conrad and Schneider, p. 204.

[10]Cited in Conrad and Schneider, p. 208.

[11]For a discussion of how punishment, disingenuously called therapy, is often used to control mental patients in institutions, see Murray Edelman, "The Political Language of the Helping Professions," *Politics and Society* 4, no. 3 (1974): 295–310.

Chapter 18

The Search for Meaning in Modern Medicine: The Patient Speaks

Most of the medical cultures and healing scenarios we have looked at in this book attempt to put serious illness and death in a meaningful framework. Illness is typically related to morality and is often said to be caused by spirits, gods, or ancestors. One of the principal tasks of the healer in these cultures and scenarios is to help sick people understand their illness in terms that make some kind of religious, spiritual, or moral sense. Often the healer plays the role of interpreter, guide, and teacher to the patient, and the healing process itself is understood to involve primarily the proper understanding of the illness.

In modern medical culture, framing illness in a meaningful context is a muted theme. Although medicine and morality are intertwined and modern medical professionals often define and arbitrate morality, there is a strong inclination in modern medicine to avoid setting serious illness in a spiritual, religious, or moral framework. Medical professionals are often explicit about this, refusing to indulge patients' questions concerning the ultimate meaning of an illness. It is true that certain individual medical professionals will assume the role of the traditional healer and seek to help patients understand the religious, spiritual, or moral implications of their illness,[1] but it is much more typical for doctors and nurses to avoid the role of teacher, guide, or interpreter. In the context of modern scientific medicine, the possible religious, spiritual, or moral meaning of an illness is held to be beyond the scope of medical treatment, and probably irrelevant to the disease and healing processes. These are matters belonging to other types of professionals: social workers, counselors, or clergy. It is not the business of physicians, nurses, or other medical professionals. A very common position, firmly articulated by nurses in my classes for years, is that seriously ill patients should not be further troubled with moral or religious theories of illness that blame them for their sickness. In the training of both physicians and nurses in Ontario, the trend seems to be toward delinking illness and morality. If there is time, it is all right to listen sympathetically to patients' musings on such subjects, but patients should not be encouraged to think that they have brought about their own illness through moral shortcomings or turpitude. In modern, scientific medicine, patients are given little explicit help from their doctors in trying to understand their illnesses in a meaningful framework. Modern medical professionals seem reluctant to take on the role of guide or mentor to patients while treating their illness.

Modern patients, however, are like people suffering from illness in other cultures that we have looked at. They, like sick people everywhere, are prone to ask such questions as: "Why me?" "What is the meaning of this for me?" Relatives, spouses, friends, and many doctors and nurses also ask these questions. That is, the need to make sense out of serious illness and dying persists, even though attempts to do so are muted or avoided by medical professionals.

"PATHOGRAPHIES": THE VOICE OF THE PATIENT

The extent to which the need to make sense of serious or terminal illness persists among modern patients is evident in a relatively new genre of literature in which individuals write about their personal experience with illness. These accounts, primarily a phenomenon of the past thirty years, have been termed *pathographies*.[2] What is so valuable and interesting about these works is that they allow us to view the disease, healing, and dying processes from the patient's point of view. They give clear, rich, detailed voice to the patient. And what is striking about most of these works is the urgent need on the part of the authors to make sense out of their predicament. While the modern medical establishment and its personnel may be reticent or silent (preferring what is often referred to as scientific agnosticism on such issues), it is clear that patients are often consumed by the search for meaning. These personal accounts of the illness experience are not primarily concerned with accurately documenting the disease or curing processes. They are concerned, rather, with making sense of illness. They are not objective descriptions as much as creative formulations by means of which chaotic, destructive, terrifying events are perceived to form part of a meaningful whole.

Some of these works, as we might expect, resort to traditional biblical, Jewish, or Christian themes and images to provide a context in which to understand serious illness.[3] It is striking, however, that most pathographies do not draw upon such religious materials. The dominant images and themes in these works are at once archaic, reflecting themes apparent in ancient literature and traditional cultures, and modern, in the sense of being compatible with modern culture, including rational, scientific medicine. The images and themes, that is, although archaic in nature, do not fit awkwardly or uncomfortably with modern medical culture and are sometimes used by medical professionals themselves. Most of the authors of pathographies, furthermore, are not active, practicing members of traditional religions such as Christianity or Judaism; indeed, they do not describe themselves as very religious or spiritual. They are secularly minded individuals. This makes their search for meaning particularly interesting.

It is not just religiously minded people who are wont to frame their life experiences in a meaningful framework; secularly minded individuals have the need as well.

ILLNESS AND RENEWAL

A frequent theme in modern pathographies is the idea that serious, life-threatening illness brings about a crisis that results in renewal or transformation. As a result of a heart attack, cancer, or some other serious malady, many authors experience an awakening of consciousness, or a change in outlook, that is sometimes described as a rebirth. They perceive their lives as being dramatically transformed as a result of the illness and usually speak of this transformation as positive. This theme was put succinctly and dramatically by Patricia Hingle in her book *A Coming of Roses*, an account of her experience with cancer. She began her book with the words: "Cancer saved my life."[4] Hingle, like many other authors of pathographies, thought of her life as consisting of two distinct phases: life before the onset of serious illness and life afterward. For Hingle and others, the illness experience serves as a crisis that calls into question many basic aspects about one's life. In coming to terms with illness, pathographers often discover that they have basically, often radically, changed their self-perception. They have been renewed or reborn.

This theme is particularly evident among patients who have suffered severe heart attacks. In many cases, the heart-attack patients attribute their illness to a lifestyle that was stressful or otherwise "pathological." Authors describe their lives prior to the heart attack as hectic, frantic, entirely focused on work, and preoccupied with deadlines. Authors often refer to their "type-A personality," someone who is too aggressive, competitive, and "up-tight" and supposedly "coronary prone." One author described himself prior to his heart attack in appropriately modern, technological terms: "As a 'type A' personality my radiator ran hot all the time."[5] The heart attack is often understood as a kind of conversion experience that results in an attempt to change one's life. Authors tell about shifting their focus to their families, becoming less preoccupied with work and career, and adopting habits that force them to relax. The heart attack, in pathographies of this type, is affirmed as the critical event that brought about personal transformation or rebirth. As one author put it: "God was blowing the whistle on me, trying to get my attention."[6] A terrifying, life-threatening event is placed in a framework in which it becomes a highly positive, life-transforming experience.

This approach to serious illness in pathographies is also seen, although not as often or consistently, in people afflicted with cancer. As in the case of heart-attack victims, several authors suffering from cancer expressed the conviction that it was their lifestyle or personality that had led to the onset of cancer. A particularly vivid example of this approach is found in Anthony Sattilaro's account of his experience with cancer:

> I had lived a life of selfishness, greed, self-centered ambition, and fear. I was bent on satisfying my own appetites, and was intractable in my dealings with others. I viewed life as a dog-eat-dog existence; it was the contest of getting what one could for one's self,

and the hell with the rest of the world. . . . This clutching for pleasures of the senses, and for material possessions, is what gives rise to cancer, I believe.[7]

The remorseful description of one's life prior to the onset of serious illness as in some sense reprehensible and misguided is reminiscent of confession as part of religious conversion. Several authors describe themselves prior to the onset of illness as "the chief of sinners," as it were, reckless of their well-being and health, and deserving of serious illness as a kind of punishment or just reward for their heedless, indulgent, self-ish actions.

Confession is followed by conversion in some of these works. Having acknowl-edged the bankrupt state of their lives prior to serious illness, several authors resolve to change their lives and cultivate values that subvert and challenge the old values that led to illness. Dr. Anthony Sattilaro spoke of an awakening, saying "I went from focus-ing my attention on viruses and cells under a microscope to sitting back and con-templating the vast interwoven mosaic of the universe."[8] Anne Hargrove, suffering from cancer, spoke of her illness as "turning me into a new creature. I have chosen to exchange the ways of death for a new life and have felt the stirrings of a new crea-ture within me, myself newly conceived."[9]

For many authors, their illness is understood to be an opportunity to learn something valuable about themselves and life in general. They speak of discovering a new person or identity. They speak of awakening to insights that redirect and reorient their lives. In many ways, they speak as though they have undergone a con-version, as if they have been born again.

ILLNESS AS A JOURNEY

An image that fits very well with the theme of renewal or rebirth is the illness expe-rience as a journey. The importance of journey imagery in pathographies is seen in the following titles: *Climbing toward the Light: a Journey of Growth, Understand-ing, and Love*; *Voyage and Return*; *Beyond AIDS: A Journey into Healing*; *The Doctor/The Patient: The Personal Journey of a Physician with Cancer*; *Mind, Fan-tasy, and Healing: One Woman's Journey from Conflict and Illness to Wholeness and Health*; and *Coming Back: One Man's Journey to the Edge of Eternity and Spiritu-al Rediscovery*.[10] The journey as described in these works is into dangerous, foreign territory, a journey away from the familiar, comfortable, and comforting surroundings of one's normal life. It is a trip into the "kingdom of the ill," as Susan Sontag has termed it,[11] where there is a "more onerous citizenship." One pathographer described being seriously ill as like living on another planet. Another, suffering from AIDS, said that he felt as though he were in exile "on the moon."[12] Robert Murphy, an anthro-pologist suffering paralysis from a spinal disease, said that he felt as if he were on an "extended anthropological field trip. . . . Through [illness and disability] I have sojourned in a social world no less strange to me at first than those of the Amazon forests."[13]

The foreign land into which the seriously ill venture is marked by disorder, fear, pain, and strangeness. While physically remaining in the same world as before, pathographers experience the world as entirely different. It is as if they have discovered an alternative world lying beneath the surface of, or lurking behind the façade of, the normal world of health.[14] The new, foreign world of illness puts the normal world in a new light, a different perspective. It is seen as fragile, fleeting, insubstantial, and impermanent. The strangeness of the world of sickness, the kingdom of the sick, is often described in terms of an immersion in medical culture. The strange language of medical diagnosis and treatment, the mysterious and often dehumanizing rituals of the hospital, the at-once impressive and frightening technology, and the hierarchical and authoritarian world of modern medicine are described as an alien environment in which the patient is disoriented, overwhelmed, and often powerless.

In many ways, the journey that pathographers describe is similar to the three-stage rite of passage found in almost all cultures to mark the transition from one stage of life to another. Birth, puberty, marriage, and death are often marked by rites of passage having three distinct phases: separation, in which people are cut off from their normal, familiar circumstances; transition, liminality, or marginality, in which people find themselves in transit, betwixt and between stages, in a world in flux and without clear structures or boundaries; and incorporation or completion, in which people either return to the world they have left—which has changed in some important way—or move on to a new stage in life.

In the case of pathographies, the stage of separation is illustrated by leaving the familiar world of being healthy and entering the "kingdom of the sick." Patients leave the familiar world of home, family, and work and enter the realm of the modern hospital with its strange rituals, customs, and peculiarities. Patients are reduced to anonymity, stripped of status and particularity. Everyone must be divested of personal clothing and wear the same, plain, white hospital gown and don an identity bracelet. Patients are subjected to many rules and requirements that seem to make no sense but are explained as "standard procedure." The hospital staff are dressed in uniforms and speak a language that seems foreign to patients. Patients are also treated differently from in the normal world, objectified and observed and identified more as a disease than as a person. Pathographers often complain of the dehumanizing process that they experience in hospitals.

In this strange, often painful and hostile, world of illness and medical culture, pathographers struggle to discover meaning, understanding, and renewal; they seek to be renewed or reborn, to be reincorporated into the normal world of health, although inwardly transformed. The worlds of illness and medical culture challenge the voyager to make sense out of experiences that are threatening and disruptive, potentially fatal, and completely disorienting. Thinking of the illness experience as the critical midway point in a journey of discovery stresses the positive potential to be found in illness; illness becomes an opportunity to learn, mature, and wake up to truths difficult to grasp in the normal world. In the imagery of illness as a journey, the patient becomes an explorer, a pilgrim, a traveler who develops positive expectations.

ILLNESS AS BATTLE

Another common metaphor found in pathographical literature is that of battle. This metaphor is particularly congenial to allopathic medicine with its aggressive approach to disease. Modern, scientific medicine often thinks of disease as something separate from the patient, as an alien entity that invades the individual. Disease is not thought of as intrinsic to the individual, the result of interior imbalance or disharmony between individuals and their environment. Objectified as a foreign presence, disease becomes a fitting object of aggression; it is the enemy that must be fought and defeated. Military language and images are commonly used by both medical professionals and pathographers.

Perceiving disease as an enemy to be battled is quite common in the case of cancer. One pathographer, suffering from leukemia, used vivid military language: "It's like going to war, only the battlefield is inside my body. I have to fight a battle with the enemy and destroy it. This damn disease is my enemy—it is trying to kill me."[15] Gilda Radner said: "Now here I was, deeply embroiled in the battle of my life—a war against cancer taking place in my own body."[16] Cornelius Ryan, a military historian suffering from cancer, resorted to military imagery frequently and consistently. He described himself as the commander-in-chief consulting his doctor-generals on strategy and weapons to be used against the enemy.[17]

When the illness experience is perceived in terms of a battle, patients (and patients' allies such as medical professionals) are often pictured as warriors or knights. Many pathographers claim that it is crucial in fighting illness, particularly cancer and AIDS, to have a fighting spirit, not to "give in" to the disease, not to accept defeat. Authors speak of being aggressive, alert, thorough, unyielding, and persistent in combating their diseases. It is also interesting that in visualization therapies, such as those introduced by the Simontons, the most popular image used in picturing the body's fight against cancer cells is that of white knights who attack and destroy the enemy invaders.[18] The white knights represent the immune system, which battles the invading cancer cells, and therapy is aimed at strengthening and reinforcing the knights. Chemotherapy and radiation are often referred to in military terms. The chemicals and radiation are used to "attack" and "bombard" the malignant cells. Surgery also is thought of as an attack on the enemy.

The image of white knights and the metaphor of combat give cancer patients a feeling of control over their illness experience. It allows them to organize their feelings and experiences; it allows them to galvanize their efforts in the classic metaphor of good versus evil.

MAKING SENSE OF DEATH

In most of the medical scenarios and cultures we have looked at, death is understood within a larger framework of meaning. Death is usually seen as a transition to a new state of being. One becomes an ancestor, travels to another world, is united with a deity in heaven or punished in hell, or transmigrates and is reborn. Rarely is death thought of as the ultimate and absolute end to the individual's existence. Healing in many cases is the process of achieving a "good death," and the role of the healer is to guide the sick person through this dramatic transition from life to death. In modern medical culture, death is not consciously perceived in a wider framework of meaning. Medical professionals rarely play the role of guides who help patients die. There are no appropriate rituals for guiding patients through the dying experience in a meaningful way. Preserving life is the principal task of modern medical professionals; easing patients through dying to a meaningful death is not what they are trained for. It is someone else's task. It is relegated to clergy or, as many pathographies demonstrate, is left to patients and their families and friends.

Coming to terms with death in a positive way is clearly a difficult achievement in pathographic literature. With a few exceptions, most pathographies do not resort to traditional religious images and themes to make sense of death, nor do most authors seek help from clergy. Lacking or rejecting such a framework, pathographers often struggle to find images or metaphors to help them think of dying and death as meaningful or redemptive. In many cases, pathographers think about dying and death primarily in terms of finding an easy death, by which is usually meant a relatively pain-free death. But this approach is not very effective in putting dying and death in a meaningful context. Among recent pathographies, two stand out as impressive attempts to deal in a meaningful way with dying: Virginia Hine's *Last Letter to the Pebble People: "Aldie Soars,"* an account of her husband's death from lung cancer, and Peter Noll's *In the Face of Death*, an account of his dying of bladder cancer. The two works illustrate what might be called victorious death and heroic death, respectively.

Aldie Hine was diagnosed with lung cancer at age 54. With the help and encouragement of his wife, he undertook a series of therapies aimed at halting the cancer. In addition to radiation treatment, the Hines organized a group of relatives and friends and sought to treat Aldie by focusing their love and concern on him. Each member of the group who agreed to take part in this project signified participation by placing a pebble in a pool in the Hines's home. The radiation therapy and the work of the "pebble people" brought about a remission of Aldie's cancer. During this period, the Hines also attended clinics in Texas run by the Simontons that taught people the art of visualization in the treatment of illness. Aldie's cancer returned, however, and despite his experiments to control it, eventually he realized that he would soon die. Throughout this period of active treatment, the Hines emphasized the importance of taking responsibility for and control of one's illness.

This theme persisted in their approach to Aldie's death.[19] The Hines chose to confront the fact of Aldie's imminent death and take responsibility for making the experience "victorious," by which they seem to have meant an experience that enhanced rather than diminished all those involved in Aldie's dying and death. In this sense, the Hines's approach to death was reminiscent of the medieval tradition of *ars moriendi*, "the art of dying," in which the dying person sought a "good death." A basic emphasis in Aldie's dying was the presence of family and friends who openly acknowledged his imminent death and his interaction with them. About fifteen to twenty family members and friends surrounded Aldie during his dying weeks in a "house party atmosphere."[20] The Hines thought that death should not be a solitary event. It should affirm and invigorate one's most important human relationships. It is an intensely social act, as it strongly affects the family and friends of the dying person.

Another important emphasis in the Hines's approach to Aldie's dying concerned what might be termed its liminal potential. In the *ars moriendi* tradition, dying people were understood to have unique wisdom as a result of their special perspective. They were deemed qualified to impart insights and knowledge to the living. They were attended by the living as sources of wisdom. Their last words were often noted carefully. In the case of Aldie, he was also attended by friends, to whom he imparted, according to Virginia Hine, "a healing quality in [a] strange nonverbal communication." His death became, for those who witnessed and participated in it, a "solvent for their angers, their griefs, their jealousies, and tensions."[21] His death became a blessing to them, a final gift to them. In this sense, death squarely faced, undertaken as a social and relational ritual, can be victorious for both the dying person and the survivors. Healing is not pain relief or heroic therapies to keep the physical body alive; it is the process of resolution and transformation.

Peter Noll was a Swiss professor of law. He was diagnosed as having bladder cancer and resolved to refuse the heroic surgical therapies suggested by doctors, realizing that his life was ending. Noll was an experienced writer on several topics, including law, religion, and philosophy, and decided to write about his own dying. His book, *In the Face of Death*, gives a vivid account of his gradual death from cancer. A central theme throughout is Noll's insistence on refusing therapies that would diminish his quality of life and surrender his life to medical professionals. He realized that taking this decision to reject a "medical death" or an "easy death" might make his death very painful. He thought it was important in his circumstances, however, to resist intense medical attention with its temptations to deny the dying process. In rejecting medical attention, he chose to look death squarely in the face and experience it as fully and completely as possible. Noll self-consciously adopted the attitude of the medieval *moriens*, the dying person who learns the art of dying and in the process gains wisdom that may be given to others. Noll imparted his wisdom not only to his two daughters, who attended him throughout his death, but also to his readers. Noll said that he decided to write his journal "to give meaning to my dying and death, a meaning also for others in the same situation."[22] He wrote his will, planned his own funeral and memorial service, and wrote his funeral oration.

Although Noll tended to eschew traditional Christian themes in his understanding of his own dying and death, his emphases on facing death self-consciously, on cultivating a heroic, triumphant spirit in the face of death, and on seeking meaning in agonizing physical pain and suffering suggest Christian themes. Noll also, at times, did reflect on certain Christian themes and for his funeral chose passages from Bach's B Minor Mass concerning resurrection. He insisted, however, on working out his own dying rituals and exploring for himself the meaning of death with very few references to explicit traditional teachings.

Both Hine's and Noll's pathographies affirm the human need to frame death in a meaningful context. They both also affirm how difficult this is to do in a secular context. Both pathographies stress how ill-equipped and even detrimental modern medical culture is in helping people in this process. These pathographies (and many others that stress the same theme) are an indictment of modern medicine's inadequacy in dealing with this basic human need. The standard response, of course, is that death and dying are not concerns of modern medicine, that modern medicine is concerned with treating disease and maintaining life; death and dying are concerns for clergy, family, or friends. That this distinction is artificial, and in many ways tragic, is vividly attested in much pathographical literature.

PATHOGRAPHY AS A MEANINGFUL ACT

Finally, writing about one's illness and death can be a meaningful act in itself. In many pathographies it is evident that the authors have taken the occasion of writing a journal of their experiences as an opportunity to reflect on the meaning of their illness. A pathography is almost never written simply to record the illness experience. It is written, to a great extent, as a way of coping with and making sense of one's illness. The act of writing a pathography becomes part of the healing process in the sense of helping patients find meaning in their predicaments.

In several cases, the authors of pathographies are also consciously taking on the roles of mentor and exemplar. Several authors are explicit in saying that they have written about their experiences in order to help others in similar situations. For them, the meaning of an illness can be found in helping others by relating, confessing, and pondering the illness experience; the authors consider this therapeutic for others. Bernice Kavinoky, the author of *Voyage and Return*, which recounts her experiences with cancer, wrote:

> This was a book that *had* to be written. I wrote it originally for myself, because it clarified my thinking and emotions. Then I began to ponder over it and felt perhaps it was for everybody—not only those who had my operation but everyone who had been through an experience of shock and loss, and who eventually—after the flying of flags and lifting of the chin—had to face it, in his own waiting room, alone.[23]

Maintaining a semblance of human dignity when confronted with life-threatening illness and death, maintaining a sense of meaning and purpose in the face of increasing disability and bouts of great pain and fear, is a perennial and intense human need that arises in every society and culture. Pathographical literature testifies to the persistence of this need in our own culture. In most societies and scenarios we have looked at, it is met in the context of medical treatment. Healers are also often religious specialists who understand that healing must help patients make sense of their illness. Modern medical professionals do not easily play this traditional role. It is not surprising, therefore, that when we hear the voice of the modern patient, we find the need being addressed by the patients themselves. Scientifically sound and technologically sophisticated modern medicine is stunning in many ways. That it often lacks the basic healing strengths of older, nonscientific, traditional medical systems, however, is also clear when we listen to the voices of some of its patients.

ENDNOTES

[1]See, for example, the works of Bernie S. Siegel, *Love, Medicine, and Miracles* (New York: Harper & Row, 1986), and *Peace, Love, and Healing* (New York: Harper & Row, 1989).

[2]Anne Hunsaker Hawkins, *Reconstructing Illness: Studies in Pathography* (West Lafayette, Ind.: Purdue University Press, 1993). The following discussion is based primarily on this excellent study of autobiographical accounts of serious illness.

[3]See, for example, Shireen Perry, *In Sickness and in Health*, Terry Jones, *Venom in My Veins*, and Clifford Oden, *Thank God I Have Cancer!*; cited in Hawkins, pp. 53–56.

[4]Cited in Hawkins, p. 26.

[5]Cited in ibid., p. 39.

[6]Cited in ibid.

[7]Anthony J. Sattilaro with Tom Monte, *Recalled to Life: The Story of My Recovery from Cancer* (Boston: Houghton Mifflin, 1982), pp. 201, 207; cited in Hawkins, p. 41.

[8]*Recalled to Life*, p. 178; cited in Hawkins, p. 42.

[9]Anne C. Hargrove, *Getting Better: Conversations with Myself and Other Friends while Healing from Breast Cancer* (Minneapolis: CompCare Publishers, 1988), p. 44; cited in Hawkins, p. 42.

[10]Cited in Hawkins, p. 80.

[11]Susan Sontag, *Illness as Metaphor* (New York: Vintage, 1979), p. 3.

[12]Paul Monette, *Borrowed Time*; cited in Hawkins, p. 81.

[13]Robert Murphy, *The Body Silent*, p. ix; cited in Hawkins, p. 81.

[14]Hawkins, p. 82.

[15]Daniel Panger, *The Dance of the Wild Mouse* (Glen Ellen, Calif.: Entwhistle Books, 1979), p. 160; cited in Hawkins, p. 66.

[16]Gilda Radner, *It's Always Something* (New York: Avon Books, 1989), p. 124; cited in Hawkins, p. 66.

[17]Cornelius and Kathyrn Ryan, *A Private Battle* (New York: Simon & Schuster, 1974); cited in Hawkins, p. 67.

[18]Carl O. Simonton and Stephanie Matthews–Simonton, *Getting Well Again: A Step-by-Step Self-Help Guide to Overcoming Cancer for Patients and Their Families* (New York: Bantam, 1980), p. 153, fig. 3; cited in Hawkins, p. 63.

[19]Hawkins, pp. 149–50.

[20]Hine, p. 104; cited in Hawkins, p. 108.

[21]Hine, pp. 118, 119, 106; cited in Hawkins, p. 108.

[22]Noll, p. 210; cited in Hawkins, p. 121.

[23]Kavinoky, pp. 71–72; cited in Hawkins, p. 25.

Conclusion

Throughout this book, we have sought to illustrate the ways in which religious and moral concerns impinge on or relate to healing in a variety of cultures and traditions. Certain themes have emerged as central in all three parts of the book. By way of concluding this book, let us summarize these themes.

1. At the most general level, healing in traditional cultures, the Christian tradition, and modern medical culture involves making sense of illness. Healing means attempting to place a patient's illness in a meaningful context. To heal often means to make sense of a patient's life and death. This theme is more explicit in traditional and Christian materials, and often muted in modern medicine. In traditional and Christian materials, illness usually is directly related to moral law, custom, taboos, or sin, to use the traditional Christian term. Even though modern medicine has sought to isolate illness from moral culpability, the cause of illness is often linked to "lifestyle," which has moral overtones. In addition, illness is frequently thought of in metaphors that are redolent with moral and ethical connotations. By relating illness to a meaningful framework, by trying to set illness in a moral context, healing almost always implies an explicit or implicit theological or moral cosmos.

2. Healing in all three types of contexts that we have covered is symbolic and ritualistic. The common practice of objectifying, externalizing, and naming illness by identifying it with a hostile, invasive spirit, deity, or ancestor is highly symbolic and particularly easy for us to identify as such, since we are part of a scientific and "rational" medical culture. But in modern medicine, giving illnesses Latin names, objectifying and externalizing illnesses and speaking of them as invading the body, and using combat imagery and metaphors in therapy are symbolic also. Navaho chantways, Zinacanteco pilgrimage, and exorcism of ghosts by North Indian Hindu healers are thoroughly ritualistic approaches to healing from the point of view of mod-

ern medicine. But in modern medicine, visiting the doctor, induction into a hospital, taking prescription medicines, and a host of other details also have ritualistic overtones. The symbols and rituals that so dramatically mark healing in almost every culture and tradition relate to an ordered cosmos, a reality that is implicitly accepted in a culture or tradition and that almost always has religious or moral aspects to it.

The symbolic nature of healing is especially clear in studying other cultures, where it is obvious to us that many illnesses and therapies are culture specific and that illness is culturally constructed. It is not so much that certain types of societies cause particular diseases as it is that societies stamp reality (including illness and healing) with their distinctive assumptions and textures. While *susto* among Mexican Americans or *koro* among the Chinese may appear vividly culture specific to us, our stress-related ailments, seasonal affective disorder (SAD), and hyperkinesis are equally culture specific. Because illness and healing are symbolic, and because most societies' symbol systems are permeated with religious and moral features, illness and its treatment are naturally infused with religious aspects. Illness and healing express, willy-nilly, a given culture's cosmological, theological, and ethical assumptions about reality.

3. A central part of the healing process in almost every culture and tradition, including modern medical culture, involves combating patients' demoralization. In a variety of ways, healing techniques, symbols, rituals, and overall strategies aim at dispelling patients' feelings of malaise, fear, and depression that stem from illness. By implication and association, healing strategies also seek to alleviate similar feelings on the part of patients' relatives, friends, and community. Healing often explicitly aims at galvanizing patients' own healing powers. Rituals dramatically engage patients (and their families and friends) in the healing process and thereby invest patients with a sense of power and control over illness. Pilgrimage, sacrifice, prayer, incantation, song, diet, exercise, and taking medications engage patients in their own healing and discourage feelings of demoralization and resignation. Put another way, a crucial part of the healing process often involves engendering hope in patients.

4. Another aspect of the healing process that is especially apparent in small, traditional cultures, but is also present in modern medicine, is the mustering of community support on behalf of the patient. Many healing procedures, rituals, and strategies focus the family's or community's concern on the patient. In many cases, family or community tensions are implicated in the cause of illness, and healing involves the airing and mending of relations between family or community members and the patient. Serious illness not only affects the patient but threatens the family and community. Healing rituals and procedures that involve the community often relate directly to the restoration of social harmony and order in the face of the disruption represented by serious illness and death. Healing procedures and rituals often aim at affirming the underlying principles and values of a culture. This is particularly clear in the case of the Kung healing dances and the Navaho chantways, but it is also suggested in modern medical treatment of heart attacks, for example, when family members are involved in helping patients adjust to a new lifestyle.

5. In traditional cultures, the Christian tradition, and modern medical treatment,

serious illness provides the occasion for reflection and discernment. It often stimulates questions about the nature of things in general and the meaning of one's life in particular; that is, it provides the context for religious or moral brooding. The healing process often involves the working out of religious or moral problems. This may take the form of a narrative about the patient that frames his entire life in a way that is meaningful, perhaps even redemptive. The healer in such cases plays the role of teacher or guide. She helps the patient, and sometimes the patient's family or community, reflect on the place of the patient in a wider scheme of things. The patient's illness may be understood as a special message from a deity, from God, from an ancestral spirit; it may be understood as the result of the patient's actions in general; or it may reveal a special meaning for the community at large.

The intensity of serious illness and the rigors of the healing process often result in a person's discovery of new worlds or visions, sometimes involving contact with spirits or the spirit world. In this sense, the illness experience is sometimes transformative. This is especially clear in cases where healers discover their healing powers during a serious illness of their own that serves as an initiatory ordeal.

The view of things from the sick bed, which has been likened to a journey to a foreign land, is frequently very different from the view of things when one enjoys good health. Patients often feel they have been pushed to the edge of the normal world. One becomes an outsider, in many ways. One senses from the sick bed the fragility of life, for example, and experiences a certain urgency to the task of making sense of one's own life. Serious illness, that is, can represent an opportunity for self-reflection and self-definition. The healing process often involves a transformation of perspective in which the experience of illness ceases to be a curse and becomes appreciated as an opportunity for spiritual awakening. This is just as apparent in modern society as it is in traditional cultures, with the difference that traditional healers are often trained to act as spiritual guides, whereas in modern medical culture the burden is shifted from the healer (the medical doctor) to the patient, friends, or nonmedical professionals such as clergy or counselors.

6. In traditional cultures and the Christian tradition, healers are usually religious, spiritual, or moral specialists. In many cases, they are practical theologians who diagnose and heal with reference to elaborate pantheons, spiritual landscapes, and direct knowledge of the spirit world. This is the case with Kalahari Kung, Navaho, and Zinacanteco healers, as it is with charismatic Christian healers, faith healers, and clergy or lay healers in small church healing services or groups, all of whom diagnose and treat illness with reference to Christian cosmology, theology, and ritual.

The religious aspects and roles of modern medical doctors are far less apparent, to be sure. However, medical doctors often do play the kinds of roles undertaken by healers in traditional societies and the Christian tradition. Like those more explicitly religious healers, modern doctors sometimes help the patient frame illness in a meaningful context, help "make sense" of illness. It is also obvious that aspects of medical training and medical costume are replete with ritual and symbolism and that the physician is regarded as a powerful figure who presides over the mysteries of birth, life, and death.[1] It is also clear that modern medical doctors play the role of moral arbiters. In the process of defining, diagnosing, and treating illness, they often implicitly or explicitly make moral judgments. They frequently play the role of moral counselor, judge, or advocate in discussing with patients what is deemed "healthy" or "sick."

ENDNOTE

[1]See Jack Haas and William Shaffir, *Becoming Doctors: The Adoption of a Cloak of Competence* (Greenwich, Conn.: Jai Press, 1987), pp. 53–84.

Bibliography

GENERAL

GROSSINGER, RICHARD. *Planet Medicine: From Stone Age Shamanism to Post-Industrial Healing.* Garden City, N.Y.: Anchor Press, 1980.

HARPUR, TOM. *The Uncommon Touch: An Investigation of Spiritual Healing.* Toronto: McClelland & Stewart, 1994.

HELMAN, CECIL G. *Culture, Health and Illness.* London: Wright, 1990.

KIEV, ARI, ed. *Magic, Faith, and Healing.* New York: Free Press, 1964.

OURSLER, WILL. *The Healing Power of Faith.* New York: Hawthorn Books, 1957.

SANFORD, JOHN A. *Healing and Wholeness.* New York: Paulist Press, 1977.

SOBEL, DAVID S., ed. *Ways of Health: Holistic Approaches to Ancient and Contemporary Medicine.* New York: Harcourt Brace Jovanovich, 1979.

THOMSON, WILLIAM A. R. *Faiths That Heal.* London: Adam and Charles Black, 1980.

TORREY, E. FULLER. *Witchdoctors and Psychiatrists: The Common Roots of Psychotherapy and Its Future.* New York: Harper & Row, 1986.

WEIL, ANDREW. *Health and Healing: Understanding Conventional and Alternative Medicine.* Boston: Houghton Mifflin, 1983.

TRADITIONAL CULTURES

ELIADE, MIRCEA. *Shamanism: Archaic Techniques of Ecstasy.* Trans. Willard R. Trask. New York: Pantheon Books, 1964.

FABREGA, HORACIO, AND DANIEL B. SILVER. *Illness and Shamanistic Curing in Zinacantan: An Ethnological Analysis.* Stanford, Calif.: Stanford University Press, 1973.

GRIM, JOHN A. *The Shaman: Patterns of Religious Healing among the Ojibway Indians.* Norman: University of Oklahoma Press, 1983.

HALIFAX, JOAN. *Shamanic Voices: A Survey of Visionary Narratives.* New York: E. P. Dutton, 1979.

KAKAR, SUDHIR. *Shamans, Mystics and Doctors: A Psychological Inquiry into India and Its Healing Traditions.* New York: Alfred Knopf, 1982.

KALWEIT, HOLGER. *Shamans, Healers, and Medicine Men.* Trans. Michael Kohn. Boston: Shambala, 1992.

KAPFERER, BRUCE. *A Celebration of Demons: Exorcism and the Aesthetics of Healing in Sri Lanka.* Bloomington: Indiana University Press, 1983.

KATZ, RICHARD. *Boiling Energy: Community Healing among the Kalahari Kung.* Cambridge, Mass.: Harvard University Press, 1982.

REICHEL-DOLMATOFF, GERARDO. *The Shaman and the Jaguar.* Philadelphia: Temple University Press, 1975.

SANDNER, DONALD. *Navaho Symbols of Healing: A Jungian Exploration of Ritual, Image, and Medicine.* Rochester, Vermont: Healing Arts Press, 1979.

SHARON, DOUGLAS. *Wizard of the Four Winds: A Shaman's Story.* New York: Free Press, 1978.

TROTTER, ROBERT T., AND JUAN ANTONIA CHAVIRA. *Curanderismo: Mexican American Folk Healing.* Athens: University of Georgia Press, 1981.

CHRISTIANITY

CRANSTON, RUTH. *The Miracle at Lourdes.* New York: McGraw-Hill, 1955.

HAMILTON, MARY. *Incubation or the Cure of Disease in Pagan Temples and Christian Churches.* London: Simpkin, Marshall, Kent, 1906.

HARRELL, JR., DAVID EDWIN. *All Things Are Possible: The Healing and Charismatic Revivals in Modern America.* Bloomington: Indiana University Press, 1975.

———. *Oral Roberts: An American Life.* Bloomington: Indiana University Press, 1985.

KELSEY, MORTON T. *Healing and Christianity in Ancient Thought and Modern Times.* New York: Harper & Row, 1973.

MACNUTT, FRANCIS. *The Power to Heal.* Notre Dame, Ind.: Ave Maria Press, 1977.

MCGUIRE, MEREDITH B. *Pentecostal Catholics: Power, Charisma, and Order in a Religious Movement.* Philadelphia: Temple University Press, 1982.

———. *Ritual Healing in Suburban America.* New Brunswock, N.J.: Rutgers University Press, 1988.

SANFORD, AGNES. *The Healing Gifts of the Spirit.* Philadelphia: J. B. Lippincott, 1966.

SCANLAN, MICHAEL. *Inner Healing: Ministering to the Human Spirit through the Power of Prayer.* New York: Paulist Press, 1974.

SHORTER, AYLWARD. *Jesus and the Witchdoctor: An Approach to Healing and Wholeness.* Maryknoll, N.Y.: Orbis Books, 1985.

SPRAGGETT, ALLEN. *Kathryn Kuhlman: The Woman Who Believes in Miracles.* New York: World, 1970.

MODERN MEDICINE

BRODY, HOWARD. *Placebos and the Philosophy of Medicine.* Chicago: University of Chicago Press, 1980.

CONRAD, PETER, AND JOSEPH W. SCHNEIDER. *Deviance and Medicalization: From Badness to Sickness.* St. Louis: Mosby, 1980.

COUSINS, NORMAN. *Anatomy of an Illness as Perceived by the Patient: Reflections on Healing and Regeneration.* Toronto: Bantam Books, 1981.

FRANK, JEROME D., AND JULIA B. FRANK. *Persuasion and Healing: A Comparative Study of Psychotherapy.* 3d ed. Baltimore: Johns Hopkins University Press, 1991.

FRANKL, VICTOR E. *The Doctor and the Soul: From Psychotherapy to Logotherapy.* New York: Random House, 1986.

HAAS, JACK, AND WILLIAM SHAFFIR. *Becoming Doctors: The Adoption of a Cloak of Competence.* Greenwich, Conn.: Jai Press, 1987.

HAWKINS, ANNE HUNSAKER. *Reconstruction Illness: Studies in Pathography.* West Lafayette, Ind.: Purdue University Press, 1993.

ILLICH, IVAN. *Limits to Medicine: Medical Nemesis: The Expropriation of Health.* New York: Penguin Books, 1976.

INGLIS, BRIAN. *The Diseases of Civilization.* London: Granada, 1981.

PELLETIER, KENNETH R. *Mind as Healer, Mind as Slayer: A Holistic Approach to Preventing Stress Disorders.* New York: Dell, 1977.

SIEGEL, BERNIE S. *Love, Medicine, and Miracles.* New York: Harper & Row, 1986.

SONTAG, SUSAN. *Illness as Metaphor.* New York: Vintage, 1979.

Index

Zinacanteco (Mexican Indians), 54–59, 80
disease causation among, 54, 55
group solidarity in, 82
healers of, 55–56

healing rituals of, 4, 54, 55, 56–58
pilgrimages of, 57–58, 77
sacred space among, 76